HOTEL INFORMATION SYSTEMS

HOTEL INFORMATION SYSTEMS

A Contemporary Approach to Front Office Procedures

Michael L. Kasavana
Michigan State University

CBI

CBI Publishing Company, Inc.
51 Sleeper Street
Boston, Massachusetts 02210

Library of Congress Cataloging in Publication Data

Kasavana, Michael L   , 1947-
    Hotel information systems.

    1. Hotel management—Data processing. I. Title.
TX911.3.M27K38   647'.94'0285   78-9310
ISBN 0-8436-2131-1

Printed in the United States of America

Printing (last digit): 9 8 7 6 5 4 3 2

Cover and interior photographs taken at the Shera-
ton Boston.

This book is dedicated to
Dr. Albert L. Wrisley, Jr.
Hotel and Restaurant Department
University of Massachusetts

and

Brother Herman Zaccarelli, Director
Restaurant–Hotel–Institutional Management Institute
Purdue University

Contents

List of Figures

List of Tables

Preface

THIS TEXT is unique to the hospitality industry in two ways: 1) it is the first to focus specifically on computer-assisted hotel management and 2) it has avoided sex bias in an effort to indicate the opportunities for both women and men in the hotel industry. The text is designed to give insight into the manual operations involved in effective hotel administration and to introduce advancements rendering a contemporary appraisal and a prognostication of front-office procedures.

This text is intended to serve both the needs of students at the college level and persons occupying managerial positions within hospitality enterprises. It is different than other texts on hotel operations, because it focuses specifically on the monitoring and controlling of the guest cycle through effective management information systems. Although most of the major concerns of front-office procedures and the relevant problems requiring managerial expertise that arise out of these procedures are presented, they are done with an objective, economic viewpoint; not with an arbitrary rule of thumb or an industry average approximation.

Part I of the text is aimed at significant problem areas that differentiate the hotel business from other businesses and how these factors impact upon the operation of a hospitality enterprise. Such concerns as credit, room rate, budgeting and nonrevenue services are presented to illustrate the types of decisions made and the requirement of more and better information for improved management of the firm. Also, manual processes and procedures are described as a prelude to the discussion of the evolution and application of computerized technology in Part II.

The hotel manager or advanced student who fears the computer and/or refuses to acknowledge its existence and participation in the management of the operation is not well informed. The middle portion of this book is written as a historical tracing of the design and implementation of the early hotel information systems. The first applications and their cost/benefits and inherent problems within the industry are discussed.

Part III of the book is dedicated to illustrating specific hotel computer system modules presently at work or soon to be introduced into innkeeping. Several actual applications and references to hardware and software techniques are presented to enhance the reader's understanding and to persuade the reader towards contemplation of the computer as a management tool, not as a management control.

As an aid to learning each chapter begins with a list of chapter objectives, contains a summary section, and a key concepts section. The key concepts are italicized upon their introduction in the body of the chapter. The listing of questions for discussion should further generate interest in the topics covered.

Acknowledgments

THE author wishes to express special thanks to Professor Harold Lane, Mr. Raymond Schmidgall, CPA, Mr. Gerald St. Amand, and Mr. Dennis Kolodin of EECO for their guidance and/or screening of many chapters of this text.

Special indebtedness to Dr. Albert L. Wrisley, Jr. and to Brother Herman Zaccarelli, to both of whom this book is dedicated. Dr. Wrisley gave the inspiration for pursuit of management information system applications to the hospitality industry, while Brother Herman provided encouragement and invaluable suggestions throughout this entire undertaking.

The author acknowledges Ms. Pamela Steckroat, Dr. Robert L. Blomstrom, Dr. David Ley, and Mr. Steven Lerner for their continued support. Ms. Gail Whiting deserves special mention for her dedicated and professional typing and secretarial skills in the preparation of numerous drafts of the manuscript.

The author also wishes to express his heartfelt appreciation to his parents for their moral support during all phases of this text.

HOTEL INFORMATION SYSTEMS

PART

HOTEL CONCEPTS
AND SYSTEMS

The Hotel Business

Chapter Objectives:

1. To introduce the hotel segment of the hospitality industry.

2. To identify the unique characteristics of the hotel business.

3. To introduce the overlay of the hotel information system upon the organization.

4. To define the guest cycle and some of its subcomponents.

THE HOSPITALITY industry is a broad classification encompassing those commercial facilities furnishing either food and beverage service, room accommodations, or both. The industry is a vast array of operations including hotels, country clubs, ocean liners, restaurants, cocktail lounges, hospitals, and health care facilities. The hotel industry, normally segmented into resort, commercial, and residential properties, typifies almost all of the hospitality industry traits and will therefore serve as the main focal point of this text. It should be noted that many of the techniques discussed in later chapters are applicable to several related operations.

Hotel Characteristics

Nearly all facets of the hospitality industry require large volumes of paperwork and communications in order to insure the proper coordination of services and internal control, and the hotel is no exception. Hotels are differentiated from most other business enterprises based upon: 1) their treatment of the customer; 2) the goods and services they offer; 3) the number of points-of-sale they maintain; and 4) their unique accounting and information systems structure.

The Customer

The customer is perceived as a *guest.* This basic assumption has far-reaching ramifications both in terms of products and services offered and in the area of credit transactions within the hotel. No other business allows the customer an immediate *line of credit* or strives to provide so many varied services. The simple registration of the guest enables the construction of a sequence of financial charges throughout the facility; none of which must be paid for at the *point-of-purchase.* Charges in restaurants, lounges, and valet services are examples of the deferred payments the hotel affords the guest. These assumptions of implied guest status and credit allowances have led to the generation of numerous communication networks and extensive written documentation to insure appropriate payments for services rendered. Hence, the treatment of the customer as a privileged guest certainly is a major distinguishing quality of establishments identified as hospitality service oriented.

Goods and Services

Economists often describe the hotel business as unique, inasmuch as it is a seller of both goods and services. More specifically, the hotel industry is capable of furnishing tangible and intangible services to its clientele. An even more unusual characteristic can be delineated, however, in the areas of production and consumption. The hospitality industry is one of the few places where production and consumption can occur simultaneously, for example, the ordering and subsequent preparation, service, and consumption of a menu item. Although this aspect of the industry may tend to isolate it from others, it also poses a special dilemma in the areas of guest credit and account reconciliation. Should a product be consumed and not paid for, there is little the hotel can do to recover the product or its worth. Hence, the goods and services that identify the hotel enterprise may be potential problems, especially in the realm of account collection.

Points-of-Sale

A point-of-sale can be defined as the time and location at which goods and/or services are purchased. The actual, physical *point-of-sale (POS)* is the cashier, or data terminal, station. The number of points-of-sale are directly related to the number of *operating departments* functioning as *revenue centers.* In other words, any hotel department that collects revenues for its goods or services is a revenue center and thereby requires a POS. Since most large hotels characteristically offer many diversions and a choice of eateries and lounges, this creates numerous points-of-sale. This is different from a department store, for example, which may have several product departments, but only one or two strategically located checkout counters for all its departments. The existence of scattered points-of-sale throughout the hotel leads to the need for many trained personnel to monitor business activity. Hence, the hotel finds itself with an extensive amount of machinery to record sales transactions and a large number of individuals handling cash and charges. *Internal control* of postings and cash flows becomes very tenuous for management.

Accounting and Information

From the viewpoint of accountability and control, there is no equal to the hotel's enormous volume of small transactions, taking place so rapidly, and at so many different points-of-sale. This quick distribution of products and services has led to complex internal accounting and recording systems to insure proper posting and documentation of sales activities. Due to the many scattered POS locations and the number of personnel involved, hotels face major difficulties in the maintenance of adequate control of revenues and in the accurate transmission of transactional information. This traditional volume and flow of paper throughout the facility has led to significant operational changes and to computer implementation. The "night audit" characterizes the intricate details required, on a daily basis, to guarantee an optimization of guest settlement and to provide visibility into who the guest is.

Hotel Segmentation

A hotel property can be organizationally segmented many different ways. The classification criterion may be: 1) traditional organizational chart positioning; 2) functional operating departmental isolation; 3) degree of guest contact; 4) identification of cost and revenue centers; or 5) individual personnel responsibility centers. Regardless of which method is employed, management's main objective for categorizing various operations is to monitor and control the volume of guests' transactions. A brief explanation of these classifications follows:

1. Traditional Organizational Chart Positioning. The hierarchy of managerial authority is usually specified on an organizational chart. Although this is the formal organization, oftentimes this is used as the guide to understanding hotel operations and the contributions of the personnel employed. Each employee and supervisory person is aware of the *line of authority* depicted by this type of chart. This perspective enables management a clear grasp of the firm, so long as the informal organization within the firm resembles the formal charting. Figure 1.1 is a typical

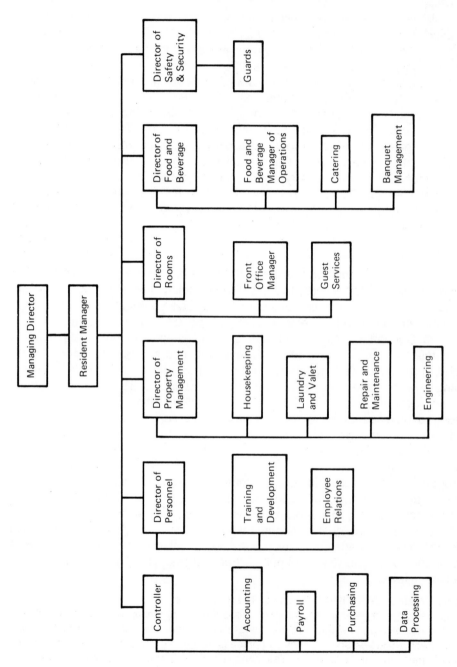

Figure 1.1. Traditional Organizational Chart Positioning

representation of an organizational chart that might be found in a moderate-size hotel. Note that the titles given to the various management personnel may vary slightly and that there is no clear consensus as to which organizational format or charting is best for all hotel properties. The chart shown is intentionally incomplete in that it does not give a thorough breakdown of all lines of authority or of all the middle and lower level managers required in a hotel of this magnitude.

2. Functional Operating Departments. The various functional departments (rooms, food, beverage, security, etc.) are analyzed as the focal point for directing the performance of the establishment. The simplicity of isolation makes this technique relatively popular. Often hotel management forgets that there are other means by which to construct their organization. Inherent in

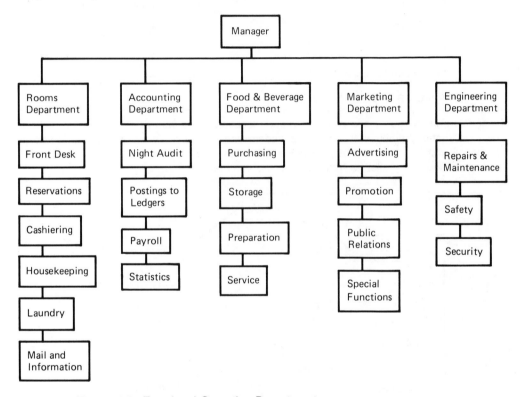

Figure 1.2. Functional Operating Departments

this type of breakdown is the problem of overlapping departments, or subdepartments. In Figure 1.2 the individual departments are illustrated. Note that the delineation of departments is based upon functional operations, not upon personnel.

3. Guest Contact Areas. Common hotel jargon includes *"front-of-the-house"* and *"back-of-the-house."* The front-of-the-house phrase refers specifically to those portions of the hotel that the guest comes directly in contact with during a normal period of *occupancy.* Food, beverage, and front-desk services qualify as front-of-the-house areas. The back-of-the-house covers those remaining areas that the guest typically never comes in touch with, for example, the payroll and

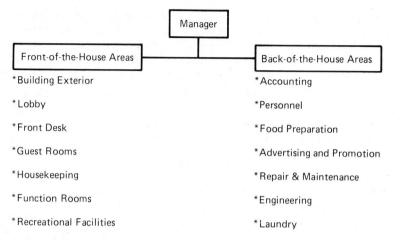

Figure 1.3. Guest Contact Areas

accounting departments and food preparation locations. The *front office,* named to coincide with the front-of-the-house, is the principal controlling factor of all guest services, and has the responsibility of coordinating the back office functions with these services. Figure 1.3 is a simple scheme of the designation of front- and back-of-the-house areas.

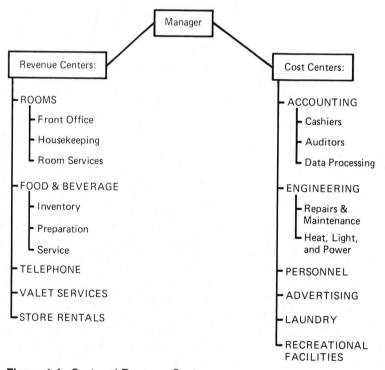

Figure 1.4. Cost and Revenue Centers

4. Cost and Revenue Centers. *Cost centers,* also referred to as nonrevenue centers, are those parts of the hotel that have minimal guest contact, are of nonservice natures, and incur costs. The outstanding characteristic of a cost center is its ability to generate costs but to collect no revenue by its operation, per se. Typical hotel cost centers include the engineering staff, the advertising department, the hotel security officers, and the accountants. Revenue centers, on the other hand, are those areas that generate revenues as a direct result of their operations. Oftentimes revenue centers are viewed from a profitability profile and hence may be called *profit centers.* A common denominator of all revenue departments is that they are also service departments, for example, the telephone operation, the food and beverage outlets, and the room sales department. This is becoming a popular means of internal structuring for hotels because of the importance of charting costs of goods sold and of holding down costs of nonrevenue centers. It must be noted that just because a department is labelled a cost center does not mean that it is any less important to the operation's success or any more difficult to construct managerial performance criteria for. Such cost centers as saunas, pools, and other gratis items certainly can be demonstrated to be a decisive factor in the guest selection of a hotel facility. Figure 1.4 is similar to Figure 1.3 inasmuch as the guest contact areas tend to be

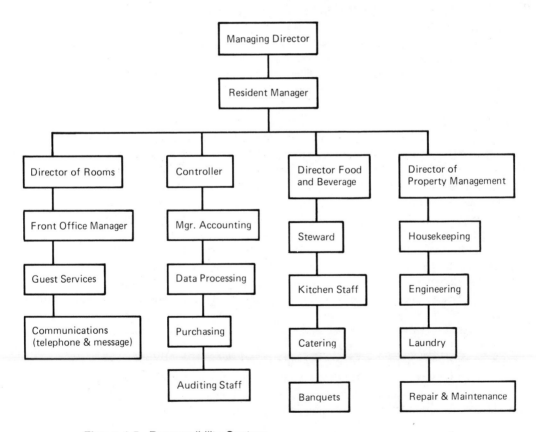

Figure 1.5. Responsibility Centers

revenue producing centers, and noncontact areas usually tend to be cost centers.
Given the trend of increasing nonrevenue producing areas (i.e., capsule elevators and large exotic lobby areas) the burden of covering the costs of these attractions must be reflected in room rates.

5. Responsibility Centers. Since most hotels are not large enough to employ a different individual for each of its operational areas, the hotel administration often assigns several areas (some of which may be either cost or revenue centers) to one person. The organization of the hotel, then, is not perceived by any other differentiation than by the responsibilities assigned to the managerial staff. This is an uncommon approach to innkeeping, but one that may become more popular soon. The major merits of this approach are in the area of managerial appraisal. The direct performance of an individual is more easily assessed if the immediate domain of responsibilities charged to that staff member can be accurately delineated and evaluated. Figure 1.5 is a sketch of some hotel personnel titles and their corresponding areas of responsibilities.

Importance of Organization

It is crucial to the understanding of the hotel operation and the construction of the management information system that the organization of the establishment be clearly comprehendible. If the line of authority is unclear or jumbled, then the identification of information and communication links may also be difficult to decipher. The functions of managerial reporting require that the flow of information for input and the dissemination of the documents and reports of output be known. These important points will be covered in detail in later chapters. Suffice it to say that the hotel is organized along the most effective design capable of charting the guest's cycle.

The Guest Cycle

Due to the increasing complexity of the hotel business and also due to the construction of very large hotels, the conceptualization of a *guest cycle* has become an effective means for enabling management to better monitor, chart, and control the guest's transactions. The guest cycle is defined as that period of time from when a potential customer first contacts the hotel, through to *checkout* and reconciliation of account. Conceptually, the guest cycle is an overview of the physical contacts and financial exchanges between the hotel and the client. From a practical point of view, the guest cycle serves as a clarification of an intricate series of communications within the hotel network. This entire process is loaded with cash and/or charge transactions in most hotel operating departments, and requires accurate posting and billing to insure appropriate settlement. Although the cycle is typically segmented by arrival-occupancy-departure phases, a more correct division can be applied. The cycle originates with a series of pre-sale events (i.e., reservations, prepayments, construction of guest account, etc.). This is followed by the guest's stay which is composed of point-of-sale transactions (i.e., purchases in the bar, restaurant, rooms department, etc.). At the time of checkout, post-sale calculations and reconciliations occur. The fact that an overwhelming volume of hotel transactions are charged against a guest's *in-house* line of credit during occupancy and then to a national credit card at completion of the stay, surely must be reflected in post-sale activities.

Similarly, the hotel's recordings, communications, and basic flow of information must coincide with the guest's movement through the cycle.

Although the entire cycle has traditionally been charted manually, there is an increasing preference toward monitoring by computer-assisted management information systems. A basic overview of the functional parts of the guest cycle will be introduced here, with more detailed descriptions in later sections. Figure 1.6 illustrates the simple chronological flow of the components of the cycle.

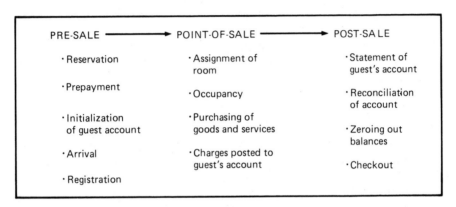

Figure 1.6. Overview of Guest Cycle

Reservations

A request for available room space can either be accepted or denied by the hotel. Upon acceptance the *reservation* is processed and a record of the expected arrival and departure dates, guest data, required accommodations, and any additional information is recorded. There are both single and group reservation techniques, designed to accelerate the reservation process. Additionally, sales representatives, agents, and referral/ reservation networks often intervene and lead to a booking and therefore a note of *commissioned sales* may need to be made. A letter of reservation confirmation is sent to the guest as the completion of this phase of the cycle.

Manually, the reservations may be displayed on a wall chart, blocked out on the room rack, or recorded in a calendar notebook. Ordinarily, hotels with manual systems will only prefer to handle a four- to six-month planning horizon and may even refuse reservation requests for later dates. With the advent of the recent computer systems, hotels are now able to accept reservations within a two-year horizon with little problem and at no great expense. Some electronic systems even purport to provide a one hundred-year reservation forecast schedule. Regardless of the documentation employed, generally, an enormous amount of time and paperwork can be consumed and a constant updating of information is imperative to an effective pre-sale system. The maintenance of accurate room availability status and identification of the guest and the guest's specific needs are critical to the coordination of hotel services.

Registration

Possibly the first face-to-face contact with the hotel takes place at the time of *registration.* The actual registration involves the completion and/or verification of a registration card. Room selection, rate determination, and room assignment are made by the desk clerk at this time. The creation of a room rack slip and the construction of the guest folio immediately follow the registration phase. Registration can take several minutes and there is usually a waiting line at the check-in counter. The major thrust of the registration procedure is to obtain accurate data concerning who the guest is and the address at which the guest wishes to be billed, should the need arise. One of the objectives of the guest cycle concept is to provide management with immediate visibility of who the guest is, what the guest's requirements are, and to establish data for future purposes. The registration process begins the POS, occupancy phase of the cycle.

Occupancy

Following the assignment of a room, the guest begins to enjoy the facilities and services afforded by the property. As the guest frequents the various operational departments of the hotel, many transactions may take place. All cash and charge transactions need to be recorded so that the appropriate postings or calculations can be made. The *guest folio* is manually updated to show the balance of the guest's account and amount of settlement. Through computer technology, the hotel has acquired the capability for automatic postings to the guest's electronic folio. This type of system provides for immediate updating of guest accounts and insures that all charges are posted.

Guest accounting is a complex procedure composed of vouchers, checks, charges, and transfers. The night audit is a tedious job and the struggle to balance departmental and guest charges can be a nightmare. Also, charges often do not reach the front desk until after the guest has departed, and thereby require *late charge* billings. Unless the guest folio is balanced out the hotel may experience unpaid accounts. Guest accounting is an essential investigation accompanying point-of-sale activities. Should the hotel be unaware of amounts owed, or should the hotel accept charges to an unoccupied room, the likelihood of collection is slim, at best.

Housekeeping must be notified of the status of occupancies and report on the condition of all rooms. Since an accurate report of *room inventory* is essential to optimal room sales, communication between the front desk and the housekeeping department is important.

As the guests enjoy their stay in the property, several documents, records, audits, and inspections are being carried out to insure proper charting and posting. In the occupancy phase of the cycle numerous forms are completed and many communications are relayed. Management information systems have made a significant impact upon both the hotel's POS operations and the realm of accounting.

Checkout
The guest's occupancy is followed by the checkout procedure. The guest folio is reconciled, room rack status is changed, and the room keys returned. The checkout can be extremely slow and awkward as examination of the folio may bring debate and/or result in evidence of error. Also, the posting of recent charges may not have been completed prior to checkout, and this needs to be done simultaneously. The folio balance must be brought to zero to clear the account. These post-sale activities are critical to the development of billings and to the development of accurate hotel statistics.

Summary
Important factors differentiating the hospitality industry from other industries are:

1. Hotels are unique in that they sell both products and services and that production and consumption may take place simultaneously.

2. The goods and services sold by hotels typically have no lasting physical value or permanent properties. Hotels supposedly sell many intangibles, often referred to as experiences.

3. Customers are seen as guests and not as clientele. This leads to an implied superior status of the customer and an increased leverage in the freedom to conduct numerous transactions without suspicion.

4. Short-term credit is available to all customers simply because they are registered.

5. No other business has so many small transactions occuring with such rapidity.

6. Control of internal income and accounts receivable is difficult to maintain since there are so many different points-of-sale and personnel involved.

The organization of the hotel is critical to the design and development of an effective management information system. Hotels are usually segmented in one of five ways: 1) the traditional organizational charting, 2) the functional operating departments, 3) the degree of guest contact, 4) the cost and revenue center identifications, or 5) the responsibility centers. Regardless of which method of organization is employed, the objective of the hotel segmentation is to enable management to better monitor, chart, and control the guest cycle.

The information system parameters, an important part of the hotel organization, identify:

1. lines of authority.

2. communication and information links and flows.

3. report dissemination channels and summarization locations.

The guest cycle begins with the guest's first contact with the hotel and continues through to checkout. The cycle involves pre-sale, point-of-sale, and post-sale activities and requires an intricate link of communications and information. The guest cycle is critical to effective management and to the minimization of errors and omissions. The application of computer technology to the guest cycle has made a significant impact on management's ability to govern and coordinate the services and collection of accounts for the hotel.

Key Concepts

Back-of-the-house

Check in

Checkout

Commissioned sales

Cost center

Front office

Front-of-the-house

Guest

Guest accounting

Guest cycle

Guest folio

Housekeeping

In-house

Internal control

Late charge

Line of authority

Line of credit

Occupancy

Operating department

Point-of-purchase

Point-of-sale (POS)

Profit center

Registration

Reservations

Responsibility center

Revenue center

Room inventory

Questions for Discussion

1. What are some of the problems associated with the unique characteristics of the hotel business?

2. How does the transient nature of the guest place pressure upon effective hotel management?

3. Discuss the importance of the relationships between the hotel organizational structure and the information system.

4. Explain the pre-sale, point-of-sale, and post-sale segments of the guest cycle. Relate these segments to the accounting and informational flow of the hotel.

5. How many standard types of forms can you list alongside the subcomponents of the guest cycle? (Hint: next to reservations could be the letter of confirmation or reservation file card.)

6. Define the term "hospitality industry" and explain the representativeness of the hotel sector.

7. What are the three segmentations of the hotel industry?

8. Why is there a large volume of paperwork generated in the hotel business?

9. What are the effects of treating the hotel customer as a guest?

10. What is an operating department? What is a revenue center? What is a cost center?

11. What are some of the major factors that have led to hotel computer assistance?

12. What are five forms of hotel organization segmentation?

13. What is meant by a profit center?

14. Why is the concept of a guest cycle important?

15. What are the segments of the guest cycle and what differentiates one segment from another?

The Front Office

Chapter Objectives:

1. To introduce the central artery of the hotel, the front office.

2. To enumerate the front-office functions and their relationships to the overall hotel operation.

3. To present the basic pieces of equipment used in the front office.

4. To highlight the flow of front-office functions.

REGARDLESS of how the hotel is organized, the *front office* is always an essential focal point. It is strategically located in the lobby area and is a major point of guest contact. The *front desk* represents the hotel to the guest and is the key source of information pertaining to *guest services* and guest accounts. It is the place where the check in and checkout takes place, and typically serves as a sounding board for guest complaints. From the hotel's perspective, the front office is the liaison between management and the coordination of all guest services. The more information the desk assembles about the profile of the guests, the easier it becomes to monitor and chart the hotel's business. Hence, the front office is that area connecting guest services with back office operations. It serves as the main channel of communication and information dissemination for the hotel and is the central point of the hotel's business activity.

The front desk is normally organized along functional lines and the degree of specialization within each of these areas is dependent upon the volume of the hotel's transactions. Some hotels even provide a different employee (or clerk) for each function performed at the front desk, whereas other operations may provide only one individual who is responsible for carrying out all the necessary front-office procedures.

Front Office Equipment
Most of the following pieces of equipment are common to hotel front offices.

1. *Room Rack*—an organization of file pockets that contain rack slips displaying room status and availability.

2. *Folio Well*—also called folio rack or bucket; a file designed to hold the guest folios. May be arranged alphabetically according to the guest's last name, but usually indexed sequentially by room number.

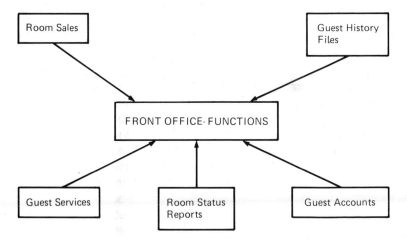

Figure 2.1. The Flow of Front-Office Functions

3. *Posting Machine*—a registering machine used to record transactions (charge posting or cash adjustments) onto guest account folios.

4. *Cash Register*—a machine to record and maintain cash transactions and balances at the front desk area.

5. *Key Rack*—a series of numbered compartments used to maintain guest room keys.

6. *Telephone Switchboard*—also called the *PBX;* used to direct incoming calls for guests and to control guest room telephone traffic and charges.

7. *Reservation Record*—also called the reservation file or rack; contains information on advance reservations. Usually arranged chronologically and then may be sorted alphabetically.

Front Office Functions

Regardless of the number of employees, the two major purposes of the front desk are: 1) to monitor the guest cycle; and 2) to coordinate all guest services. The functions that correspond to these broad purposes include:

1. the sale of rooms

2. dissemination of information

3. coordination of hotel services

4. charting of room status reports

5. maintenance of guest accounts

6. settlement and collection of guest accounts

A closer analysis of each of these essential front-office functions will provide further insight into the larger and more complex overlay of a hotel information system. The overall information system is, however, dependent upon the functions and procedures that occur at the front desk. It is here that important decisions (e.g., pricing, accounting, assignment, etc.) that impact upon the entire hotel are made. Hence, each of the specific functions and their subfunctions is highlighted in Table 2.1 and discussed below.

Room Sales

The most obvious and important function performed at the front desk is the sale of hotel rooms. The measurement of the desk clerk's performance normally can be derived from an analysis of the number and rate (price) at which rooms were sold. Since guest rooms usually generate the highest profit margin within the hotel, this further increases the pressure on the front office to sell rooms. Within the realm of selling rooms the desk clerk will be concerned with four aspects of rooming the guest: 1) handling guests with reservations; 2) handling walk-ins; 3) carrying out the registration procedure; and 4) assigning the guest a specific room.

Although profiles vary from hotel to hotel, the number of guests arriving with reservations has been generally increasing and will continue to increase in the future. The guest with a reservation simplifies the role of the *desk agent* or *clerk* in the sales procedure since reservation requests typically deal with a specific room type and are

I. **SELL GUEST ROOMS**
   A. Accept reservations
   B. Handle walk-ins
   C. Perform the registration procedure
   D. Assignment of the room

II. **PROVIDE INFORMATION ON HOTEL SERVICES**
   A. Concerning internal hotel operations
   B. About external events and locations

III. **COORDINATE GUEST SERVICES**
   A. Liaison between front- and back-of-the house areas
   B. Handle guest problems and complaints

IV. **CHART ROOM STATUS REPORTS**
   A. Coordinate room sales and housekeeping
      1. Occupied status
      2. On-change status
      3. Out-of-order status

V. **MAINTAIN GUEST ACCOUNTS**
   A. Construction of folio and account
   B. Posting to folios (updating)
   C. Supervision of credit levels
   D. Documentation of guest's transactions

VI. **SETTLEMENT OF GUEST ACCOUNTS**
   A. Preparation of guest statement
   B. Reconciliation of folio
   C. Perform the checkout procedure

VII. **CONSTRUCT GUEST HISTORY FILE**
   A. Record the guest's personal data for future reference

Table 2.1. Summary of Front-Office Functions

answered with a rate quote. Hence, the price and type of accommodation may be known in advance of check in. Any request for different accommodations or other deviations from the original reservation, however, may void the pre-specified quotation and free the clerk to sell a higher priced room.

There are usually three common reservation statuses with which the desk clerk comes in contact. The most common is the simple *advance reservation.* This implies that a room request was made sometime prior to the guest's arrival and that the room will be held until the guest registers or the hotel's reservation hold time has elapsed. A *confirmed reservation* is one made far enough in advance to permit the hotel to respond to the reservation request in writing. Typically the guest forwards an advance deposit as a prepayment and as insurance that the room will be reserved as per the request. This facilitates the construction of the guest account, enables the hotel to verify some relevant personal data (i.e., address) of the customer, and may provide the hotel with some cash flow prior to the stay. Some hotels even extend a greater line of credit to guests holding confirmed reservations because of the verification of the future whereabouts of the guest, with regard to account collection. Another frequent status is the *guaranteed reservation.* From the hotel's perspective this is perhaps the most desirable since the hotel is assured of the room sale even if the guest fails to arrive.

Guests not holding reservations are called *walk-ins.* The walk-in guest presents some additional work for the front desk inasmuch as the clerk must ascertain the guest's requirements and select an appropriate room rate. Although the determination of the rate is normally specified by management, there are usually variations within each room category and this requires the clerk to act as a sales agent. Since hotels know the least about walk-in guests, there is usually a lower floor limit of credit extended to that type of customer. In addition, the clerk must capture the relevant guest data and may only assign a room from those remaining available for sale. In the case of the walk-in, versus the reservation, the desk clerk is called upon to interact more with the guest (at check in) and try and sell the most appropriate room available.

The *registration procedure* is critical to the capturing of guest information and to the initialization of the guest account. Almost all of the paperwork produced throughout the guest cycle is predicated upon the data recorded and verified at, or prior to, check in. Although the filling out or complying with the hotel's demand for personal data may not always fulfill a legal requirement (i.e., a legal hotel/guest relationship), it is mandatory for charting the guest cycle effectively. The registration card, or more recently the display of its equivalent on a television-like screen, is the basis for the construction of the *room rack slip,* the guest folio, and the eventual entry into the guest history file. Also, with the ever increasing application of electronic data processing to hotels, the need to collect guest information only once, and at the beginning of the guest cycle, renders the registration function basic to efficient computerized hotel operations. Hence, the attainment of visibility as to who the guest is, what the guest's requirements are, and the status of the guest's account, originate at the point of registration.

The front-desk clerk will attempt to satisfy the guest's request for a specific room type from an up-to-the-minute inventory of available rooms. Upon the location of an agreeable *room assignment* the clerk will furnish the guest with a room key, and the occupancy phase of the guest cycle will commence. Although closely aligned with room rate differentials, the guest may make special demands or request a room elsewhere in the hotel. The guest may even decline the room offered. In any case, the room rate and assignment technique will be an important function performed in the front office. From an economic perspective it becomes obvious that the quantity of room types sold, and their respective rates, will certainly be reflected in the overall financial profile of the establishment.

Informational Service

The front office is certainly the main source of guest information and serves as the focal point of the entire property. The desk not only serves as a sales representative for rooms but is also an important marketing tool for other on-the-premise services and activities. The desk clerk's answers to questions concerning recreational facilities or foodservice will certainly be important to the guest's selection among alternatives. In addition to information about the internal opportunities, most hotel front desks are normally called upon to furnish information about the surrounding community. Persons who are staying at a particular hotel for more than just one night may seek a change of scenery and/or eatery. Hence, one of the important support functions of the front office is to provide accurate information concerning the internal and external happenings about the hotel.

Guest Services

One of the most essential roles of the front office is to serve as the liaison between the guest and the service departments of the hotel. The coordination of guest services is a direct responsibility of the desk and is the branch of the hotel organization that meshes the front- and the back-of-the-house areas. When a room is sold, for example, the paperwork generated at the front desk flows to the housekeeping department, which recognizes the need for and schedules the cleaning of the room the following morning. Similarly, the hotel's foodservice department, if any, may rely on the *house count* (the number of guests) to forecast their production and staffing schedules. Another crucial outgrowth of the front desk's registration of the guest is the establishment of a guest directory for the purposes of the switchboard and message and mail services. All in all, the front office performs the documentation function that leads to the coordination of the service and nonservice departments with the guest's demands.

Additionally, the front office also serves as a sounding board for guests' complaints and as a reporting booth for guests' problems. Once the desk becomes aware of any guest dissatisfaction or unrest, corrective action can be initiated which may enhance the stay, or at least reduce the guest's discomfort.

Room Status Reporting

The front office also is required to provide the hotel with an accurate status of each room at any point in time. One of the most common, and relatively simple, ways to maintain *room status* is through the use of a room rack. The room rack is usually assumed to be the most important of all front office equipment. It may be a simple arrangement of vertical slots sequentially numbered to represent the guest rooms or it may be filed in a computer memory disc pack. No matter how sophisticated or facile the room rack design, its basic function is merely to provide an up-to-the-minute inventory of rooms occupied, rooms being prepared for sale (on-change), and rooms not to be sold (out-of-order). The status of each room is essential knowledge to the workings of the front desk (especially in terms of assignment) and the housekeeping department. Should a room appear to be occupied according to its status report, but in actuality be vacant the error is termed a *sleeper* and the room will be listed as sold until the mistake is found and corrected. A guest who checks into the hotel and then leaves without paying is called a *skipper* and similarly is disruptive to the proper functioning of the room status reporting system.

Although up-to-the-moment status is a desirable goal, in reality some hotels are often twenty to fifty minutes late (or even longer without the aid of a rapid communications network) in learning of changes in room inventory. Since the loss of hotel room sales due to erroneous inventory listings of available rooms is expensive, hotels are beginning to adopt computer assistance in the front office room status system. This may lead to the room rack, as it exists today, becoming obsolete.

Guest Accounting

The guest approaches the front desk, is sold a room, and then registers with the hotel. The subsequent construction of the guest folio (or guest's account record) begins the monitoring of the financial transactions of the occupancy phase of the guest cycle. Monitoring of the guest's account transactions are usually performed in the front office and later audited by the accounting department staff. The running balance of guest receivables (debits) must be accurately recorded to the proper accounts and normally the desk clerk will be responsible for overseeing or actually performing the postings. Cash payments made against the accounts receivable balance are also posted at the desk, but cash purchases made anywhere in the hotel do not appear as folio entries. Hence, the folios are posted only for items that are charged by the guest.

Closely associated with the maintenance of the guest accounts is the supervision of credit lines to guests. Typically the hotel will have a standard *floor limit* to which the guest is authorized to make charges merely contingent upon the fact that the guest has registered with the desk. The posting clerk must be aware of the credit limits allocated to each folio and must notify management and/or the guest (depending upon the hotel's policy) of balances approaching the limit of their credit line. Such accounts are designated as *high risks* and normally cause management to demand either partial or full settlement of the account. Guests that closely approach or exceed their lines of credit usually lose their right to charge in the hotel until some retribution has been made to the establishment.

The hotel is notorious for generating volumes of paperwork that document the guest's transactions (i.e., restaurant checks, telephone vouchers, cash pay-out slips, etc.) and often finds itself inefficient due to overloading. The source documentation that proves the specifics of a guest's charges and/or payments is the minimum requirement for data input into an effective hotel information system. What normally happens is that a record of a given transaction (a charge to an account in a restaurant) is made at least once in the service department (the restaurant's sales journal) and then is sent to the front desk for posting to the guest's folio (updating of receivables balance). During the daily or nightly audit an additional entry or recording of the same transaction may be made in the trial balancing of all accounts. When the daily report of operations is produced an additional record of the same transaction may be made. Hence, the redundancy in the processing and the unnecessary reentry of the same piece of data at several interrelated stages in the flow of hotel information needs to be resolved. Here, as in other aspects of the front office, sophisticated data processing technology is evolving with the intent of minimizing the handling and tedious processing of hotel transactional data.

Settlement of Accounts

Prior to the guest's departure the folio must be reconciled and any outstanding balance either paid for in cash or charged to a suitable vehicle for future billing (major credit card, or business address, for example). The preparation of the guest's balance merely revolves around the tabulation of the receivables balance. Any payments made against the folio during occupancy will appear as credits and only the remaining debits are brought forward for settlement. Once the account has been satisfactorily zeroed out (brought to a zero receivable balance) the guest returns the room key and departs.

Guest History File

The collection of registration card information, after departure, is recorded and assembled in an inactive guest file for future analysis. The data normally is used as a marketing tool by the hotel. Such questions as: Who were our guests? Where does our market come from? How many persons, on average, occupy our rooms? can be answered by simple evaluative techniques. The development of long-range marketing strategies should be enhanced given that the hotel has some knowledge of who it is catering to and attracting. One of the uncommon applications of the guest history data is the delineation of weak market penetrations. Perhaps the convention market penetration, for example, is not working, and/or the average age of the guests is fifty years old; this type of information certainly can be of significant value to the hotel. Management may be unaware of the existence of the data found in the guest history file and the front office may have to initiate the classifying and profiling of the hotel's clientele.

Summary

The front office is strategically located in the high traffic lobby area and represents the hotel and all of its services to the guest. The front office is the central liaison connecting the front- and back-of-the-house, and its structure is contingent upon the required functional operations and the hotel's volume of business.

All of the guest services emanate from or begin at the front desk. The front desk performs several functions, all of which are oriented at coordination of the guest cycle. The selling of rooms and the establishment of registration are the most obvious roles of the desk. As important, however, is the maintenance of room status information, guest accounts, and the settlement of guest accounts. Figure 2.1 outlines the basic functions served by the personnel at the front desk. Attention should be given to the fact that almost all phases of the guest cycle are accompanied by written documentation and this volume of paperwork can make the workings of the desk cumbersome.

Key Concepts

Account settlement	Guest services
Advance reservation	High risk
Cash register	House count
Confirmed reservation	Key rack
Desk agent	PBX
Desk clerk	Posting machine
Floor limit	Reservation record
Folio well	Room assignment
Front desk	Room rack slip
Front office	Room status
Front office equipment	Skipper
Guaranteed reservation	Sleeper
Guest folio	Switchboard
Guest history file	Walk-ins

Questions for Discussion

1. What are some of the advantages that the front office provides to the efficient operation of the hotel?

2. What is the most important single function of the front office? Why?

3. How is the flow of hotel information effected by the front office structure?

4. What other pieces of front office equipment exist, other than those mentioned herein?

5. Discuss some of the basic characteristics of the front office area.

6. Why is the front office the "focal point" and "liaison" of the entire hotel operation?

7. What are the two major purposes of the front office?

8. List the basic functions of the front office and relate these to the overall organization and operation of the hotel.

9. Explain the difference, from a managerial viewpoint, of a walk-in versus a guest with a reservation.

10. What are the three types of reservation statuses and how does each effect the hotel?

11. What is a room rack and of what importance is it to the hotel?

12. What is a sleeper? What is a skipper? What effects do these two guest situations have upon the hotel?

13. What function does the guest folio serve? Why is its accuracy so essential?

14. What is meant by a high risk account and what threat does it pose to the hotel's financial operations?

15. What is an example of the redundancy or reentry of information found in hotel operations?

16. Of what importance is the guest history file? Where does this information file come from?

Hotel Industry Economics

Chapter Objectives:

1. To demonstrate the use of hotel information in some economic decision-making areas.

2. To define the economics of room rating, rate cutting, over-booking, and cash flow.

3. To present basic mathematical room rate determination models.

4. To introduce the concept of cash flow as it relates to a hotel's financial position.

THE TYPE of information that flows through the hotel's arteries is likely to be a function of the degree of emphasis management has placed on the microeconomics of the firm. Although almost all managerial decisions are economically oriented (e.g., pricing, purchasing, budgeting, and staffing), some hotel information systems may not be providing management with timely or accurate feedback; they should be. Some of the most basic and essential economic principles of the hotel industry are found in the areas of *room rating, rate cutting, overbooking,* and *cash flow.*

Room Rating

One of the few controllable factors in the hotel business is the determination of price structures for available rooms. Since room revenue tends to make the largest contribution to overall profitability, the rate-setting methodology becomes a critical managerial function. Those hotel operators who depend primarily upon the attire or mode of transportation of the arriving guest, as a determinant of rate differentiating, are usually not aware of the consequences of their pricing behavior. Aside from the ethics of such practices, the economical soundness of arbitrarily flexible rating is certainly questionable. Although the needs of the hospitality property may suggest some minimal rates (through a break-even analysis) and competition might identify maximum expectations, the hotel can usually distribute its rates within a fairly reliable range. If the flexible pricing scheme mentioned above considers this spread then perhaps there is little loss of revenue. Oftentimes, however, this is not the case.

Room rates must not be so exorbitant that they dissuade the clientele, or so small that they fail to cover expenses. An *optimal room rate* can be defined as one that incorporates and adequately reflects all of the following internal and external factors.

Internal Considerations

1. *Capital Investment Costs.* A reasonable rate of return should be expected for taking the risks of going into the hotel business versus merely investing in a guaranteed deposit account, for example. The costs that went into constructing the entire rooms physical plant (such as the building, land, and parking lot) and its furnishings (such as guest room furniture and fixtures, public areas, lobby decorations, and back office equipment) must be represented in the rating structure to insure a proper return on the total investment.

2. *Availability of Nonrevenue Services.* Those services that incur costs but do not receive direct remuneration (for example, housekeeping, security, and maintenance) must be considered in the overall cost composite. Not only do these services indicate the class of the hotel operation, but they also provide the guest with a more pleasurable experience. Although this is justification for their presence, their expense must be covered by the room revenue, at least in part, if the hotel desires to continue to offer them gratis. Other less obvious nonrevenue items are swimming pools, saunas, fountains, floral decorations, capsule elevators, and expansive lobby areas.

3. *Allocatable Indirect Expenditures.* A multidepartmental hotel normally has some executive salaries and groups of expenses (accounting services, personnel department, advertising, and energy) that may not be directly charged to any one departmental account. Often, these items are allocated on a proportion to total sales basis for all departments. The fractional component of these indirect cost items assigned to the rooms department must be included in the overall cost profile used to formulate the room rates.

4. *Profile of the Customer.* Reduced or special rates are usually offered to guests with special considerations:

- *commercial rate*—a reduced rate offered to a frequent guest
- *complimentary rate*—a free room compliments of the management to promote business
- *group plan rate*—a reduced rate offered to a large group of persons staying overnight
- *family plan rate*—although these plans vary, typically children stay free if they are in their parent's room
- *day rate*—a rate for the rental of a room for less than an overnight accommodation
- *package plan rate*—a room rate that includes or is included in a special combination of activities and/or events (transportation, entertainment, and so on).

External Considerations

1. *Competitive Factors.* In any geographic area, the supply and demand for hotel rooms will certainly impact upon the rate that can be levied for any particular type of accommodation. The *intensity of competition* and the *market share* (of rooms sold) are the two most important market considerations that management must contend with. These factors tend to require subjective evaluation and are not groups of expenses (accounting, personnel, or energy) that may be easily distinguished and/or quantified. Measuring intensity is often done intuitively by each manager. There are no hard and fast guidelines for evaluation.

Elasticity Equation

$$e_{rooms} = \frac{\Delta \text{ room rate}}{\Delta \text{ no. rooms sold}}$$

2. *Elasticity of Demand.* Although closely related to direct competitive market forces, the elasticity of demand for room sales is a more abstract concept. Two adjacent establishments may have similar market shares but not the same elasticity configurations. The change in room price (rate) as related to changes in the number of rooms sold is defined as *elasticity of demand* for room sales. If the movement of price affects an inverse movement in the number of rooms sold, then the situation is said to be elastic. In other words, if the price of a room is lowered and more rooms are sold, then this would surely demonstrate an *elastic demand* for the product. The hotel industry is presumed to possess an *inelastic demand* for rooms within a small range of occupancy percentages. Hence, if a hotel operator is aware of the elasticity of demand, or the inelasticity, then the room rating procedure will be much more reliable in attaining workable

pricing figures. In the elasticity equation the change in price divided by the change in the number of units sold is required to derive the *coefficient of elasticity*.

The optimal room rate is derived through a combination of subjective and objective calculations designed to provide the management with effective operational information. The optimal rate is not, necessarily, the rate the hotel would offer at any given point in time, but rather it is an average figure that should be achieved throughout the accounting period for which the input data is applicable.

Additional Factors Influencing Rates

A few other factors need delineation in order for the complexity of the rate setting problem to be properly perceived. Such key variables as location within a market area and the assignment of the room within the hotel should be considered.

The location of the hotel, within a given market area, certainly effects the rate that can be successfully charged for its rooms. Two identical suites located in two different sections of the same city, for example, can have significantly different rates simply based upon locale. The five traditional geographic locations for hotel properties are: a) highway, b) airport, c) center city, d) suburban, and e) resort.

These areas vary with respect to the:

1. proximity to their customers

2. degree of direct marketing exposure

3. advanced guest planning

4. length of the guest stay

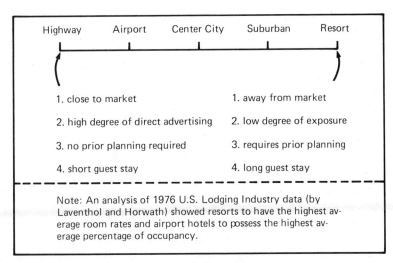

Figure 3.1. Continuum of Market Differentials

Resorts, for example, are usually located far away from the market they service, necessitate prior reservation planning, and involve more than a one-night stay. Highway properties, on the other hand, may attract the transient, weary traveller by along-the-road advertising and the physical appearance of the facility. Suffice it to say that, in general, the hotel locations can be ranked along a continuum for each of the four differentiation factors (Fig. 3.1). Hence, market location within a geographic area does influence the demand for rooms and the rate that can be charged for accommodations.

The specific assignment of a room, within the same hotel, may provoke different rate schedules. Rooms offering scenic views, located on higher floors, or closer to recreational facilities are qualifications that have become acceptable critera for rate differentiation within the same building structure. The more obvious separation of prices by useable square foot area, the number and types of beds, and/or the number of conveniences within a room are also prevailing factors effecting what the guest will be charged.

Room Rate Determination

The hotel industry has three reliable formulations for determining room rates. The inherent problems associated with many of them (which often can be reduced or corrected for) revolve around: 1) the *occupancy mix,* 2) the *construction costs* of the physical structure, and 3) the ability to accurately estimate *costs* and other departmental *contributions* to overall hotel profitability. The mathematics of most of these models are based upon the assumption that an occupancy of 65 percent will lead to the hotel breaking even, regardless of anything else. Although the hotel may be quite new, or very old, the original construction costs are pieces of historical data that are inputs into several of the rate calculations. Additionally, the generation of an accurate room rate is predicated upon the manager's ability to accurately estimate *fixed* and *variable cost* levels for the coming accounting cycle (or other planning horizon). Hence, the accepted formulas used to determine room rates (or average room rates) have most of their shortcomings in the validity of assumptions and their dependence on historic data. The models to be discussed are the 1) Rule-of-Thumb Method, 2) Hubbart Formula, and 3) Horwath and Toth Break-Even Formula.

Average Room Rate

The average room rate is a weighted average that reflects the *room sales mix* (i.e., number of singles, doubles, and so on) and the prices charged for those accommodations. As the more expensive rooms, or a higher percentage of rooms are multiply occupied, the average room rate will tend to increase. Although the average room rate is assumed to represent the overall quality, services, and class of the hotel, in reality it is a better measure of the hotel's ability to sell higher-rated rooms than it is an index of comparative stature among hotels. Also reflected in the average room rate are rooms sold at a discount (for whatever reason). Even with all the complexities associated with the average room rate, the pricing formulations employed throughout the industry

I. INTERNAL CONSIDERATIONS

   A. Capital investment costs
      1. Attainment of a return on investment

   B. Availability of nonrevenue services
      1. Recovery of nonrevenue service expenditures

   C. Allocatable indirect expenditures
      1. Reflection of component costs to rooms department

   D. Profile of the customer
      1. Selection of rate category

II. EXTERNAL CONSIDERATIONS

   A. Competitive factors
      1. Intensity of competition
      2. Market share

   B. Elasticity of demand
      1. Elastic demand coefficient
      2. Inelastic demand coefficient

III. ADDITIONAL FACTORS

   A. Location within market area
      1. Highway
      2. Airport
      3. Center city
      4. Suburban
      5. Resort

   B. Room assignment criteria
      1. Proximity to recreational facilities
      2. Availability of scenic views
      3. Size of the room
      4. Services available within the room

Table 3.1. Summary of Room Rate Determination Factors

specify average rates, not specific rates. The whole point is that regardless of what the average rate is, it can only be evaluated in conjunction with a level of occupancy.

Methodologies

1. *Rule-of-Thumb.* This is the easiest to apply, and perhaps the oldest known, rating formulation that gives the hotel operator an instant estimate of room rate based upon construction costs.

This method simply specifies that the hotel should charge one dollar of average room rate for every one thousand dollars of construction costs per hotel room. The justification of this rule rests with the fact that the greatest portion of the cost-of-goods sold (hotel rooms) certainly is determined when the hotel is built. Since taxes, insurance, depreciation, operating expense levels (heat, light, power), and interest charges are all a function of the initial investment, this formula has withstood almost a fifty-year period of testing.

This would mean that a hotel that cost $4 million and contains one hundred rooms has an average construction cost of $40,000 per room and will necessitate a $40 average room rate. The identification of an average room rate may be somewhat misleading, in that it is not the rate the hotel quotes, but reflects rather a weighted average of all room rates. The application of this rate may be more difficult than first appears.

The reasons that the rule-of-thumb is still employed after so many years is that: 1) it is simplistic in nature, and 2) although construction costs have risen significantly, so have average room rates, thereby rendering the one dollar per one thousand dollars cost ratio still valid. Properties that were built in different decades can update construction cost figures on a per room basis by adding any redecorating or remodelling expenditures. Those older establishments having no new additions or modifications simply can charge a lower rate since that best reflects their cost structure. One factor to be kept in mind, however, is that maintenance costs are higher for older properties and this should also be reflected in the cost per room.

A few of the disadvantages of the rule-of-thumb method are: 1) room rates may not be completely dependent upon initial construction expenses, and 2) the formula produces an estimate of an average room rate that may be difficult to strive for and/or attain. The common problem with identifying room construction costs is that oftentimes hotel space goes for large public areas, retail stores, foodservice outlets, and/or offices. Should the guest support all or most of these areas? Also, unless construction costs represent fair market values and/or the actual costs of the project, the resulting rate may be in error. With regard to the nonimplementary nature of the average rate, suffice it to say that this can only be resolved by management having a clear understanding of the profile of the hotel's business and trying to adjust to an average rate only after analysis of occupancy levels. Additionally, it is mandatory to acknowledge that this formula does not have anything to do with the marketplace and/or the consumer's willingness to pay the rates, it merely is concerned with the needs of the hotel. Hence, the rule-of-thumb method should be used with caution and recognized as a viable approximation to room rate determination. The formula being: RT = $1 Average Room Rate / $1,000 Room Cost.

2. *The Hubbart Formula.* This is a popular method for determining the minimum average room rate required to achieve a desired return on investment (ROI). In its simplest form, the Hubbart model merely is the division of the sum of expected operating costs (EOC) and ROI by the expected number of rooms to be sold (RMS). Hence, the quick formula can be stated as: Average Room Rate (minimum) = (EOC + ROI) ÷ RMS.

It should be noted that several practical problems may arise from either lumping all rooms together (RMS) and/or specifying a desired return on investment. Although the specification of operating costs may be difficult to project, normally this variable is the one best understood by management.

In its more sophisticated format, the Hubbart rating scheme incorporates a biased break-even approach that requires the rooms department to support all the other hotel departments. The extended Hubbart approach can be divided into five steps that lead to a solution.

STEP ONE. *Compile Operating Expenses*
> The sum of all departmental operating expenses should be used to arrive at the total operating expenses.

STEP TWO. *Determine a Desired ROI*
> The total present market value of all capital assets and equity should be multiplied by a reasonable rate of return factor (10 to 15 percent).

STEP THREE. *Calculate Income from Sources other than Rooms*
> The income derived from all departments, except rooms, should be summed.

STEP FOUR. *Generate Amount of Sales to be Realized by Rooms*
> The subtraction of income from other sources (Step Three) from the sum of operating expenses (Step One) and the desired ROI (Step Two) will yield the amount of business that must come from the rooms division.

STEP FIVE. *Find the Average Room Rate*
> The average room rate is found by dividing the amount of sales to be realized from rooms by the number of rooms available (the number of rooms times the expected occupancy percentage).

An illustration of this method (Table 3.2) will shed some light on the derivation of the room rate and its limitations. This example assumes that a new hotel costs $10 million (for land, building, furnishings, and fixtures) and that management considers a 12 percent return on their equity of $1 million to be reasonable. The application of the Hubbart formula in Table 3.2 shows an average room rate of approximately $10.50 to insure that all operating expenses are covered. It is for this reason that the Hubbart formula is referred to as a determinant of the minimum acceptable average room rate.

One of the major shortcomings of this model lies in the number and kind of required assumptions that need to be made. The level of operating expenses, selection of an acceptable return on investment, and a projection of future occupancy all are complicated factors involving several overlapping and interrelated facets of the hotel. Additionally, the Hubbart method places a tremendous burden on the rooms department to support all the other hotel departments, even though they may be operating inefficiently and at a loss. This is not necessarily good business judgment. This formula is fine for illustrating some of the complexities that enter into the rate determination scheme, but, like all formulas, it may not necessarily generate the optimal room rate. In most cases the Hubbart method produces the minimal rate for the rooms.

3. *Break-Even Analysis.* The break-even approach is not unique to the hotel industry nor is it limited in application to only pricing. Although similar in nature to the Hubbart formula, the break-even analysis affords management the opportunity to select any starting point (from required occupancy levels to room rates or vice versa) and to determine what percentage of each dollar of room rate contributes to fixed or variable costs. The Hubbart model merely attempts to project operating expenses, and fails to detail or permit any flexibility in cost levels due to fluctuations in room sales.

Fixed costs are costs that do not vary with sales levels (for example, rent, salaries, or interest expense), are incurred regardless of business activity (at least within some reasonable range), and must be covered through the pricing formulation. The variable cost segment of the room rate is that portion that fluctuates with sales, such as housekeeping costs or room costs. Although some cost items (semivariable) have to be apportioned according to what percentage

STEP ONE: **COMPILATION OF OPERATING EXPENSES**

Rooms Expenses	$300,000
Food and Beverage Expenditures	85,000
General and Administrative Expenses	210,000
Advertising and Promotion	110,000
Heat, Light, and Power	80,000
Repairs and Maintenance	75,000
Total Operating Expenses	$860,000

STEP TWO: **DETERMINATION OF ROI**

given: equity investment = $1,000,000
reasonable return rate = 12%

Hence, ROI = (.12)(1,000,000) = $120,000.

STEP THREE: **CALCULATION OF INCOME OTHER THAN ROOMS**

Income: Food and Beverage	$275,000
Other excluding rooms	37,500
Total Other Income	$312,500

STEP FOUR: **GENERATION OF ROOM SALES REQUIRED**

Return on Equity (STEP TWO)	$120,000
(plus) Operating Expenses (STEP ONE)	+860,000
(minus) Income from Non-Room Sources (STEP THREE)	−312,500
Room Revenues Required	$667,500.

STEP FIVE: **FINDING AVERAGE ROOM RATE**

Expecting a 70% occupancy for
the 250 room hotel yields 63,875
rooms sold in a 365 day year.

Hence, Average Room Rate $= \dfrac{\$667,500}{63,875} = \$10.45$

Table 3.2. Hubbart Formula Example

of their level is fixed and what is variable, the break-even analysis forces management to acquire a better grasp of the respective expenditure levels.

The break-even level of sales is *not* the sales volume that equals the total of all costs, but rather it is the level that equates the movement of cost levels with revenues. For example, a hotel with $15,000 per month in fixed expenses and $12,000 in variable costs will not necessarily break even at a monthly sales volume of $27,000. Why? Because as sales levels change so do variable costs, by definition (they vary directly proportional to sales). So if a firm has a

$$BE_{sales} = \frac{\text{fixed expenses}}{1.00 - \dfrac{\text{variable costs}}{\text{sales}}}$$

Hence,

$$BE_{sales} = \frac{\$15,000}{1.00 - \dfrac{\$12,000}{\$20,000}} = \frac{\$15,000}{1.00 - .60} = \$37,500$$

Table 3.3. Break-even Sales Level

$$BE_{room\ rate} = \frac{BE\ sales}{(\text{no. of available rooms})\ (\%\ \text{occupancy})}$$

Hence,

$$BE_{room\ rate} = \frac{\$37,500}{(200 \times 30\ \text{days})(.50)} = \frac{\$37,500}{3,000} = \$12.50$$

Table 3.4. Break-even Room Rate

$$BE_{occupancy} = \frac{(BE\ sales)/(\text{room rate})}{(\text{no. of available rooms})}$$

$$BE_{occupancy} = \frac{(600,000)/(10.50)}{63,875} = \frac{57,143}{63,875} = .895$$

Table 3.5. Break-even Occupancy Rate

monthly sales volume of $20,000 and fixed and variable expenses of $15,000 and $12,000, respectively, then the break-even sales level is found using the break-even formula in Table 3.3. In this example the monthly break-even sales for the hotel will be $37,500 so long as cost profiles remain similar to their present nature. Since the hotel requires $37,500 in sales to cover its financial obligations (break even) and there are two hundred rooms available in the thirty-day month involved, management assumes a realistic 50 percent occupancy and then tries to determine the break-even room rate. The break-even room rate can be found by using the formula in Table 3.4.

Conversely, if the hotel wanted to analyze its room rate in light of its occupancy, it would use the formula in Table 3.5. To illustrate this formula, assume a 250-room hotel, having a $10.50 room rate, similar to the one used in the Hubbart example. Knowing this hotel has a break-even sales level of $600,000, its break-even occupancy level must be about 90 percent.

It is important to note the flexibility of the break-even approach to a hotel's economic analysis. In addition to it being a quick method for determining an average room rate, it also can be useful in illustrating the relationships between occupancy levels and the movement of actual average room rates. If, for example, the hotel under scrutiny had its actual average room rate at $12 and not the Hubbart rate of $10.50, this would mean that instead of the hotel breaking even at an occupancy level of 90 percent, the occupancy requirement would fall to about 80 percent. Hence, a $1.50 variance in the average rate would require a 10 percent change in occupancy level to achieve a break-even point.

To analyze deviations, like the one above, merely place the new data in the BE (occupancy) equation and perform the necessary mathematics (Table 3.6). Other variations can be evaluated in a similar manner so long as the proper equation is selected, and the correct data is inputted.

$$BE_{occupancy} = \frac{\$600,000/12}{63,875} = \frac{\$50,000}{63,875} = .79$$

Table 3.6. Break-even Occupancy Variation

Akin to the weaknesses of the Hubbart and rule-of-thumb methods, the break-even analysis is dependent upon some critical assumptions involving cost levels and occupancy characteristics. The break-even approach requires a separation of fixed and variable cost components and an assumption concerning their validity and duration of their consistency (How long will fixed costs remain fixed or become semivariable?). The assumption concerning the level of projected occupancy is not much different than the one required by the Hubbart formula. Caution should be given to the employment of the break-even analysis results, especially if the basis for the required assumptions change.

Pricing Dynamics

Although hotel managers have at least three somewhat simplistic mathematical approaches to the determination of average room rate, room rates are often decided intuitively, competitively, or psychologically. Pricing methods based on original construction costs, industry occupancy statistics, and/or assumptions of cost expenditures have been criticized for being too static and biased. The belief that pricing must be dynamic has led to the development of pricing philosophies rather than a strict adherence to mathematical models.

Intuitive pricing, or what economists might call charging what the market will bear, is usually used when little is known about the complete cost of constructing and/or maintaining a room. Also, especially attractive to the hotelier is the fact that the intuitive pricing method also works well when little is known about the demand for rooms. In either case, intuition is a very undependable basis for pricing, but one that an experienced manager may be able to rely on.

Competitive pricing approaches seem to make a lot of sense initially, but lose much of their validity upon close inspection. In competitive pricing, one hotel simply prices its rooms as all the other hotels in the marketplace do. The inherent problem with this approach is that the pricing of similar rooms at a reasonably identical rate says nothing about similar hotel cost structures. Although this practice is fairly common among hotel operators, it must be remembered that more efficient firms acquire price advantages, especially when all rooms are priced similarly. Another variation of this approach has been a follow-the-leader technique. One hotel will be recognized as the price leader in a market area (usually based on percent of market share or number of rooms sold) and all the other hotels will follow price changes initiated by the leader. Again, caution must be taken when practicing this type of pricing philosophy.

A psychological price is one that is based upon management's predetermination of what the customer will be expecting to pay. This type of pricing scheme usually reflects a whole array of tangibles and intangibles (for example, location, decor, services, and furnishings) and has had some relative success in the lodging industry. If management can incorporate some notion of cost with a knowledge of the consumer then this approach can be viable.

Fixed Room Rates

A recent trend that may have a tremendous impact on lodging industry pricing is the concept of a fixed room rate. In other words, all rooms of similar configuration (design, beds, and decor) are priced the same. Hence, a hotel offering singles, doubles, and suites may only have three rates; one for each room type. The determination of the rate is thus a function of the size of the room (in square feet) rather than the traditional index of number of occupants. Most establishments that have tested the fixed room rate have limited the number of persons that may rent a room for the fixed rate. Few other problems have arisen. Standardization in accounting procedures, certain marketing advantages, and an increase in the effectiveness of check ins and checkouts have been cited as some of the advantages of this pricing scheme.

The realization that there is only a marginally different variable room cost regardless of whether two or three or four persons stay in a room with two double beds, for example, has led to the development of fixed rates. Marginal cost analysis supports the proposition that pricing a room slightly above its average rate will insure that a reasonable rate is recovered. The fixed rate, especially in seasonal or cyclical markets, may even lead to a better all-around revenue picture. Hence, the establishment of a fixed room rate may become a very common practice, given a marginal cost analysis of guest rooms.

Rate Cutting

Once a room rate is established, management may not be satisfied with the corresponding occupancy percentage, and might lower (or cut) the rate. The belief that a reduction in room rates will automatically lead to an increase in the number of rooms sold is prevalent throughout much of the hotel industry. This theory has not been proven for most segments of the lodging economy. Innkeepers' attempts at reducing prices as a means for increasing occupancy levels, and sales in other hotel departments, has instead usually resulted in a decline in sales.

The basic inverse relationship between price and quantity can be found in any introductory book on economics. Quite simply stated: as the price of a product declines (or rises) the quantity demanded of that product will rise (or decline). So why is this not found to be true in the hotel market? It seems that the best explanation of the unusual economic outcome in the hospitality industry is found in an analysis of the *elasticity of demand* for hotel rooms.

By definition, a product is said to have an elastic demand if demand reacts to changes in price in an inverse manner. In other words, the lowering of the price of an item should trigger demand for that item so long as its demand is elastic in nature. An example of this can be found in the fast food industry. Should a fast food restaurant lower the price of its hamburger by only a few cents, this may generate a substantially large increase in demand. An important characteristic of products with highly elastic demands is that consumers are indifferent about whom they buy the product from, or what its brand name is. Hence, products of similar utilities will tend to be perceived as homogeneous. The consumer may desire a hamburger and will not care who the vendor is, so long as it is sold at the lowest price. Most items in our economy fall into this category.

Inelasticity of demand, on the other hand, is quite different. Products for which price changes do not effect changes in quantity demanded are termed inelastic goods. If a specific brand name product or a unique experience is desired, and there is no other product perceived as a substitute for it, then its demand is most likely inelastic. Where do hotel rooms fit in the discussion of elasticity? Research has illustrated that there is only an indirect relationship between price and demand, and that within certain percent changes in price, demand may be totally uneffected.

One pricing strategy that has been tried and found to be marginally effective is a trial-and-error pricing scheme. The hotel simply maintains a price for a given period of time and then changes it and studies the effect of changing prices on demand for rooms. This has not been a completely effective method of pricing, not only because its foundation is arbitrary, but also because it fails to take into account the elasticity of demand for the product being sold. Several dimensions to the inelasticity of hotel rooms serve to compound the issue. Questions concerning: 1) the fixed quantity (inventory) of rooms, 2) the magnitude (percentage) of the price change, 3) the timing of the price change, 4) the exposure (advertisement) of the price change, and 5) the price versus convenience within a given market. Since hotels cannot sell more than a finite number of rooms, it is obvious the experiments with pricing can be detrimental to the continuity of business. Similarly, the size of the change may combine to further explain the ineffectiveness of price changes on sales. Also, if the price change is unnoticed or unknown to the guest, then a measurement of its effect may be spurious, at best. Hotels often are unable to determine if the demand for their rooms is based on a matter of convenience or simply on price advantages. The guest who travels from property to property shopping for the least cost room, appears to be the exception rather than the rule.

Effects of Rate Cutting

An important evaluation that must be made by management is a study of price changes on the level of occupancy required to generate identical revenues. For example, at 60 percent occupancy, it takes a 5.5 percent increase in occupancy (to 63.3 percent) to offset a 6 percent reduction in the room rate. The formula in Table 3.7 can be used to calculate the effects of changes in room rate on occupancy levels.

STEP ONE: CALCULATE THE NUMBER OF ROOMS SOLD

No. of Rooms Sold = (Present Occupancy Percentage) × (No. of Rooms Available)

Example: No. of Rooms Sold = (60%)(100) = 60 rooms

STEP TWO: DETERMINE PRESENT ROOM REVENUES

Revenues = (No. of Rooms Sold)(Present Room Rate)

Example: Revenues = (60)($20.00) = $1200

STEP THREE: FIND NEW NUMBER OF ROOMS TO BE SOLD

$$\text{New No. of Rooms Sold} = \frac{\text{Room Revenues}}{\text{New Room Rate}}$$

Example: New Rooms = $\dfrac{\$1200}{\$18.80}$ = 63.3 rooms

STEP FOUR: CALCULATE NEW OCCUPANCY PERCENTAGE

$$\text{New Occupancy \%} = \frac{\text{New No. of Rooms To Be Sold}}{\text{No. of Rooms Available}}$$

Example: New Occupancy % = $\dfrac{63.3}{100}$ = 63.3%

STEP FIVE: DETERMINE PERCENT CHANGE IN OCCUPANCY

$$\text{Percent Change} = \frac{(\text{New Occupancy \%}) - (\text{Original Occupancy \%})}{\text{Original Occupancy Percentage}}$$

Example: $\dfrac{63.3 - 60.0}{60.0} = \dfrac{3.3}{60} = .055$

Table 3.7. Kasavana's Rate Cutting Trade-Off Analysis

Similar use of the formula further dramatizes the effects of a larger change in price on occupancy. With a 50 percent occupancy, a 15 percent reduction in price (from $20 to $17) necessitates an increase of 17.6 percent in occupancy (from 50 percent to 58.8 percent). It should also be noted that when the room rate is lowered, the costs of the room and of its maintenance and/or repairs *do not* change correspondingly. Hence, even achieving similar revenues at lower rates may not lead to an increase in profitability.

The Relationship with Occupancy

As the problem of declining occupancy becomes apparent management should not react with an initial lowering in room rates. The obvious solution to an insufficient house count is to raise occupancy. Realizing that rate cutting may not attract more guests, management must grasp the concept of semi-inelasticity. One possible solution is to increase advertising and promotion so that the property receives greater exposure and the hotel caters to a wider base of clientele. In any case, the innkeeper is warned that a rate cut should not be a first means of raising occupancy because cost levels, revenue levels, and demand levels do not support this behavior.

Overbooking

Hotels sell more rooms than they have available because persons holding reservations often do not show up or cancel out. The practice of *overbooking,* or overselling, is basically a hedge against *no-shows.* The no-show, or nonarriving guest, problem is a large one for the hotel and airline industries and there is much interest in its control and/or extinction. Often hotels overbook in the neighborhood of 12 to 15 percent while airlines have been found to maintain a 20 percent factor. From the consumer's point of view, it is an insult to show up with a reservation, only to learn the hotel is full and that you have been bumped (transferred) or bounced (deleted). Hotels are aware of guest reactions and have presented many consolations (dinners, gift certificates, free lodging elsewhere) to the guest. Although these consolations may be costly, they may not approach the possible lost revenues the hotel may experience if it turns away a large percent of its walk-in guests, in lieu of reservations that may not materialize.

Hotels normally set a reservation hold or a cancellation hour. At this time all reservations, except those classified as "guaranteed," are defunct and the hotel will fill its remaining rooms on a first-come, first-served basis. Guaranteed reservations insure the hotel that the room rate will be paid regardless of whether anyone occupies the room or not. From a financial/economic viewpoint, the no-show problem is one that has tremendous impact on the cost structure of the hotel and the hotel's ability to maximize its revenues.

The three common causes of the overbooking problem arise out of: a) unexpected departures by registered guests, b) walkouts, and c) stayovers. The departure of a guest who had reserved the room for an additional night or more is becoming more popular. The problem with the prematurely departing guest revolves around a lack of advance notice. The hotel may be unable to resell the room only because of an inability to foresee its availability early enough. These persons are called *understays.*

A walkout is a guest who leaves the hotel without formally checking out. In other words, the guest occupies a room for the stated duration and then leaves without going to the desk. The hotel, not sure if the guest plans to return, or has vacated, often does not decide to make the room available for sale until late in the day, thereby reducing the probability of selling the room. Guests who are presently in the hotel and decide to remain for additional nights are called stayovers. Those guests who stay longer than the time for which their reservations covered may have to be relocated elsewhere in the hotel, but the hotel typically will afford them priority over an incoming guest. This may create many problems in terms of overbooking, but at least the hotel is assured of the guest's presence and of making the sale.

Many hotel companies and independent organizations have sought to educate the consumer about the dysfunctional effects of overbooking; but have met with marginal success. Educational and promotional programs and slogan contests have not had the impact that hotel demands for payments from no-shows have had. Some hotels have gone to the extremes of contacting customer's homes and offices both as a precautionary measure prior to the stay, and immediately after a failure to check in. Although hotels are only collecting about 50 to 60 percent of their no-show debts by calling the guest, this is far superior to the smaller or nonexistent revenues collected up until a few years ago.

The best method for insuring collection might be a recent concept that incorporates a credit card and cancellation coding. When the guest phones or writes the hotel for a reservation, the hotel also requests the guest's bank or retail credit card account number. Prior to the guest's arrival, the credit card company is contacted and a voucher in the amount of the room rate is preposted. Should the guest not show, the hotel pursues collection from the credit card company (just as if the guest had stayed). The cancellation code is devised as a verification to both the hotel and the guest that a proper cancellation was made in advance of the no-show. The hotel will be able to settle guest billing disputes by requesting the guest's cancellation number. If the guest has no record of one, then the hotel can easily establish justification for the charge. This idea will insure the hotel of payment and make the guest very aware of the overbooking issue.

Cash Flow

Perhaps the single most important economic factor effecting any business is its cash flow position. The cash flow cycle is that period of time from when goods or services are provided until the business receives cash for such functions. Therefore, cash flow is best described in terms of available cash. The hotel's ability to plan and project cash flows will enhance its ability to meet financial obligations on time. The firm's creditors, and employees, count on the hotel as a source of funds and the hotel, in turn, is dependent upon its clientele for cash. Since a large percentage of hotel transaction payments are deferred through credit card billings, this leads to potential cash flow problems.

The level of cash that will reach the establishment is a function of the firm's pricing structure, and the discounted cash flows resulting from credit card companies' settlement. The length of the cash flow cycle should be minimized and this can be accomplished by:

1. speeding up collections
2. slowing down disbursements
3. securing additional cash sources
4. liquidating some assets

The speeding up of collections simply relates the point-of-sale charge and the time from services rendered to account reconciliation, in cash. Some credit card companies have facilitated a shortening of the collection period by offering higher discounts for faster payment turnarounds. This means of increased cash flow may be at the cost of cash balances and should be viewed as a trade-off requiring extensive comparative analysis. Bank credit cards have provided the hotel with significant advantage, inasmuch as their vouchers can be immediately deposited in a local bank with the discounted amounts soon to be credited to the lodging establishment's account.

An additional factor, which may effect a favorable change on cash flows, will be the proposed Electronic Funds Transfer (EFT) card. The concept of the EFT is centered around its instant transfer of cash balances from one account to another. Instead of imprinting vouchers, mailing them or carrying them to a bank or processing center, the guest simply furnishes the hotel with an EFT card, and the expenses incurred during the stay are switched from the guest's account to the hotel's account. Although the legalities of such a card are presently being scrutinized by the government and the Federal Reserve System, it appears that EFT transactions may eventually be widely used and lead to a large volume of cashless transactions.

The slowing down or discontinuing of disbursements surely will have an impact on the requirements for cash balances. This approach to cash flow management is not typically thought of as the best, primarily because it is not aimed at bringing more cash to the hotel (it is directed at retaining present balances). However, the analysis of spending patterns and the effects of these disbursements against account receivable balances is one factor the hotel need analyze more regularly. The securing of additional cash balances is a constant attraction to management and when the internal cash budget is not sufficient for meeting obligations, the firm may seek additional cash from private or public lending institutions. The borrowing of cash balances, from a bank, involves interest expense and should be done with caution lest the money borrowed be more expensive than the cash owed to the hotel from its clientele. This could leave the cash flow budget in a deficit, which would certainly hurt the financial health of the property.

The fourth technique that can be employed to increase the hotel's cash flow is in the area of selling off some assets. By liquidating fixed assets the hotel may be able to generate some useable cash for pressing transactions. This may be a sound avenue only for those firms in the process of planning or constructing an expensive addition to their facility. In other words, the conducting of the hotel's normal business should not warrant the sale of assets to generate large enough cash balances to operate. Hence, capital expansions or financing of new ventures may necessitate the liquidation of assets, the guest cycle should not.

Summary
This chapter dealt with a few of the essential economic characteristics of the hotel industry. One such area is room pricing. The determination of a room rate is critical to the financial well-being of the hotel since a large portion of the room revenues are used to support the other hotel departments, and usually make the largest contribution to the hotel's profitability. Although the room rate is critical to the achievement of profit, it can not be adequately discussed in the absence of a satisfactory occupancy level. The inherent problem with objective formulas aimed at room rating is that they require numerous assumptions. Along with the three mathematical models presented in this chapter, several subjective adjustments to the rate were discussed as pricing dynamics.

The rule-of-thumb method is a rather static estimation based solely on construction costs. Although it is very simplistic, the rule-of-thumb is believed to be as valid today as it was in its initial use in the 1930s. The application of the Hubbart formula adds concern for the receipt of a reasonable return on investment in addition to reflecting costs. The formula incorporates many varied cost accounts and revenues and produces a minimum average room rate, which must be achieved if the hotel is to cover its projected costs.

The break-even analysis method of pricing is sensitive to changing cost levels as related to variable revenue levels. The delineation of fixed and variable cost components for hotel expenses more accurately develops a price based on flexible conditions than either the Hubbart or rule-of-thumb methods can. Also an important facet of the break-even analysis lies in its multiple potential uses. The fact that occupancy levels and room rates can be analyzed clearly and any trade-offs arising from price or quantity alterations can be reflected is surely beneficial. Overall, the break-even analysis appears to incorporate the most useful information, and forces management to analyze cost structure in order to generate prices.

Intuition, competition, and psychology are also important to pricing since the best that any of the mathematical formulas does is to produce a minimum average rate which, by itself, is nonimplementable. Since the average rate is not the hotel's quoted rate, but a weighted average of an array of rooms and prices, management normally will use the average rate as a point of departure. Since the hotel manager may feel confident in knowing the market, several adjustments to the base price are made subjectively. An educated guess, or charging what everyone else is charging, or believing the customer will be willing to pay much more, have led hotel operators to price their products more dynamically. This has been especially successful in the cases where management has a firm understanding of cost structures within the hotel.

Besides room rating, the hotel faces critical decisions in the areas of rate cutting, overbooking, and cash flow. The typical assumption that reduction in room rates leads to increases in occupancy simply has not been found true in all segments of the lodging industry. Hotel room demand is classified as being semi-elastic because no inverse relationship exists between room price and quantity. Hence, management's attempts at increasing occupancy through lowering room rates have led to losses in sales due to the maintenance of, or even a decline in, the number of rooms sold. The best method for increasing revenues, however, given a fixed number of rooms sold, is to increase room rates. The only other obvious means by which to improve the hotel's position is by increasing occupancy levels.

Overbooking is an industry problem created by the large number of no-shows. Guests who hold reservations and fail to cancel do not enable the hotel to resell the blocked room. Instead, the hotel may have to let the room go vacant and then try and seek retribution from the nonappearing guest. Recently, educational programs aimed at the no-show community had little penetration in the marketplace. The innovative union of the credit card, as insurance against the no-show, and the reservation request, appears to be helping hotels recover their no-show money. Perhaps by requiring reservations to be guaranteed, the industry will be better able to control the guest cycle and to forecast future occupancies with a higher degree of confidence.

The cash flow position of any business is surely one of the most important managerial concerns. If the flow of cash into the hotel is insufficient then the hotel may have to reduce its spending or else find other means by which to generate cash balances (for example, selling off fixed assets or the borrowing of funds). The ability to accurately project cash balances is extremely critical in a service-oriented business since the hotel comes in contact with numerous vendors and employees.

Key Concepts

Average room rate	Inelastic demand
Break-even analysis	Inelasticity of demand
Cash flow	Intensity of competition
Coefficient of elasticity	Intuitive pricing
Commercial rate	Market share
Competitive pricing	Occupancy mix
Complimentary rate	Optimal room rate
Construction costs	Overbooking
Contribution to	No-shows
profitability	Package plan rate
Day rate	Psychological pricing
Elastic demand	Rate cutting
Elasticity of demand	Room rate
Family plan rate	Room rating
Fixed costs	Room sales mix
Fixed room rate	Rule-of-thumb
Group plan rate	Understays
Hubbart formula	Variable costs

Questions for Discussion

1. Why are room rate calculations such an important managerial responsibility?

2. What are the characteristics of an optimal room rate?

3. What are the internal and external considerations that should be incorporated into a room rate calculation?

4. If things like swimming pools, saunas, and capsule elevators are high-cost luxuries that produce no direct revenues, why do hotels offer them?

5. What is a day rate and what impact does this have on the hotel's business?

6. What does the elasticity of demand refer to and how does it effect room rates?

7. What are the general factors differentiating one market area from another?

8. What differences would resorts have to overcome in their advertising that an airport property might not have to face?

9. What are some of the room assignment factors that might further influence the rate the guest will be charged?

10. List the three inherent problems associated with room rate determination and explain what effect each may have on a mathematical formulation of pricing.

11. What is the average room rate? Why is it an important index of operations? What makes the average room rate a difficult figure to strive for?

12. Why has the rule-of-thumb calculation of room rate remained valid for so many years?

13. What are the advantages and disadvantages of the rule-of-thumb method?

14. What does the Hubbart formula require of the innkeeper in order to generate an average room rate?

15. What are some of the weaknesses of the Hubbart formula approach to room rating?

16. What is the major difference between the Hubbart formula and the break-even analysis approach to room rates?

17. Is the break-even sales level the level of sales that equals the total of all costs at some point in time?

18. What has led to the development of pricing dynamics in the hotel room rating process?

19. What does psychological pricing encompass?

20. Why has the concept of a fixed room rate been so acceptable to only a small percentage of the hotel industry?

21. What are some of the assumptions of consumer behavior for products having high elasticities of demand?

22. What effect does a 6 percent reduction in room rate have on the occupancy level that produces the equivalent revenues?

23. Explain the concept of overbooking and discuss possible solutions to the industry's no-show problem.

Hotel Accounting
Systems

Chapter Objectives:

1. To establish the basic relationships between the hotel accounting and information systems.

2. To present the aspects of internal control and reporting of hotel accounting.

3. To identify the hotel accounting cycle and to give a simplistic overview of accounting procedures.

4. To illustrate the flow of transactional accounting between an operating department and the front office.

THE HOTEL information system is composed of *input data* collected from the operating departments and *output information* generated by the *back office.* Although the front office is responsible for monitoring the guest cycle and related services, the accounting department determines the quantity and kind of information required to flow to and from the desk, and to the *financial statements* and other *managerial reports.* Hotel accounting is unique in that the demand for summarized output is made on a daily basis and guest accounts must be maintained on an instantaneously updated, perpetual basis. The function of the *night audit,* for example, would not necessarily be as appropriate in the construction or forestry industries, but it is essential to the financial well-being of the hotel industry.

The need for some types of information on a daily (or more frequent) basis has necessitated the evolution of a standardization in input data and output reports. The hotel industry has developed its own methodology in terms of *vouchers, folios, ledgers, journals, operating statistics,* and *financial statements* in an attempt to minimize losses due to insufficient or inappropriate information. The informational stream of the hotel, therefore, is dependent upon the requirements of the accounting department and the collection of data at the front desk. This chapter deals with the basic *accounting cycle* and Chapter 5 is concerned with managerial reporting.

Hotel Accounting Elements

The development of a hotel accounting system is predicated on three factors: 1) to provide effective *internal control*, 2) to enhance *cash flows*, and 3) to produce essential, analytical *reports of operations.* The concept of internal control deals with protecting the hotel against dishonest employees, omissions in source documentation, and inaccuracies during the accounting cycle. Should an employee be engaged in pilferage, or several restaurant checks disappear, or a charge be posted to the wrong guest account, the hotel accounting system should be capable of detecting these problems and of identifying the nature of their occurrence.

Cash flow is critical to the hotel's ability to meet its obligations to pay its employees and creditors. The cash operating cycle is basically the time from when a guest charge is incurred until the hotel receives payment. One of the most important considerations in any business is the ability to receive cash in order to meet expenditures and this is an essential objective of the hotel accounting process.

The production of essential hotel statistics and financial statements is important feedback information for management. The hotel accounting system must be designed in such a manner that accurate reports can be produced in a minimum amount of time. Reports that are not timely or that are heavily biased will serve little purpose in the total information system. It should be noted that the information system is also responsible for generating external reports for government and stockholder purposes.

The hotel accounting system is made up of a myriad of vouchers, journals, ledgers, and folios. The accounting segment of the hotel information system tries to chart the guest's financial transactions and to summarize outstanding balances in a perpetual (running) balance. Daily audits of the guest folios and operating department transactional sheets help guarantee accuracy in the accounting system and insure the hotel of a higher probability of collection. The frequent omissions and/or erroneous postings to guest folios may not be completely eliminated, but a well-structured auditing procedure will provide better data, more rapidly, for analysis.

The account receivables, in the guest accounting branch of the total accounting process, are charges made by the guest throughout the hotel's operating departments. These charges represent balances for goods and services that will be paid at a later than point-of-purchase time. The balance of the receivables is limited to the line of credit, or floor limit, afforded each guest. As the guest approaches this limit, either settlement in part or in full may be requested and no other charges will be accepted, by the hotel. Typically, transient guests (those currently registered with the hotel) will have a tighter or lower limit on their line of credit than a city ledger (non-guest) account. Hence, the ledger of guest folios, and the city ledger of non-guest folios, are account receivable listings that must be regularly audited to insure proper payment.

Transactional Accounting

The enormous volume of paperwork maintained in a hotel is a function of the number of operating departments and the *degree of verification* required for internal control. The business transactions that take place within the hotel can be classified as being either: a) *cash transactions* (sales), b) *account receivable transactions* (charges), c) *account payable transactions* (debts), or d) *cash payout transactions* (short-term loans). When an operating department sells a product or service, a record of the revenue transaction and a notation of whether it was paid for in cash or charged is made. At this point the operating department's sales journal, the cash register tape or POS terminal record, and the guest check are all used to document the transaction. If the purchase was charged then it is an account receivable for the hotel and a voucher, or the guest check itself, is transmitted with the necessary information to the front desk for posting to the guest folio. These balances represent monies owed the hotel (account receivables). Account payable transactions involve the hotel incurring debts to a vendor, or a guest, for goods or services rendered. These balances are monies the hotel owes and are also charted in the accounting cycle.

Accounting Cycle

The accounting cycle is a chronological sequencing of transactions, postings, and the development of financial information and statements. In more specific terms, the hotel accounting cycle can be broken down into the following five phases:

1. *Transactional Analysis.* A business transaction is evaluated so that the nature and monetary value of it is understood.

2. *Supporting Documentation.* Once the transaction has occurred a record of it will be made in the operating department and a voucher prepared for transmittal to the proper individual folio or account.

3. *Account Posting.* The vouchers are posted to the proper accounts to insure accurate billing and

settlement. Some transactional data may necessitate postings in more than one account or ledger.

4. *Accounting Procedures.* The postings to various accounts are audited and summarized for transfer to other accounting records and/or statements.

5. *Financial Reporting.* All the information in the accounting system is compiled and several financial statements and operating statistics are prepared.

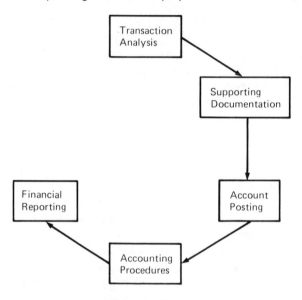

Figure 4.1. Transactional Accounting Cycle

The accounting cycle is concerned with the recording of all transactions and the analysis of how each transaction effects the hotel. It is for this reason that the hotel accounting structure is composed of numerous folios, ledgers, journals, and vouchers and that the accounting data is the principal component of the overall hotel information system. The accounting cycle is depicted in Figure 4.1.

Debits and Credits

The recording of transactions to individual accounts is accomplished through the use of debits and credits. The basic accounting technique for maintaining perpetual account balances is to reflect purchases (or payments) in terms of account increases (or decreases). The accounting rule that every debit also produces a credit (and vice versa) insures the business of an accounting equation balance throughout the entire accounting cycle. It is this double entry concept that facilitates the detection of errors and/or omissions. When a guest charges a purchase to a folio, an addition to that account also generates a subtraction in another account, elsewhere in the hotel's accounting system. Charges to guest folios, or city ledger accounts, are debits (additions) and payments against those balances are credits (subtractions). The source of folio debit is guest purchases charged in the hotel, while the source of folio credits arises from cash payments and/or adjustments (allowances or transfers) to the guest's account. Hence, when a guest account is settled the outstanding debit balance should be negated by the settlement credit balance and render the account zeroed out (with a zero balance due). Guest folios that are not zeroed out when the guests depart are transferred to the city ledger for billing.

Guest and City Accounts

Although each operating department will probably require at least one account, the hotel also must maintain at least one account for every guest room. The guest room account record is called a folio and serves to provide a running balance of the guest's financial position with the hotel. These accounts are maintained in a guest ledger.

Non-guest accounts are called city accounts and these are maintained in a different ledger. Hence, folios are accumulated in a guest ledger, while city accounts are found in the city ledger.

The guest folios are constructed primarily for the maintenance of account balances but they also serve as central records of guest data. Folios are typically assigned on a per room basis but individual guest records or master folios (for aggregating two or more rooms on one folio) are possible. The collection of registered guest folios combine to form a transient type of ledger that necessitates daily auditing.

City accounts are maintained for local customers as an incentive for them to patronize the hotel's departments. Local business concerns, dignitaries, and civic organizations are usually extended this charge account type of billing. Obviously important are the assurance of eventual payment and the understanding of inherent time delays in cash flows. The hotel must evaluate these considerations prior to granting city accounts. Hence, the transient ledger of guest folios, and the city ledger of non-guest accounts, are account receivable listings that must be routinely inspected to insure proper receipt of payment by the hotel.

Source Documents

In a transactional accounting system it is critical that all transactions be posted accurately and as soon as possible. The hotel employs numerous source documents in its attempt to chart the financial aspects of the guest cycle, through an accounting cycle. Some of the traditional documents found in the lodging industry are discussed below. The implementation of computer-assisted hotel information systems has either reduced or eliminated the need for some of these documents, at least in their traditional format.

Guest Checks. The guest check, or ticket, is the original record of an order and statement of purchase in an operating department. The restaurant check, for example, is the basic document used to track the guest's item purchases and the corresponding prices (see Fig. 4.2).

Vouchers. Although the hotel may have several different types of vouchers, the basic purpose of a voucher is to serve as a support document for an original record. In other words a charged

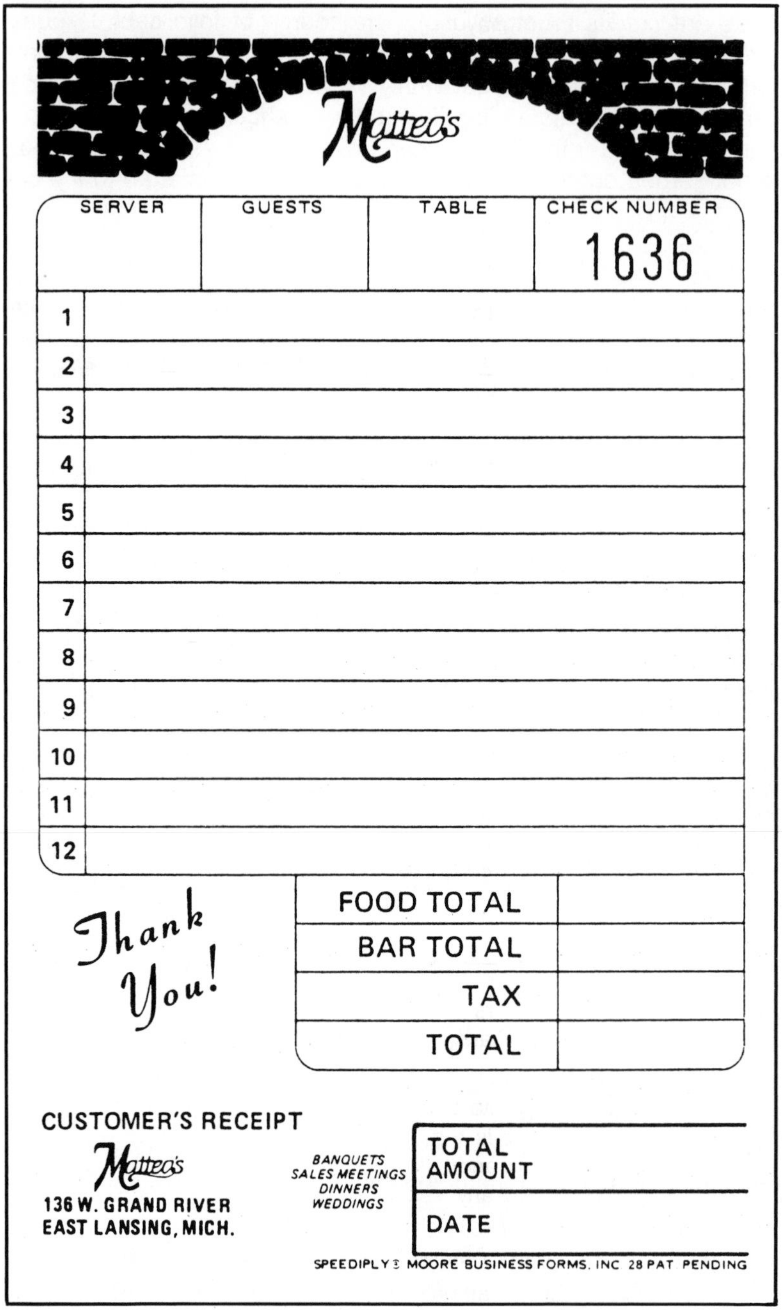

Matteo's

SERVER	GUESTS	TABLE	CHECK NUMBER
			1636

1	
2	
3	
4	
5	
6	
7	
8	
9	
10	
11	
12	

Thank You!

FOOD TOTAL	
BAR TOTAL	
TAX	
TOTAL	

CUSTOMER'S RECEIPT

Matteo's

136 W. GRAND RIVER
EAST LANSING, MICH.

BANQUETS
SALES MEETINGS
DINNERS
WEDDINGS

TOTAL AMOUNT

DATE

SPEEDIPLY® MOORE BUSINESS FORMS, INC 28 PAT PENDING

Figure 4.2. Guest Check
(Courtesy of Matteo's Restorante)

sale, in a foodservice outlet for example, may be communicated to the guest folio by transmittal of a voucher; not a guest check. Vouchers provide back-up for recording transactions and present the posting clerk with a written communique. They can be either a debit (charged sale) or a credit (payment) (see Fig. 4.3).

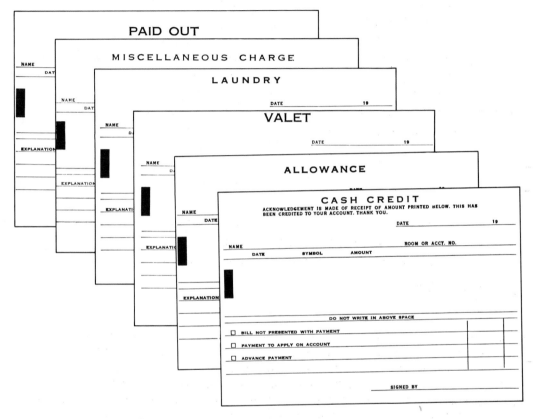

Figure 4.3. Assorted Hotel Vouchers
(Courtesy of Kellogg Center, East Lansing, Michigan)

Registration Cards. When the guest checks into the hotel a completed registration card is an important source of information. Not only is the guest's personal data there, but also the length of stay, number in party, room rate and assignment. This document serves to inform the hotel as to who the guest is and what, if any, special considerations have been made (see Fig. 4.4).

Register Tapes. The use of a cash register or POS terminal in an operating department will provide a written record (paper tape) of all transactions. This can be helpful in insuring that all sales are accounted for.

Sales Journals. Operating departments maintain daily journals for recording and summarizing all

208454-7   REORDER No. 70205   DATAFORMS COMPANY, JACKSON, MICH. 49204

ROOM	LAST	(NAME)	FIRST	INITIAL

GUEST INFORMATION

VALUABLES must be placed in the office safe otherwise we cannot accept responsibility for them.

LOCAL PHONE CALLS may be placed directly from your room. There is a charge of 30¢ for each call.

We hope you enjoy your stay at

MICHIGAN STATE UNIVERSITY AND THE

KELLOGG CENTER

RATE	CITY	STATE

TAX	IN DATE	OUT DATE

Room Clerk | Conference

— ☐ CASH (Including Check or Credit Card)   ☐ CHARGE

East Lansing, Michigan 48824

MEMO	EXPLANATION	CHARGES	CREDITS	BALANCE DUE	PICK-UP

SIGNATURE

X _____

ADDRESS

CITY   STATE   ZIP

CHARGE INSTRUCTIONS (For Clerk Use Only)

FULL NAME
COMPLETE ADDRESS

FOR CLERKS USE ONLY

☐ SINGLE   ☐ JOINER

☐ DOUBLE   ☐ SINGLE IF POSSIBLE

☐ WILL SHARE

☐ WILL SHARE WITH _____ NAME

SIGNATURE OF APPROVAL

ATTENTION

Figure 4.4. Combination Registration Card/Folio
(Courtesy of Kellogg Center, East Lansing, Michigan)

sales transactions. The compilation of this data can serve as an audit cross-reference and/or as a base for forecasting.

Payroll Journal. A back office personnel record designed to document the hours and salaries of employees.

Purchase Journals. A record of all purchases on credit are maintained by each of the operating

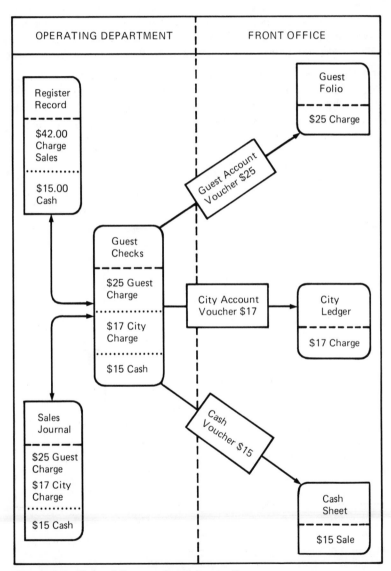

Figure 4.5. Flow of Transactional Accounting

departments. This document serves as a support record for the purchase invoices that may be directly handled in the accounting office.

Ledgers. Ledgers vary from journals in that they are more permanent and complete in nature; and are not all given daily attention. The city ledger, for example, is a listing of outstanding charges made by nonresident guests. This ledger is not normally reviewed and/or audited daily.

Cash Sheet. The front office normally maintains a cash sheet for processing all cash transactions. Cash payments against folio accounts and cash payouts will appear on the front office cash sheet. This sheet serves as a cross-reference document of funds transferred to the desk from the operating department and those collected from the guests at the desk itself.

The general flow of transactional accountings for purchases in an operating department is depicted in Figure 4.5. Figure 4.6 depicts this same transactional process but in terms of debits and credits for the same transactions. The accounting symbols "cr" and "dr" stand for credit and debit entries, respectively. The "T" account format is used to show the type and amount of entries per account.

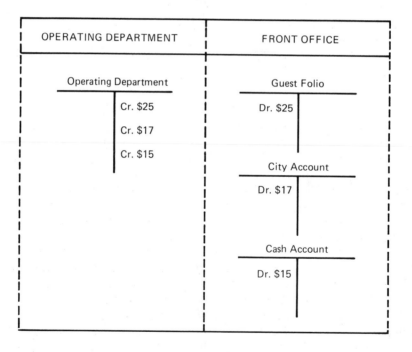

Figure 4.6. Flow of Accounting Entries

Hotel Accounting Procedures

Posting

All the vouchers that emanate from the operating departments flow to the front office for posting to the respective guest folios. Similarly, payments made against a guest's outstanding balance are also posted at the front desk area. A transactional accounting system (which most hotels employ) is wholly dependent upon a competent posting procedure. In fact, computerized guest accounting systems focus much attention on instantaneous posting (posting usually occurring simultaneously with the recording of transactions at the POS terminal). Postings can be performed: a) pre-occupancy, b) in-occupancy, and c) post-occupancy. The establishments of the guest folio and the recording of prepayments and/or advanced deposits are examples of pre-occupancy postings. Should a posting be made at the same time a transaction takes place (a cash payout or settlement of account) or following a charge purchase, the posting is performed while the guest is in the occupancy phase of the guest cycle. Late charges, charges posted after the guest's departure, are detrimental to the hotel's collection since billings are not nearly as effective as in-house reconciliation. Typical late postings are telephone calls and breakfast charges that may not reach the desk until after the guest has completed occupancy and departed.

Zeroing Out

Postings are either of a debit or a credit nature. Charge purchases, and other transactions that increase the account payable balance to the hotel (by the guests) are debit entries. The payments or partial payments against account balances are credit entries. At the conclusion of the guest cycle (and the accounting cycle) the folio balance should be zeroed out. The zeroing of an account necessitates that credits and debits equal out. Guest accounts not having a zero balance, following the checkout, are transferred to the city ledger for billing and collection.

Control Information

The accounting system is dependent upon source documentation to establish accurate account records and to maintain effective control of operations. At the time of an account review, or audit process, the ledger accounts are checked against the respective source documents in an attempt to prove totals and proper postings. Any discrepancies found by the auditor must be reconciled, and the hotel's control information enables a complete review of guest transactions. The room revenue report, for example, is constructed from data found on the registration card in the room rack, and serves as an important piece of control information.

Cross-Referencing

Efficient accounting system design requires that there be some additional, independent documentation available to prove the account totals constructed from control information. Hotels have traditionally produced such large volumes of paper, in a manually audited environment, that it is possible to identify supporting documents, produced by different individuals, capable of serving as cross-reference sources. Although the auditor may receive information on room revenues from the room rack, a check on the accuracy of postings may be found in the housekeeping report produced by that operating department. Similarly, food and beverage postings are usually constructed from vouchers or guest checks, and the register tape, and/or sales journal of the operating department serve to support these entries.

Daily and Supplemental Transcript

The daily transcript is basically a worksheet analysis aimed at early detection of erroneous records in the posting of departmental transactions to the guest ledgers (folios). The intent of the transcript is to facilitate the eventual complete audit procedure by identifying those out-of-balance figures in advance of a thorough, detailed review. Hence, the transcript is the final step in the preparation for the audit and serves as a preliminary screening, by account totals, used to find department-level errors. Some accountants consider the transcript preparation part of the audit itself. This is also an acceptable procedure.

The supplemental transcript is basically the same a priori treatment but for the city ledger accounts. Not all city accounts have daily activity. Those that do, on any particular day, must be reflected in the overall daily transcript, if all accounts and totals are to be proved. The omission of a restaurant sale charged to a city account, for example, will be obvious when the sum of the guest account restaurant debits is compared with the charge sales total found in the operating department. It is this inequality condition that initiates an investigation, or audit, into the accuracies of the posting procedures. Hence, this transcript renders the daily account totals accurate.

Auditing

The audit procedure serves as a verification of the accuracy of the transactional postings made during an accounting period. Typically the hotel, due to the transient nature of its guests, performs the audit on a daily (or more than once a day) basis. Because the daily audit has been traditionally done during the slower, late night business hours, it is known as the night audit. It need not be limited to a nighttime performance; as a matter of fact many computerized guest accounting systems are capable of performing an audit upon demand.

The degree of accuracy required in the audit is a function of: 1) the frequency of errors, and 2) the number and types of accounts and source documents that require checking. Although the total of outstanding account balances (debits) in specific categories must equal the sum of the respective operating departments' charged sales (credits), the identification of specific out-of-balance figures may not lead to the location

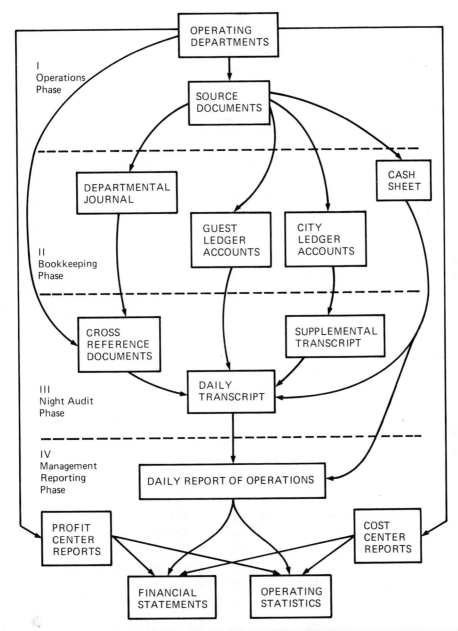

Figure 4.7. Overview of a Hotel Accounting Information System

of the error. The discovery and correction of the error is truly the auditing function. The auditor might have to carefully compare the daily transcript, folios, source documents, and vouchers with the cross-reference documentations that are independently produced at the operating department level. An overview of the hotel accounting information system is presented in Figure 4.7.

Summary

This chapter presents a simplification and an overview of the hotel accounting system. Basically, the accounting system is dependent upon accurate transactional recordings to the appropriate ledger account during the accounting cycle. The accounting cycle is a five-phase sequence of procedures that begins with transactional analysis and posting and continues through to the production of managerial reports and operating statistics. Source documents help communicate charged sales data to the desk and provide control information for postings. A daily transcript is performed on all guest ledger accounts, and a supplemental transcript is prepared for those city accounts having activity. The daily transcript serves as a trial balance of guest accounts and city accounts with the departmental control information. The transcripts identify transactional accounting errors prior to the beginning of the auditing process. The daily audit, or night audit, is a verification of all account entries and balances based upon the comparison of the transcripts with departmentally prepared cross-reference documentation. When all account balances are proved and all errors corrected, the audit is complete.

Key Concepts

Account payable transaction	Guest account
Account receivable transaction	Input data
Accounting cycle	Internal control
Auditing	Journal
Back office	Ledger
Cash flow	Managerial reports
Cash operating cycle	Night audit
Cash payout transaction	Operating statistics
Cash transaction	Output information
City account	Postings
Credit entries	Report of operations
Cross-referencing	Source document
Debit entries	Transactional accounting
Degree of verification	Transcript
Documentation	Trial balance
Financial statements	Voucher
Folio	Zeroing out

Questions for Discussion

1. What are the basic components of a hotel information system?

2. How does the hotel accounting system interface with the information system? Why is this interface so important?

3. What are the typical account receivables that the hotel has to deal with?

4. Describe the concept of a double entry system of accounting and relate it specifically to the hospitality industry.

5. What are the five phases of the accounting cycle?

6. What is a city account and how does it differ from a guest folio account?

7. What are the essential hotel source documents?

8. What is meant by cross-reference documentation and what contribution do these documents make to the hotel accounting system?

9. Relate the flow of hotel documents to the flow of accounting entries in the transactional framework.

10. Why is a hotel that employs a transactional accounting system so dependent upon an accurate and expedient posting function?

11. Of what value is the daily transcript? When is it normally prepared and by whom?

12. What is the purpose of a supplemental transcript? Give some examples of possible supplementary transcripts.

13. When is the (night) audit complete?

Managerial Reporting

Chapter Objectives:

1. To introduce the concepts of reporting and the impact reporting makes upon the management function.

2. To describe the use of the Uniform System of Accounts for hotel record standardization.

3. To present the development of budgets, operational reports, the income statement, and the balance sheet.

4. To explain basic financial terminology used in reporting.

ONCE THE hotel's basic operations have been defined and the accounting information system implemented, the accounting cycle leads to the generation of reports for management. The purpose of a management report is to assist management in carrying out the basic functions of planning, coordinating, and controlling the hotel. All management reports are not of the same format and normally vary with regard to the degree of concentration and completeness. Managers rely on reports to enable them to: 1) make more intelligent and informed dicisions, 2) better monitor and plan the business activities, and 3) attain important feedback concerning the status of operations. Reports that are timely and concise tend to make more impact on the managerial process than reports that are overly redundant or unnecessarily cumbersome. This chapter and Chapter 6 combine to form the complete discussion of managerial reporting.

Uniform System of Accounts

Throughout the hotel industry there is a standardization of format and content developed in a manual entitled, *The Uniform System of Accounts for Hotels,* published by the American Hotel & Motel Association. Although there are many important reasons for the uniformity in financial statement preparation, one of the most essential is to provide an industry-wide interpretation of financial results without regard to the individual whims of any given operator. With the uniform system, many operators are able to evaluate their operations against national or regional averages or trends. This system also may help them be consistent in their own record keeping from year to year.

The Reporting Function

Hotel managers usually receive reports of either a statistical nature (e.g., occupancy percentage or inventory turnover) or of a financial nature (e.g., balance sheet or income statement). The manager's ability to interpret the information contained in these two kinds of documents will certainly influence the value of the report on the hotel's operations. The main objective of the reporting function is to give management control over the *assets* and *liabilities* of the business. The hotel's accounting information system is generally concerned with all transactions that occur, while managerial reports are usually focused on specific segments of the firm (profit and cost centers) or summarized status reports dealing with classifications of accounts (daily report of operations and financial statements). The reporting system should be constructed in accordance with the organizational stratifications of the firm and should be aimed at those individuals responsible for effecting the outcome of different areas of the hotel. Basically, financial statements are oriented toward management control while operating statistics tend to report efficiency and productivity rates.

Financial Terminology

Based upon the needs and operations of hotels over the past years, several common financial terms have become mainstays on lodging industry statements of financial position and profitability. Some of these phrases are:

1. *Current Assets.* Business resources of value (assets) that are or will be converted to cash during the next accounting period (or fiscal year). Included in this category are such items as: cash, account receivables (guest and city ledger accounts), inventories, marketable securities, and prepaid expenses.

2. *Noncurrent Assets.* These include intangible, fixed, and other assets. These resources are usually of a permanent nature and have a significant monetary value. Land, physical plant, furnishings, fixtures, and equipment are examples of a hotel's noncurrent assets.

3. *Current Liabilities.* Outstanding financial obligations (liabilities) due within the next accounting period (or fiscal year). The hotel will have to meet its payroll, accounts payable, taxes, and the like, within a given period and hence, these liabilities are categorized as current.

4. *Long-Term Liabilities.* Debts incurred but will not require payment within the coming year. Such items as long-term loans and mortgage payments are examples of these obligations.

5. *Owners' Equity.* The capital investment and retained earnings portion of the firm, combined with any outstanding stocks, forms the equity segment of the firm.

6. *Total Revenues.* The aggregation of all departmental sales, plus any other sources of income, will sum to the hotel's total revenues. Room sales, food sales, beverage sales, and telephone add up to this revenue summary.

7. *Operating Expenses.* Indirect, allocable costs of doing business. In other words, these costs are not directly a result of a department's sales, but rather are incurred by the overall operations. Examples: advertising, administrative salaries, insurance, rent, and maintenance.

8. *Cost of Goods Sold.* The directly allocated cost incurred from the sale of an item. If the product was not sold then this cost would not be incurred. The realization that the cost of food is a direct expense in generating food sales is an example of a direct expenditure to generate a sale.

9. *Net Income.* Income derived by subtracting direct and indirect costs of sales from total gross revenues, and after taxes.

10. *Retained Earnings.* Those earnings kept in the firm to replenish the assets, and to encourage investment for new projects (e.g., expansion or redecoration).

Financial Reporting

Although there are many levels and types of financial reports employed by various hotel companies, only four key documents will be discussed herein. The concept and structure of budgets, the (daily) report of operations, the income statement, and the balance sheet will be highlighted because they are representative, essential, and common to hotel operations. Although hotel reports may be on a departmental, account, responsibility center, or cost and profit center basis, management should select the format that reflects most favorably on the hotel's performance.

Budgeting Systems

A budget is a management tool used to communicate planned or expected levels of financial performance for the next accounting period. Although a budget can be developed for various planning horizons (short term, intermediate, or long term) and for variable levels of sales, its main utility lies in its ability to serve as a base for comparison with actual operating results of the hotel. Typically, business firms will generate three types of budgets that compose their overall budgeting system. An *operating budget,* detailing planned operations for the forthcoming accounting period; a *cash budget,* depicting anticipated sources and uses of cash; and a *capital budget,* concerned with planned changes in fixed assets, are the component subsystems of the budgeting plan.

CASA VANA INN
1980 Operating Budget

REVENUES:
    Rooms   _____
    Food   _____
    Beverages   _____
    Telephone   _____
    Valet   _____
    Other   _____

        Total Revenues . . . . ._____

COST-OF-GOODS SOLD:
    Rooms   _____
    Food   _____
    Beverage   _____
    Telephone   _____
    Valet   _____

        Total Cost-of-Goods Sold . . . . ._____

GROSS OPERATING INCOME . . . .=========

OTHER EXPENSES:
    Admin. and General Expenses   _____
    Advertising and Promotion   _____
    Heat, Light, and Power   _____
    Repairs and Maintenance   _____
    Wages and Salaries   _____
    Insurance, Interest, and Taxes   _____
    Depreciation   _____

        Total Other Expenses . . . . ._____

NET INCOME . . . .=========

Table 5.1. Operating Budget Format

Operating Budgets

An operating budget can either be constructed for each operating department, or for responsibility centers (persons responsible for carrying the plan out), or both. This type of budget is useful in that it describes the distribution of financial resources throughout the operating departments. Operating budgets are usually reflections of cost percentages by items, based upon some forecasted level of sales. Since operational revenues usually are not forecasted with complete accuracy, and any deviation from the targeted sales level might render a static budget irrelevant, the concept of a variable budgeting format has become popular. Basically, assumptions are made concerning a forecast of sales volume, then deviation percentiles are calculated to yield a multirevenue, or dynamic budget, analysis. For example: The Casa Vana Inn forecasted rooms sales to be $500,000 next year and then calculated all the requisite costs of sales to come up with a static expenditure plan, based upon the anticipated sales level. Now, suppose the Inn experiences an actual level of $550,000, can management determine whether or not cost levels are potentially accurate? With a static plan this is a difficult analysis to achieve, but with a variable budget more than one sales level is budgeted. If the Casa Vana had a $500,000 expectation, then they may also have calculated several sales levels, say at 10 percent incremental deviations, on either side of the expectation. Hence, an 80 percent, 90 percent, 110 percent and 120 percent of planned revenues levels might be made up to highlight various cost profiles.

All in all, the operating budgets are essential to departmental decision-making, specification of desired performance levels, and serve as motivational incentives to managers. Since sales are the major premise upon which most allocations of expenditures are based, a dynamic budget is preferred to a static plan. Since sales can fluctuate throughout an infinite number of levels usually management selects percentage brackets for computation. The use of a computer-assisted budgeting system allows management the flexibility of having any sales level, with specified cost relationships, displayed. This significantly enhances management's ability to plan, coordinate, and control operations. Table 5.1 presents a typical format for an operating budget.

Cash Budget

The operating budget, prepared in terms of revenues and expenses, can be translated into cash receipts and disbursements to produce a cash budget. The resultant cash plan represents an analysis of cash flows for the hotel and serves as a projection of future cash balances. It simply reflects the time lag between the point-of-sale and the point-of-payment (the accounts receivable collection period). Short-term cash forecasts are usually made on a monthly basis and longer term prognostications only serve to show cash available for more permanent capital purposes. The generation of a cash budget is basically to alert management to a possible shortage of cash. This early notification is to enable the negotiation of loans, or other sources of funds, for working capital, in something less than a crisis situation. Hence, cash-on-hand, cash in the bank, and anticipated account collections give a reasonable expectation of the source of funds; while the accounts payable, and operating expenditures are illustrative of the uses of funds. The

CASA VANA INN
1980 Cash Budget

CASH ON HAND (and bank balances)

(plus) ESTIMATED COLLECTIONS (from cash sales, account receivable collections, etc.)

TOTAL SOURCES OF FUNDS
(minus) ESTIMATED CASH DISBURSEMENTS (operating expenses, etc.)

ESTIMATED CASH BALANCES

Table 5.2. Cash Budget Format

variance between uses and sources of funds is what the concept of cash budgeting is wholly concerned with. See Table 5.2 for the basic format of a cash budget.

Should management discover that forecasted cash balances are going to be too low (deficit balance), then either: 1) the accounts receivable (A/R) collection process must be accelerated; 2) the level of expenditures and payouts slowed; 3) some excess fixed assets must be sold off; or 4) funds must be borrowed to meet impending commitments. In any case, a forecasted cash deficit should be avoided since the hotel's inability to pay creditors will surely be detrimental to its financial well-being in the long run.

Capital Budget

The capital budget reflects management's projections for the acquisition of new assets. The construction of a new facility, the redecoration of a dining room, or the refurnishing of guest rooms are examples of capital expenditures that may require a capital budget. Although the capital budget depicts an expenditure plan over different time periods, it is not all that common in the lodging industry. Some large chain operations may require management to work within the confines of a capital budget, but basically the smaller operators usually do not use a capital budgeting tool. A capital budget is similar to an operating budget except that it deals with one specific project and not with an operating department.

Report of Operations

The report of operations is usually produced daily from the accounting department records and the (night) auditor's work. The accounting department functions as the hotel's data collection center and the audit provides some updated and verified balances in the departmental accounts. The generation of a daily report presents management with a quick reference of some essential financial indices and facilitates the eventual compilation of to-date information. The report, also referred to as the report of income or

CASA VANA INN
Report of Operations

1. ROOM ACTIVITY
  Rooms Sold _____
  Rooms Available _____
  No Shows _____
  Turnaways _____

2. REVENUES
  Rooms _____
  Food _____
  Beverage _____
  Telephone _____
  Valet _____
  Other _____

    Total Revenues ...._____

3. ACCOUNTS RECEIVABLE
  Previous Remaining Balance _____
  Plus Recent Transactions _____

    Net Balance..._____

4. CASH ACTIVITY
  Deposit _____
  Balance _____

5. STATISTICS
  Occupancy % _____
  Single Occupancy % _____
  Double Occupancy % _____
  Average Rate/Room _____
  Average Rate/Guest _____
  Food Sales % _____
  Beverage Sales % _____
  Room Sales % _____
  Payroll/Sales % _____
  Others _____

Table 5.3. Report of Operations Format

the auditor's daily report, is basically a recapitulation of overall guest transactions, a summary of banking activity, and a collection of departmental statistics. This report often tends to replace some departmental journals, especially in smaller properties, summary journals, and may even substitute for departmental worksheets.

The types of information usually contained in the report of operations are:

1. *Room Activity Summary*—information concerning the number of rooms available and sold; the profile of single and multiply occupied rooms; and the number of no-shows and turnaways, are important components of the report.

2. *Revenue Activity Summary*—an itemized summation of departmental (e.g., rooms, food, beverage, or telephone) sales from departmental sources are included to reflect the volume of business transactions.

3. *Account Receivable Summary*—a differentiation between departmental total sales into charged and cash categories. The charged sales represent accounts receivable and are shown on the report.

4. *Cash Activity Summary*—the internal volume of cash transactions and the external activity with the hotel's banking institution are important reflections of the hotel's cash position. Bank deposits, balances, and cash-on-hand information represents the cash flow status of the firm.

5. *Statistical Analysis*—a quick ratio of occupancies, payroll costs, food and beverage sales, and average room rate.

Also, common to the operations report is the presence of month and year to-date figures for comparisons of present operations with business in the past. The usefulness or utility of the daily report is surely increased by the presence of to-date information. Table 5.3 depicts an abbreviated report of operations form for the Casa Vana Inn. It should be noted that all of the information in this report can be used to indicate the short-term sources and uses of funds. Although labor costs are usually reflected in the daily report, it is imperative that management realize the infeasibility of computing up-to-date cost figures in all departmental areas. Hence, the report of operations is primarily a quick form of an income statement that does not contain significant information (on costs) to be of equivalent value to the hotel's management.

Income Statement

The purpose of the income statement is to report upon the profitability of the hotel for some period of time, usually one fiscal year. This statement is a summary of revenues received (from selling goods and services) and costs incurred (by cost of goods sold and operating expenses). Although this document is also referred to as the profit and loss statement, or the earnings statement, the hotel industry has preferred the income statement heading. The net profit (or loss) of the hotel is found by simply matching sales against the respective expenditures incurred. If revenues exceed expenses, net earnings results; but should the reverse be true, then a net loss is determined. A condensed version of an income statement can be found in Table 5.4.

An alternate format for the income statement and one that illustrates the flow of

CASA VANA INN

Income Statement—1980

SALES:

Rooms   _____

Food and Beverage   _____

   Total Sales .... _____

COST OF SALES:

   Cost of Goods Sold   _____

   Operating Expenses   _____

   Depreciation   _____

      Total Costs .... _____

OPERATING PROFIT .... _____

LESS: Interest and Taxes .... _____

NET INCOME (Profit) .... _____

Table 5.4. Condensed Income Statement

hotel information to the report can be found in Table 5.5. Note the identification of a contribution margin in Table 5.5. The contribution margin refers to those Gross Operating Profits that remain to cover the indirect, allocable expenditures and net profit. One basis for sound operating departmental comparisons might be on a contribution margin basis because most departments may not be adequately appraised against a net profit criterion.

CASA VANA INN

Income Statement—1980

SALES (and other income)

(minus) COST (direct) OF GOODS SOLD

CONTRIBUTION MARGIN

(minus) OTHER (indirect) OPERATING EXPENSES

NET PROFIT (or loss)

Table 5.5. Alternate Income Statement

The income statement provides data for the calculation of these important ratios:

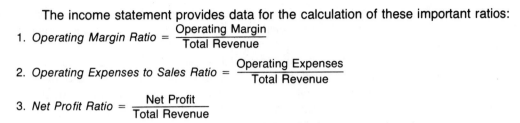

1. *Operating Margin Ratio* $= \dfrac{\text{Operating Margin}}{\text{Total Revenue}}$

2. *Operating Expenses to Sales Ratio* $= \dfrac{\text{Operating Expenses}}{\text{Total Revenue}}$

3. *Net Profit Ratio* $= \dfrac{\text{Net Profit}}{\text{Total Revenue}}$

4. *Operating Efficiency Ratio* $= \dfrac{\text{Total Income Before Fixed Charges}}{\text{Total Revenue}}$

5. *Number of Times Interest Earned Ratio* $= \dfrac{\text{Net Profit Before Income Taxes and Interest Expenses}}{\text{Interest Expense}}$

CASA VANA INN
Balance Sheet—June 26, 1980

ASSETS	LIABILITIES
Current Assets:	Current Liabilities:
Cash	Accounts Payable
Accounts Receivable	Notes Payable
Inventories	
Marketable Securities	Long Term Liabilities:
Notes Receivable	Mortgage
	Long Term Debt
Long Term Assets:	
Building	Owners' Equity:
Equipment	Capital Stock
Furnishings	Retained Earnings
Land	
Total Assets	Total Liabilities and
. . . . . ___	Owner's equity . . . . . ___

Table 5.6. Condensed Balance Sheet

Balance Sheet
The balance sheet reflects the soundness of the hotel by presenting its statement of financial position, for a stated period of time. By equating the firm's valuable resources (assets) with its financial obligations (liabilities) and its sources of interest (owner's equity), this report is simply a representation of the basic accounting equation:

assets = liabilities + owners' equity. The balance sheet provides a detailed summary of the hotel's net worth and enables the calculation of some important financial ratios (see Table 5.6).

Such ratios as the current ratio and the quick asset ratio can be derived from the balance sheet. These are good indices for finding how much current indebtedness the hotel has and also for determining what is a reasonable cash flow for the business. The current ratio (or working capital ratio) is found by dividing current assets by current liabilities; while the quick asset ratio (or acid-test ratio) is found by dividing the quick assets (cash, accounts receivable, notes receivable, and marketable securities) by the current liabilities. Both of these ratios are concerned with the working capital (current assets minus current liabilities) of the hotel. Additionally, the solvency ratio (total assets divided by total liabilities) and the debt-equity ratio (total debt to total equity) are two other important indices that can be derived from the balance sheet.

Combined Statements

A combination of the income statement and the balance sheet data can be used for the following ratios:

1. *Inventory Turnover Ratio* (calculated separately for food and beverages) $= \dfrac{\text{Cost of Sales}}{\text{Average Inventory}}$

2. *Accounts Receivable Turnover Ratio* $= \dfrac{\text{Total Credit Sales}}{\text{Average Accounts Receivable}}$

3. *Average Collection Period Ratio* $= \dfrac{365 \text{ Days}}{\text{Accounts Receivable Turnover}}$

4. *Fixed Asset Turnover Ratio* $= \dfrac{\text{Total Revenue}}{\text{Average Total Fixed Assets}}$

5. *Return on Owner's Equity Ratio* $= \dfrac{\text{Net Profit After Income Taxes}}{\text{Average Stockholder's Equity}}$

Summary

The purpose of managerial reports is to assist in the planning, coordination, and control of the hotel. Managers might rely on reports to enhance their ability to make decisions, monitor the hotel's activities, and provide necessary feedback in operations. Timely and concise reports have more chance for effecting the managerial process because they reduce uncertainty, delete unnecessary information, and minimize redundancies. Reports are usually of a statistical and/or financial nature. Standardization in reporting is a result of the *Uniform System of Accounts for Hotels* being widely accepted and its terminology perceived as the most correct.

The main objective of the reporting function is to give management control over the assets and liabilities of the hotel.

Financial statements are typically oriented toward managerial control while operating statistics are oriented at efficiency and productivity rates.

Key Concepts

Allocatable expenses

Assets

Balance sheet

Budgeting

Capital budget

Cash budget

Debt

Direct expenses

Efficiency rates

Financial reports

Income statement

Liabilities

Operating budget

Owners' equity

Productivity rates

Statistical reports

Uniform System of Accounts for
  Hotels

Questions for Discussion

1. What are the advantages of dynamic budgeting techniques (flexible sales level forecasts) over static or single level projections?

2. Which of the financial reports contains the best analysis of the financial position of the hotel?

3. What is the major shortcoming of the daily report of operations (which is common to the hotel industry)?

4. Explain the importance of the *Uniform System of Accounts* to the overall industry.

5. What criterion helps determine where the required report information comes from and where the reports are to be distributed, once they are generated?

Statistical Analysis of Operations

Chapter Objectives:

1. To emphasize the value of statistical analysis to hotel management effectiveness.

2. To illustrate the application of analysis techniques during various phases of the guest cycle.

3. To define the relevancy of contribution margins to specific areas of the hotel operation.

STATISTICS do not establish cause and effect relationships; they merely show relationships among data. Statistics serve as a guide for supplemental judgment in problem analysis and may be oversimplifications of a total situation. The most common uses of statistical analysis are in these three areas:

1. *Reducing Uncertainty.* The quick calculation of a ratio or percent often generates enough information to reduce uncertainty about a given problem situation.

2. *Removing Bias.* Subjective evaluations are usually biased and prejudiced and the objectivity of quantitative analysis is believed to be a sound method for removing much of an analytical bias.

3. *Delineating Decision Alternatives.* The reduction of decision choices, through mathematical analysis, is one of statistics' best attributes.

Basic Statistical Tools

Probabilities

Also important to managerial effectiveness is an insight into the likelihood of an event occurring. If the hotel has forecasted 100 percent occupancy for next Sunday, and someone calls up wishing to book an additional room, the reservation clerk may over-book the hotel knowing the probability of all reservations materializing is something less than perfect. Probabilities range from zero to one and are determined either subjectively or objectively. Subjective probabilities are those weights or factors produced by an educated guess or opinion. These qualitative criteria give credence to the theory of management as an art. The quantitative or objective probability factors are derived from measurements of past events, rigorous testing, or forecasting. A combination of probability factors normally is sufficient to produce a reliable prediction of future occurrence. An example of this combined process can be found in job placement. Prior to hiring an employee for hotel accounting work, management may require the candidate to demonstrate some accounting skills and also undergo a personal interview. The applicant's professional talents and an interviewer's subjective evaluation of the person are put together to create a predictor of job success. The candidate with the highest probability of job success would most likely be hired.

Basically, probabilities may be conditional or independent, in nature. A *conditional probability* is one that is directly influenced by a previous event. If the number of guests staying in the hotel is known to be a reliable index for determining the potential number of diners in the restaurant, then the probability of the accuracy of the second event's outcome is conditioned by the first event (occupancy). Although there may be many conditional relationships within the hospitality facility, little research has been performed to substantiate this claim. Unconditional, or *independent probabilities* are those that have no relation to and are not influenced by the occurrence of any preceding events. The tossing of a coin is the typical example used to illustrate independence. The probability of a head turning up, when a coin is flipped, is .50 regardless of how many times the coin has been flipped before. Similarly, the probability of a hotel guest requesting room service is in no way directly influenced by any other occurrences within the hotel.

Sampling

All statistics are based on a *sample.* If a sample is large enough and is selected correctly, it will be *representative* of the population or universe from which it is drawn. Hence, a sample is a subset of observations selected to represent the larger population, in general. It is simply impractical to ask all guests how they enjoyed the cleanliness of the bathroom, for example, and so a survey of twenty guests may suffice to provide a reasonable opinion of how all guests liked the housekeeping work. The *size* of the sample is critical and is a function of the number of possible observations. A restaurant serving fifty portions of seafood newburg may be wise to select five platters for quality control. Is this representative? The size of the sample is usually a function of the number of irregular outcomes and the total size of the population being surveyed. The main points here being that the sample should be selected without bias from a subset of the population under analysis.

The most reliable sampling technique is called a *random sample.* Simply stated, a sample is selected from the population by pure chance. For example, every seventh guest is polled for his opinion of the hotel's courtesy toward the public. The basic test of the random sampling procedure is that every observation in the population must have an equal chance of selection. A refinement of the random methodology, making it simpler and more reliable, is to employ a stratification scheme. In other words, the population of observations is divided into several categories based upon some known characteristics. All females, or all guests who had single rooms, or all guests who dined in the hotel last night, and the like, are illustrations of stratifications. A sample drawn at random from within each group is a stratified random sample. This sample tends to reduce or explain prejudices and biases according to known characteristics in the stratification. Hence, a randomly-selected, representative, stratified sample, free from bias, is the most desirable.

Too often hotel statistics and lodging industry statistics are drawn from a sample of questionable representation. The profile of contributors to the *1977 U.S. Lodging Industry* annual report of hotel and motor hotel operations (by Laventhol and Horwath, pp. 13–14) was stated as:

> The data submitted by contributors to this report have been divided into 10 categories . . . for 42 different groups. This enables us to offer the following profile of the typical contributor, based on the use of the various measures of central tendency:

Age	Built during the period 1960–69
Size	150–299 rooms
Average Rate	$18–$23.99
Occupancy	60–69%
Sales Volume	$1,500,000–2,999,999

| Restaurant Operation | . . . food and beverage revenue is 50–74% of room sales |
| Other | affiliated with a chain . . . |

The sample is split among the major geographic areas and by the type of market served along lines quite similar to those of the lodging industry as a whole, according to the 1972 Census of Business.

Is this sample representative of the U.S. lodging market for that period? How many hotels or motor hotels make up the sample? Do any of the establishments actually have these characteristics? What is meant by the "typical contributor?" How applicable is the data in the report to the lodging establishments that are not chain affiliated; do not have sales of at least $1.5 million; and have an occupancy of less than 60 percent? These questions are difficult to answer. Hence, managerial references and statistical tools must be used cautiously, and attention must be paid to the characteristics of the sample the data represents.

Central Tendency

The most common measure of central tendency is the *average.* The main problem with using the term average is that there are three types of averages, all of which are capable of producing different statistical results. The *mean* is the arithmetic average of a set of data and is found by dividing the sum of the observations by the number of observations made. The mean is usually closely related to the median. The *median* is the geometric average; it is the middle figure of a set of data and is found by rank ordering the observations from low to high, and counting down to the middle-ranked observation. The third average is called the *mode* and is defined as the most frequently occurring observation in a set of data.

For the eleven-year sales figures presented in Table 6.1, the mean, median, and modes are calculated; note their differences. From the same sample the averages were found to be: $2,545,454; $2,600,000; and $3,000,000. So even when an average figure is given, the reader may not know very much about the data. The median is believed to be the best description of central tendency, since it is not bias due to extreme high and/or low observations (as is the mean), or because of the frequency of a value occurring (as is the mode). The 1974 version of the *Lodging Industry* report makes the following point:

> To make our analysis more precise, our computations in this report are virtually all "median" figures rather than averages. This is done because the average (or arithmetic mean) can be heavily influenced by extremes—the very high numbers and the very low ones . . . . We use the mean very seldom in the report so that most of the amounts and ratios are medians. We

will continue to use the medians because we believe that they are the most representative of the data we analyze.[1]

Hence, managers relying heavily on broad industry reports must realize that the best method for treating the report's data is as an approximation. The authors themselves comment: "The data provided by this report are not intended to be standards of performance for the lodging industry, but they do represent guidelines with which operating results can be compared. We suggest that several analyses be selected for comparison purposes, depending upon those factors which you believe most influence the results."[2]

Sample: 1967–1977 Revenues
Casa Vana Inn, Inc.

1967	$1,850,000
1968	2,155,000
1969	2,600,000
1970	2,000,500
1971	2,222,500
1972	3,000,000
1973	2,222,500
1974	3,000,000
1975	2,600,500
1976	3,000,000
1977	3,349,000
Total Revenues	$28,000,000

The averages for this data are:

1. Mean:

$$\mu = \frac{\Sigma x}{n}$$

μ = arithmetic mean
Σx = sum of observations
n = number of observations

Therefore, $\mu = \dfrac{\$28,000,000}{11} = \$2,545,454$ average

---

1. Laventhol, Krekstein, Horwath and Horwath, *Lodging Industry,* Philadelphia, PA, 1974, pp. 13–14.
2. Ibid., p. 14.

2. Median:

    m = geometric mean (middle
      ranked observation)

    Rank Ordered Data (Low to High)

1)	$1,850,000
2)	2,000,500
3)	2,155,000
4)	2,222,500
5)	2,222,500
6)	2,600,000 ← mean value
7)	2,600,500
8)	3,000,000
9)	3,000,000
10)	3,000,000
11)	3,349,000

3. Mode:

    f = most frequently occurring observation
    f = $3,000,000 Average

Table 6.1. Averages

When all three of the averages come out very close together, the data can be shown to approximate a normal distribution. The normal distribution merely implies that if the data was graphed it would be presented as a symmetric, bell-shaped curve with the mean, median, and mode all falling at the same point. (See Fig. 6.1.) If the mean and median are different, the distribution is described as being *skewed.* Skewness illustrates the effects of extreme values in the sample and a deviation in the averages. (See Fig. 6.2.)

Operating Statistics

Quantitative analysis has become a very significant portion of the hotel information system. The heavy dependence placed upon hotel statistics is characteristic of the trend toward more numbers and less qualitative or subjective evaluation. Although there are several different ratios and percentiles that hotel operators may employ as performance checks on operations, the most common denominator for these statistics is room sales. Room sales are used as a base because they are assumed to be the best indicator of profit efficiency and are a reliable index to the overall business. Because the list of statistical calculations may be extended to several dozen indicators, only some essential yardsticks for operational measures will be presented. The statistics will be segmented along pre-sale and post-sale criteria.

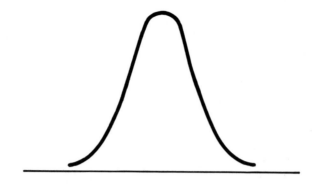

Figure 6.1. Normal Curve

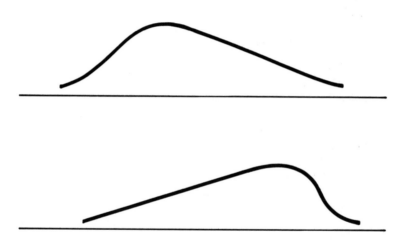

Figure 6.2. Skewed Distributions

Pre-Sale

1. *Room Availability Forecast.* The number of guest rooms that are available at any point in the future is an important fact for management to know. Primarily the calculation is a function of the reservations forecast, the hotel's no-show factor (those persons with reservations that will not register), the number of stayovers (the difference between the previous night's occupancy and the number of guests expected to depart), and the number of available rooms. This calculation (Formula One) may tend to be misleading and often leads to overbooking, but management should have an estimation of future sales to plan operations by.

   For example, the Casa Vana Inn has seven hundred and fifty rooms and desires to forecast the number of available rooms for a holiday four weeks in the future. The reservation and no-show information is received from the reservations department and the number of guests remaining from the previous night is derived from a similar review of future reservation requests.

Formula One: RAF = (AV) − [(R) − (R) (NSF) + (S)]

where,   RAF = Room Availability Forecast
AV = Number of Rooms Available
R = Number of Reservations (Forecasted)
NSF = No-Show Factor
S = Number of Stayovers
(S = No. of Occupied Rooms −
No. of Rooms to Open)

Knowing that the number of available rooms is 750 and the reservation forecast for the day in question is 250 with a no-show factor of 10 percent, the reservations department also discloses that the previous night shows 450 rooms sold, while the number of guests expected to depart represents 200 rooms. Using the formula to analyze room availability yields:

$$RAF = (750) − [250 − 250(.10) + (450 − 200)] = 275$$

So now management is cognizant of the number of unsold rooms (conditional upon the option of subtracting out the no-show factor) that remain available for sale.

2. *Forecasted Room Cost Percentage.* The number of room types and the expected sales in each category form the basis of a forecasted sales mix. The information on room availability may lead to the identification of this mix, which may lend itself to a pre-cost analysis. Should management be aware of the estimated costs per room occupancy (housekeeping, supplies, and energy costs) then a pre-cost percentage can be computed as a review of room rates prior to the sale. (See Formula Two.)

Formula Two: $FRCP = \dfrac{(FSM) \ (SROC)}{(FSM) \ (RR)}$

where,   FRCP = Forecasted Room Cost Percentage
FSM = Forecasted Sales Mix
SROC = (Respective) Standardized Room
Occupancy Cost
RR = Respective Room Rate or Price

The Casa Vana Inn estimates that single rooms cost $6.40 and double rooms cost $8.40 per occupancy. The rooms rent for $16.00 and $21.00, respectively. If the management knows that of the 475 rooms it has sold, referring to the above example, 158 are singles, then the forecasted room cost percentage will be:

$$FRCP = \frac{(158) \ (6.40) + (317) \ (8.40)}{(158) \ (16) + (317) \ (21)} = \frac{3,674}{9,185} = .40$$

Hence, the forecasted rooms cost percentqge is 40 percent or for every dollar of room revenue forty cents will go to pay for the cost of providing the room for sale. This information is valuable to management prior to the implementation of a firm set of prices. In essence it enables a before-the-sale review of costs and margins.

This same type of calculation could be employed for any other operating department such as food, beverage, phone, or valet, as an a priori feedback on cost and price profiles.

3. *Contribution Margin Analysis.* The contribution margin (CM) is defined as the difference between an item's selling price and the direct cost of the item being sold. (See Formula Three.) The $16.00 single room that costs $6.40 to maintain and prepare for sale has a CM of $9.60;

Formula Three: $CM = RR\text{-}SROC$

where, CM = Contribution Margin
RR = Room Rate or Price
$SROC$ = Standardized Room Occupancy Cost

while the double room sells for $21.00 and has a cost of $8.40 yielding a CM of $12.60. The two rooms each have a cost-of-goods-sold ratio of 40 percent; but the Casa Vana management is interested in which room type is sold. Since the CM relates to profit and fixed (or indirect) expenses, the product or room with the highest contribution is the one management will favor. This analysis can be done for any product available for sale.

4. *CM Adjustment Factor.* Knowing the contribution margin for each product (or room) enables management to evaluate trade-offs among its various product lines prior to the point-of-sale or even after the sale. Since the contribution margin percent (CMP) is the complement of the direct cost of goods sold percent, management is able to develop a contribution margin adjustment factor for evaluating product mixes among its goods and services.

Formula Four: $CMAF = \dfrac{CM_H}{CM_L}$

where, $CMAF$ = Contribution Margin Adjustment Factor
CM_H = Dollar CM of Higher CM Product
CM_L = Dollar CM of Lower CM Product

To determine how much of one product yields the same contribution margin as the sales of another product requires a two-step calculation:

STEP ONE: Determine the contribution margin adjustment factor using Formula Four.

STEP TWO: Find the contribution margin equality factor (which equates the margins of the two items for sale) using Formula Five.

For example, given the two room types and their respective contribution margins, the management of the Casa Vana Inn wants to know if they sell fifteen double rooms, how many single rooms would they have to sell to equal the derived CM?

Formula Five: $CMEF = (CMAF)(\text{No. of } CM_H \text{ Products})$

where, $CMEF$ = Contribution Margin Equality Factor
(i.e. number of CM_L
products needed to be sold)
$CMAF$ = Contribution Margin Adjustment Factor
No. of CM_H = Number of CM_H products
expected to be sold

STEP ONE: Determine CMAF
$CMAF = \$12.60 \div \$9.60 = 1.3125$

STEP TWO: Find CMEF
$CMEF = (1.31)(15) = 19.65 \text{ or } 20 \text{ rooms}$

So for the trade-off of 15 double rooms, the hotel would have to sell 20 singles to receive the equivalent contribution margin dollars. This index is not very widely used in the industry but may become more popular if selling margins continue to tighten.

Post-Sale

Most of the familiar computations of the lodging industry take place after the point-of-sale. This type of approach informs management of business situations following their occurrence and may not be as beneficial as some pre-sale analyses in avoiding problem areas.

Formula Six: $\% \text{ Occ} = \dfrac{RMS}{RMA}$

where, $\% \text{ Occ}$ = Percentage of Occupancy
RMS = Number of Rooms Sold
RMA = Number of Rooms Available for
Occupancy

1. *Percent of Occupancy.* The percentage of occupancy is the best known and most widely used statistic of the hotel business. Believed to be an adequate reflection of the hotel's ability to attract clientele in the market and a vital index of the hotel's usage, the overall occupancy figure is easily calculated. Formula Six relates the number of rooms sold to the number of rooms available, yielding the percent of occupancy.

Assume the Casa Vana sells its estimated 475 rooms on a particular evening, what is the percent of occupied rooms? $475 \div 750 = 63.3\%$

2. *Percentage of Multiple Occupancy.* Knowing the percentage of rooms sold may not reflect the

$$\text{Formula Seven:} \quad \% \ M \ Occ \ = \ \frac{\text{No. Guests} - \text{RMS}}{\text{RMS}}$$

where,   % M Occ = Percent of Multiple Occupancy
No. Guests = Number of Guests
RMS = Number of Rooms Sold

complete profile of the hotel's operation. The number of rooms sold that were occupied by more than one person (multiple occupancy) can be derived through Formula Seven.

Knowing that the Casa Vana Inn accommodated 750 guests in its 450 sold rooms yields a multiple occupancy percentage of:

$$\% \ M \ Occ = (750 - 450) \div 450$$
$$= 300 \div 450$$
$$= 66\frac{2}{3}\%$$

3. *Average Number of Guests Per Room.* Just as important as knowing the percentage of multiple occupancy is knowing the average number of guests per room. Should the hotel determine that the average room sold accommodates three or four persons, whereas the facility was only designed for single or double occupancies, this may lead to managerial action. The average number of guests can be found by using Formula Eight. The Casa Vana Inn figures show that it housed an average of 1.66 guests with its 450 sold rooms and 750 accommodated guests.

$$\text{Formula Eight:} \quad ANG \ = \ \frac{\text{No. Guests}}{\text{RMS}}$$

where,   ANG = Average Number of Guests Per Room Sold
No. Guests = Number of Guests Accommodated
RMS = Number of Rooms Sold

4. *Average Rate Per Room.* The average rate per room is the mean of room revenue dollars acquired through the number of rooms sold. This index gives management feedback on its rate schedule and its actual sales mix.

Since the desk clerk at the Casa Vana Inn was given room rate ranges, rather than structured fixed rates, the total sales mix produced an average rate per room of $19.11 ($8600 ÷ 450).

$$\text{Formula Nine:} \quad ARR \ = \ \frac{R \ REV}{RMS}$$

where,   ARR = Average Rate per Room Sold
R REV = Room Revenues (or income)
RMS = Number of Rooms Sold

The average room rate is *not* the rate the hotel advertises or charges any guest. It is a weighted average of all rooms sold and the dollars collected (or to be collected) from those sales.

5. *Average Rate Per Guest.* Some additional information about the rate scheme can be found using Formula Ten to calculate the average rate per guest. This statistic gives management a reflection of both the magnitude of occupancy and dollars collected.

$$\textbf{Formula Ten:} \quad ARG = \frac{R\ REV}{No.\ Guests}$$

where,   ARG = Average Room Rate per Guest
R REV = Room Revenues
No. Guests = Number of Guests Accommodated

Knowing that the Casa Vana Inn had 750 accommodated guests and room revenues of $8,600, the formula yields an average rate per guest of: $8,600 ÷ 750 = $11.46.

The difference between the average rate per room and the average rate per guest can be explained by multiple occupancies. Although most costs are related on a per room basis, perhaps a feasible base for more statistics should be on a per guest basis.

6. *Credit Card Volume.* Due to the popularity of credit cards, the delayed and discounted cash flows to the hotel should be analyzed and understood. One statistic that provides insight into this area is the credit card usage index (Formula Eleven).

$$\textbf{Formula Eleven:} \quad CCV = \frac{CCS}{TS}$$

where,   CCV = Credit Card Volume
CCS = Credit Card Charged Sales
TS = Total Sales of the Hotel

One of the shortcomings of the credit card volume indicator is that it does not reflect charge balances that are outstanding during the guest's cycle, which impacts upon cash flow.

7. *Account Receivable Load.* Similar to the charge card technique, some innkeepers have opted to calculate and maintain an index of accounts receivable (Formula Twelve). This is better for

$$\textbf{Formula Twelve:} \quad ARL = \frac{A/R}{TS}$$

where,   ARL = Accounts Receivable Load Factor
A/R = Accounts Receivable Dollar Levels
TS = Total Sales of the Hotel

reflecting the trend and volume of charges made during the guest's occupancy, and can be related to bad debt risks to notify management of potentially dangerous financial situations.

Assume that of the 750 guests in the Casa Vana Inn, each charged their room rate per day and paid cash for their other transactions. What then is the hotel's account receivable load for a volume of $8,600 in charge sales and $34,400 in total sales? $8,600 ÷ $34,400 = 25%.

8. *Operating Departmental Cost Percentages.* The costs incurred by all the operating departments are usually compared to the revenues of their particular departments (if they signify revenue areas), the total hotel sales, and often to room sales. The comparison to room sales is made because it is assumed that any change in room sales volume will initiate a change in other departmental costs. This may or may not be the case. Formula Thirteen shows the ratio of departmental cost percentages to total sales.

$$\textbf{Formula Thirteen:} \quad OCP = \frac{ODC}{TS}$$

$$\text{where,} \quad OCP = \text{Operating Cost Percentage}$$
$$ODC = \text{Operating Department Costs}$$
$$TS = \text{Total Sales}$$

For example, if the Casa Vana Inn had a $44,000 energy cost for a total sales volume of $480,000, this would represent a 9.17 percent cost of sales or $44,000 ÷ $480,000 = 9.17%.

9. *Productivity Index.* A sound means for evaluating labor productivity (be it in the front desk area, the kitchen, or service personnel) is to relate departmental payroll costs and/or the number of employees to departmental or total sales. This index usually produces a comparable factor for appraisal.

So although Formula Fourteen is but one variation of a few possible productivity scales, it can be used to reflect worker output with sales output. At the Casa Vana Inn, for example, the 25 foodservice employees generated food sales of $50,000 for the month of June. This gave the management an index of $2,000 sales per employee, on average, for that month. This is good considering the previous month's index was only $1,200 per employee. $50,000 ÷ 25 = $2,000.

$$\textbf{Formula Fourteen:} \quad PI = \frac{DS}{\text{No. EMPL}}$$

$$\text{where,} \quad PI = \text{Productivity Index}$$
$$DS = \text{Departmental Sales}$$
$$\text{No. EMPL} = \text{Number of Employees}$$

Industry Statistics

There are several independent sources of industry information available for the hotel sector. Although these indices have been prepared against, or based upon, different sample groups (of various sizes), most proprietors fail to identify or consider these vast and great variances. Often individual properties do not follow industry trends nor do they depend on the economic index for the country as a whole. Instead, an operator would be wise to try and compare only with similar operations based on geographic location and type of clientele. Hotels in different cities, for example, may pay different taxes, have different costs of investments, and have different room rates and configurations. All these factors point out the great diversity among hotels and the tremendous problematic situation that may arise from placing too much faith and emphasis on industry averages.

Statistical Relationships

Although the calculation of operating statistics appears useful, the interrelationship between operating departments, costs, and occupancies is hardly ever related in the hospitality area. The concept of *correlation analysis* is an attempt at summarizing relationships between variables. A large relationship is designated by a correlation value

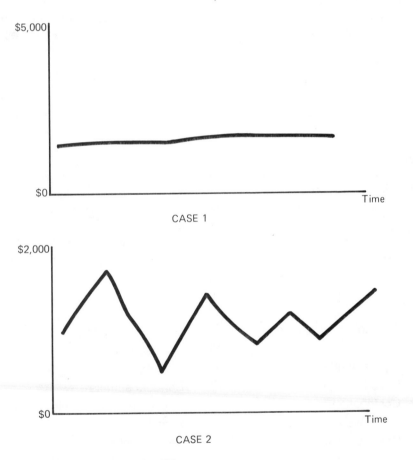

Figure 6.3. Varying Statistics

of 1.00, and no relationship is signified by a value of 0.00. If the number of registered guests, for example, has a slight or little known effect on restaurant sales, then the correlation is expressed as a value between .500 and 0.00. When a complete opposite movement is observed among two variables then a correlation value of −1.00 is appropriate. Should the price of suites be so exorbitant that no one ever rents one, then the correlation between suite prices and sales is −1.00 inasmuch as the prices actually resulted in a zero sales level. Essentially, correlations measure whether or not high values of one variable tend to move with high or low values of another variable.

Oftentimes business managers fall prey to inaccuracies in judging the importance or validity of statistical analysis. A statistical conclusion based on too small a sample, or one that is strongly biased, is termed a *spurious* relationship (not a true representation of the population it is supposed to depict). A more common error lies in the assumption that the more size, space, or amount of attention given an item, the more valuable or important the subject is. Should the media give a disproportionately large amount of copy to a given topic, the reader tends to believe it is of unequaled importance. This type of relationship is termed *semi-attachment* and is something that innkeepers need to be aware of. The use of charts and graphs that illustrate statistical relationships must be used with caution. By constructing variable proportions and altering the values along the abscissa and ordinate, a desired result or impression can usually be achieved. Figure 6.3 is an example of proving that hotel managers' salaries for the Casa Vana Inn have been stable over time (Case 1), or have been unstable over the same time period (Case 2).

Summary

The lack of sound, objective data has been misleading to management, specifically, and the hotel industry, in general. Hotel operators must realize that statistical indices are simple mathematical computations that can be very helpful in analyzing, planning, and coordinating the firm. Statistics only illustrate relationships among data; they do not link variables as to cause and effect. Probabilities are used to reflect the likelihood or chance that something might happen.

Key Concepts

Account receivable load	Multiple occupancy
Average	Normal distribution
Central tendency	Probabilities
Conditional probabilities	Random sample
Contribution margin	Representative sample
Correlation analysis	Sampling
Credit card volume	Semi-attachment
Independent probabilities	Skewness

Mean   Spurious
Median   Statistics
Mode

Questions for Discussion

1. What are the common uses of statistical information?

2. What is a probability factor and by what means can it be determined?

3. Explain the difference between a conditional probability and an independent probability.

4. What is a sample? What is a stratified random sample and how does this differ from a representative sample?

5. What are some of the inherent problems surrounding industry averages and comparison statistics among hotel operators?

6. Why might the mean, median, and mode (for a set of data) differ?

7. What does the concept of skewness involve? What does it mean with regards to the data in a distribution?

8. List some pre-sale and some post-sale hotel operating statistics and explain the data required to make each calculation.

9. When using the room availability forecasting formula, what effects do the no-show and stayover factors have on available space?

10. How is a forecasted room sales mix developed?

11. Explain the contribution margin concept and what it is a contribution towards.

12. What is the credit card volume statistic? What is its relationship to effective cash flow for the hotel?

13. What are the possible shortcomings resulting from too much emphasis on industry statistics?

14. What is the best criteria to use for productivity evaluations?

PART

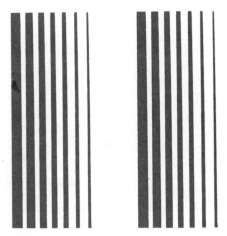

INFORMATION CONCEPTS
AND SYSTEMS

Data Processing Concepts

Chapter Objectives:

1. To introduce the concept of data processing in a general context.

2. To explain the basic underpinnings of information and systems concepts.

3. To sketch the evolution of data processing techniques from early manual procedures through to modern electronic networks.

4. To introduce the objectives of the data processing function.

ALTHOUGH data processing is not a new idea, the development of automated, electronic technology has vastly altered the concept. The lodging industry has significantly benefited from faster and more accurate means of data measurement, collection, processing, and handling. Accompanying these changes are complex suboperations required to generate desired *output,* or *input* to a system in a meaningful context. The manual tasks that once required a robot-like mentality to perform have become automated; this frees management to allocate personnel to functions requiring human capabilities. This form of *human engineering* has enabled the hotel to reorganize its *data processing* network, and has enhanced its ability to comprehend its functional operating departments. Recently, hotel data processing expanded its scope to include computer applications and *data base* management technology. As more and more advanced hotel computer systems are designed and implemented, the degree of distributed intelligence (the capability of computer processing at remote locations) throughout the hotel will significantly increase. This chapter presents some of the basic underpinnings of *information* and systems concepts and a chronological background of the data processing cycle. Chapter 8 deals with the evolution and design of computer systems, and their impact upon the business organization.

Information and Systems Concepts

Regardless of the organization, management has always generated some system of information by which to evaluate its performance. Recent pressures, however, require that a more formalized and detailed information network be utilized. Hence, general business systems have become more structured and better automated in an attempt to facilitate the flow and handling of relevant information. Traditional manual systems (the kinds common in the hospitality industry) have been ineffective in processing large volumes of data, and as the size and complexity of individual hotels continues to increase, so too does the demand for more information.

Information

Information can be simply defined as that which adds to what is known or alleged. For example, a color photograph contains more information than does a black and white one. Information can serve three general purposes. First, it can increase one's *knowledge* about a situation or occurrence. Second, it can reduce *uncertainty,* as in the case of decision-making. And third, information provides *feedback* for evaluation and future planning. Although information normally expands awareness, it should be noted that it may not make the identical impression on all who are exposed to it.

Knowledge, Uncertainty, and Feedback

As information from data of variables becomes available, management learns more about the business and its *environment.* Since information possesses the capability of reducing uncertainty, it is an essential component in the decision-making process. Historically, hotel management has suffered from the collection of too much irrelevant information and, therefore, has had trouble discerning valuable feedback on departmental operations. Information generated within the organization is affected by the delineation of specialized areas for analysis. The number of operating departments and number of employees will lead to certain parameters for information generation. If either wrong data or correct data are processed incorrectly, the resultant information will be in error.

Pressures for Information

There have been numerous reasons for an increase in the amount of information generated within the hotel. First, the increased *growth* of individual companies has been so rapid that it has rendered some operations almost incomprehensible; at least from an administrative point of view. For example, on the microlevel the construction of enormous hotel properties, with more than several hundred rooms, has certainly impacted upon the hotel's ability to adequately chart, maintain, and monitor the guest cycle. The expansion of chain operations, the development of larger franchise networks, and the popularity of conglomerate formations have decentralized operations to the point that information centralization is tedious but mandatory for corporate or macrolevel monitoring and control. Given trends in the economy, tighter costs and selling margins are becoming a reality. In order for hotel managers to meet the goals of the firm, a better understanding of costs and sales information is required.

A second important factor leading to increased pressures for information can be found in the many different forms of ownership and managerial contracting in the hotel industry. The need for *accountability* has further compounded the increasing pressure for faster and more complete knowledge. Internal reports to management and owners, as well as external reports to stockholders and the public, have become standard for most companies.

A third factor leading to additional needs has been the recent tightening of governmental *regulations* regarding reporting at the local, state, and federal levels. Firms are being required to maintain and report more information about their enterprises than they had to in the past. All in all, the lodging entrepreneur has experienced an increasing concern for information and a need for an efficient data processing network to formulate the facts.

Value of Information

The value of information can be a function of its availability, its timeliness, its comprehensiveness, and/or its accuracy. Information that is free from bias and that may be adaptable to more than one decision area is more valuable than that which is limited and prejudiced. Similarly, the degree of unexpectedness (or improbability) of a message is a key factor enhancing the amount of information it contains. Information can flow within the firm by written document, spoken message, hand or facial signal, person to machine transference, machine to machine relay, or some combination of these. The more sources the information must flow through, the greater the risk of deletion and/or alteration of the content.

The Systems Concept

A regular or orderly arrangement of component parts placed in an interrelated series, necessary to accomplish some operation, is termed a *system.* In reality, however, most systems are made up of linked subsystems and tend to satisfy more than one purpose. A complex system, for example, is one that can be factored into its respective subsystems for analysis. The hotel can be viewed as a complex system having reservations, registration, housekeeping, and accounting as some of its principal subsystems.

All systems operate in an *environment.* The environment is defined as everything outside the system that effects or is affected by the system. Hence, personnel, hardware, and software constitute a system's environment. In a business context, a system is a structure that coordinates the activities and operations of the organization, and serves to give clarity to departmental functions with regard to the overall scheme.

The term system has become overused and often misused. The advertising community, for example, has come to use the word as a product attachment; to let it mean

---

PHASE I. System Analysis
- a. fact finding
- b. fact analysis

PHASE II. System Design
- a. clerical procedures
- b. processing control
- c. data base construction
- d. forms and reports development
- e. programming development
- f. equipment selection

PHASE III. System Implementation
- a. personnel training
- b. system testing
- c. system conversion
- d. maintenance
- e. auditing

PHASE IV. System Refinement
- a. system usage
- b. updating
- c. adjusting (deleting or extending)
- d. maintenance of continuous system operation

Table 7.1. System Life Cycle

whatever anyone wants it to mean, the goal being to lend a superior scientific aura to the advertised product. The term is intended to explain real relationships; instead it has become confusing and misleading. The injector razor system and the recessed filter cigarette system are examples of inappropriate usage. More correct usage would include the solar system, a telephone system, a stereo component system, and a computer system.

General System Life Cycle

A thorough analysis of the user's needs and values is necessary for determining a system's performance requirements; while a knowledge and identification of environmental factors is crucial to an effective system design. An understanding of the hotel's available resources and its time framework is also an important consideration when constructing a system to accomplish a desired objective.

The actual system design is contingent upon the specification and isolation of a *purpose.* Once the purpose is known, the required component parts can be secured and analyzed. An interrelating and/or interfacing of the system's parts completes the system design and enables implementation, analysis and evaluation by management.

The life cycle of a general system can be thought of as a four-phase process ranging from problem situation and environmental analysis, through design and implementation, to refinement. A brief outline of the cycle is given in Table 7.1 and the individual stages are discussed in detail below.

Systems Analysis

Prior to the formal development of a system, a fact finding and fact analysis phase should be completed. The resources of the firm, the availability of input data, and the requirements of system output should be evaluated and defined. The needs of the hotel, for example, and the capability of individual system components must be equated in order to produce an optimal information arrangement.

System Design

The actual development of a system is simplified if a thorough system analysis has been performed. The identification of input data will lead to clerical specifications and the designing of forms for this purpose. A data base, or a procedural process leading to *storage,* may be required. Normally, the change in input required to produce a desired output will lead to the construction of a data base, and a determination of the size of the base. A clear statement of the flow and computational evaluations that information must undergo will not only enhance the programming of a system, but will also lead to the selection of the requisite equipment required to satisfy the system design. The largest single activity in the design of a system is usually in program development. A hotel might design an elaborate communication system between the front desk and the housekeeping department or may elect traditional procedures for exchanging and disseminating information using a telephone. In either case, a logical information flow and control should be designed to insure a proper input and output from the system.

Systems Implementation

Once a system is designed, its implementation should naturally follow. Perhaps the most important factor leading to a successful system application lies with the training and educating of personnel in the system environment. The best designed system may fail if the employees are unfamiliar or unable to properly operate it. The weakest link in any system will certainly constrain the overall performance of the whole package, and system operators and information users must be aware of this.

A system should be tested to verify its feasibility, accuracy, and reliability. Should any problems arise, the system may require conversion and therefore a flexible system design is preferred. An ongoing maintenance and auditing of the system components serves to provide continual feedback on the status of successful implementation and operation of the system.

System Refinement

During the course of system usage, it may be justifiable to either abandon or expand particular system segments. The usage of inappropriate or redundant input or output, for example, may necessitate a programming or design change. Should the system refinement fail to enhance the system operation, then a thorough review and evaluation of the original analysis and design is warranted. A major dysfunction within the system may necessitate an innovative design or simply a return to the starting point. Basically, maintenance of the system's continuous operation is an essential phase of the system's cycle.

Machines in Systems

Over the past decades systems have become very automated and machinery has been proven capable of performing almost any function that does not contain physical impossibilities or logical contradictions. Machines may be used for collecting data, making measurements, transmitting signals, performing intricate calculations, or controlling physical conditions.

There are: 1) nonautomated systems that consist only of humans (for example, the U.S. Congress), 2) semiautomated systems that are composed of people in a system's role (as in a computer system), and 3) fully automated systems in which the human capability is only required for initiation, setting criteria of performance, and deciding on corrective behavior (for example, an unmanned spaceship). Hence, the only limiting aspects of machine capabilities appear to be in the design of its control. Hotel data processing systems, for example, have become semiautomated during the past few years, whereas formerly they were strictly nonautomated.

What is a Computer?

The computer is a managerial tool capable of processing large quantities of data very rapidly and accurately. It can perform arithmetic (addition, subtraction, multiplication, and division) and logical (ranking, sorting, and assembling) operations and can dispense results in a variety of formats. Computers can repeat programmed instructions almost endlessly without error, can hold large quantities of information in storage, and can be used to simulate decision-modelling situations. There are basically two broad categories of computing machines: digital and analog.

The digital computer operates similar to a hand calculator and is based upon discrete steps. Digital computers are capable of storing programs and have a high level of precision and efficiency. The analog computer is akin to a slide rule. The number scales are not precise and it is fairly difficult to identify specific output. Hence, the digital computer has made a significant contribution to the business community while the analog machine is reserved for scientific applications.

Figure 7.1. A Simplistic Overview of a Manual-Based Data Processing System

Data Processing

Data processing can be defined as the transformation of raw, isolated, unevaluated facts to comprehensive, integrated information. A listing of individual guest accounting entries, for example, may not have much meaning per se, but a compiled summary of the ledger may lend significant understanding. It is the objective of a data processing system to take input (data) and formulate output (information) that will have a higher level of clarity and intelligibility. The basic data processing system, see Figure 7.1, consists primarily of a three-phase, input-process-output procedure. This brief overview is a simplification of a manual-based cycle that must be drastically revised and redefined so as to incorporate the advancements made through computer-based assistance. Table 7.2 illustrates some hotel functions using the three-phase data processing mode.

The Data Processing System

The new combination of data processing operations, which represents machine implementation, becomes complex. Burch and Stratler[1] delineate ten basic operations that must be performed to provide meaningful output from a data operation. They identify the following steps (typical hotel applications are in parentheses):

1. *Capturing*—the recording of data from an event or occurrence (source documentation).

2. *Verifying*—the checking or validating of data to ensure correctness (auditing).

3. *Classifying*—the placement of data elements into specific categories which provide meaning for the user (posting to guest accounts, city accounts).

4. *Arranging*—the sorting of data elements in a predetermined sequence (filing).

5. *Summarizing*—the combination or aggregation of data elements in a mathematical or logical sense (total revenues, total costs).

---

1. J. G. Burch and F. R. Strater, *Information Systems: Theory and Practice,* Hamilton Publishing Co., Santa Barbara, CA, 1974, pp. 26–27.

HOTEL DATA PROCESSING

Simplistic Overview of the Process Cycle (usually used in a manual or basic machine process).

I. **INPUT**

    A. Recording (capturing of data). The guest's registration card is the primary source document for initial input to the hotel cycle.

    B. Classifying (codes of data). Classification by type of accommodation, rate schedule, or profile of guest account (by the hotel) is designed to simplify analysis and eventual tracking of the guest's transactions.

II. **PROCESS**

    A. Sorting (arranging of data). The room rack and the indexing of guest folios are two sorting techniques hotels use to ease their data handling.

    B. Calculating (computation and/or manipulation of data). The posting and subsequent auditing procedures found in the hotel industry serve to keep guest accounts up-to-date and provide management with operational statistics.

III. **OUTPUT**

    A. Reporting (summarization of data into specified formats). The daily report, revenue center, and cost center reports are outputs of the data handling procedures designed to monitor and control hotel operations.

    B. Storage (retention of file data). The necessity to provide to-date figures, and to record historical data for future comparisons of performance, lead to the hotel maintaining a set of files concerning business and guest histories.

Table 7.2. Hotel Functions as Data Processing Items

6. *Calculating*—the arithmetic and/or logical manipulation of data (perpetual balances).

7. *Storing*—the placement of data onto some storage media for later access and retrieval (journals, ledgers, vouchers, and folios).

8. *Retrieving*—the searching out and gaining access to specific data elements from storage (support documentation).

9. *Reproducing*—the duplication of data from one medium to another, or into another position in the same medium (posting function).

10. *Disseminating/Communications*—the operation of transferring data from one place to another (managerial reporting).

The function of all data processing systems is to satisfy the user's requests in an ongoing arrangement and to report the output in a meaningful context. Figure 7.2 illustrates the flow of this extended processing cycle.

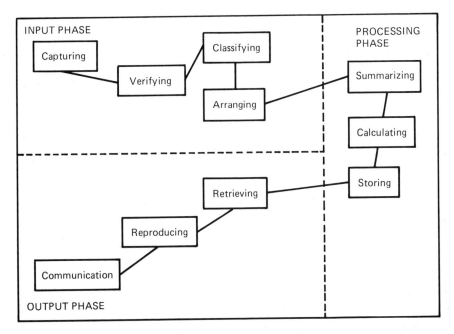

Figure 7.2. A Simplistic Overview of a Machine-Based Data Processing System

The Evolution of Data Processing Operations

Originally all hotel data operations were manual procedures that relied heavily upon repetition and extensive clerical backup. The earliest system concentrated on hand calculations and all postings and reports were handwritten. As typewriters, cash registers, and time clock devices became available, they were quickly adopted. Later keypunching, sorting, and collating machines replaced antiquated methodologies and significantly updated the processing function. Today, the data processing operation has advanced to computer automation involving such hardware as optical scanners, remote order entry terminals, central processing units, and memory units. Table 7.3 provides a very concise overview of past and present general business data processing (dp) methods. It also details the ten operating functions described above.

Data Processing Objectives

The objectives of the general data processing cycle can be summarized as:

1. to *transform* raw, isolated unevaluated facts into comprehensive, integrated information.

2. to *satisfy* the ongoing user's requests and to report output in a meaningful context to management.

3. to *reduce* the handling (and rehandling) of data.

	Operations				
Methods	**Capturing and Initial Recording**	**Classifying**	**Arranging**	**Summarizing**	**Calculating**
Manual Method	Voice; observation; handwritten records; forms and checklists; writing boards; peg-boards	Handposting; coding; identifying peg-boards	Alphabetizing; indexing; filing; edgenotched cards	Hand calculators	Human calculation; pencil and paper; abacus; slide rule
Electro-mechanical Method	Typewriter; cash register; autographic registers; time clocks	Posting machine; cash register; accounting machines	Semi-automatic (rotomàtics; gathermatics)	Adding machines; calculators; cash registers; posting machines	Accounting machines; adding machines; calculators; cash registers; posting machines
Punched Card Equipment Method	Key punch; verifier; mark-sensed cards; prepunched cards; machine readable tags	Sorter; collator		Accounting machine; calculator; summary punch	
Electronic Computer Method	Key punch; verifier; paper tape punch; magnetic encoder; OCR enscriber; collection devices; conversion devices; terminals	By systems design	Card sorter; internal computer sorting	Central processing unit	

Table 7.3. Operation and Methods of Data Processing
Reprinted from Burch and Strater, *Information Systems: Theory and Practice,* p. 28, with permission of John Wiley & Sons, Inc.

Storing	Retrieving	Reproducing	Disseminating and Communicating
Columnar journals; ledgers; index cards; paper files	File clerks; stock clerks; bookkeepers	Hand-copying; carbon paper	Hard-written reports; hand-carried, or mailed
Mechanical files (rotary or tub files); microfilm		Duplicating equipment (carbonization, hectograph, stencil, offset, photocopying thermograph); addressing equipment	Telephone; teletype; machine prepared reports; message conveyors; hand-carried or mailed reports
Card trays	Sorter; collator; hand selection	Reproducers; interpreter	Same as above
CPU, DASD; magnetic tape; paper tape; punched cards	Online inquiry into DASD; report generation	Same as above, plus on line copies from line printer; computer input/output; microfilm	Same as above, plus on line data transmission (telecommunication); visual display: voice output

Summary

Management has always constructed some system of information by which to evaluate its performance. This information serves three general purposes: 1) to increase knowledge, 2) to reduce uncertainty, and 3) to provide feedback. The demands for more information by business firms is normally a result of growth, accountability, and government regulations. All in all, management has experienced an increasing concern for information and has developed a need for an efficient data processing system to formulate the facts.

A system is an orderly arrangement of component parts placed in an interrelated series necessary to accomplish some operation. All systems operate in an environment and must be designed to meet the user's needs. A system life cycle consists of: 1) system analysis, 2) system design, 3) system implementation, and 4) system refinement.

An important objective of a data processing system is to reduce the handling of data. Historically, data had to be handled several times, now each transaction may only need to be recorded once, in a machine-usable form, and stored and retrieved whenever desired. Through advanced technology, data can be processed numerous times, without rehandling and with increased speed and accuracy. Improvements in collecting, calculating, storing, and dissemination of information have surpassed even the most optimistic expectations of innkeepers and promise even more spectacular future developments.

Key Concepts

Accountability	Input
Calculating	Knowledge
Classifying	Output
Coding	Process
Data base	Recording
Data processing	Retrieving
Dissemination	Software
Environment	Sorting
Feedback	Storage
Hardware	System concept
Human engineering	System life cycle
Implementation	Uncertainty
Information	Verification

Questions for Discussion

1. What is information and how does it impact upon the firm's management?

2. Briefly explain the concepts of decision-making and performance feedback in relation to information.

3. What additional pressures, other than those of the ordinary business environment, may affect the quantity and quality of information a firm has to deal with?

4. What are some of the characteristics that affect the value of information?

5. How can information be transmitted?

6. Define the general systems concept and list several examples of both simple and complex configurations.

7. Why is the inclusion of the system's environment so vital to system design, implementation, and operation?

8. List some examples of the inappropriate use of the system's concept. What is the determining factor as to whether the term is used correctly or not?

9. What is the value in first determining a proposed system's environmental factors?

10. What roles can machines play in the system design and/or environment?

11. What are the three relative degrees of automation?

12. Compare and contrast the simplistic three-phase data processing system with the more elaborate, sophisticated phases of the automated configurations.

13. Sketch the historic development of business-oriented data processing concepts. Relate these functions to hotel operations.

14. What are the three essential data processing objectives?

The MIS Concept

Chapter Objectives:

1. To introduce the general concept of a management information system.

2. To explicitly state the definition, objectives, advantages, and disadvantages of an information network.

3. To explain common management information system configurations and characteristics.

4. To decipher valid criticism and performance evaluation criteria for a management information system.

THE INITIAL conceptualization of a management information system (MIS) predates the development and implementation of automated and computer-assisted systems. Early MIS applications include military wartime strategy planning, mass media presentation, and the introduction of communication networks. The advent of the digital computer altered the context and extended the capabilities of the MIS to the business environment. Management information systems evolved out of the application of language and mathematics to symbolic logic. The use of symbols, in place of a complete set of operational instructions, was the initial stage of development. As knowledge increased and specialized areas of the firm became isolated, more and more information could be generated. Additional progress by management scientists paved the way for the introduction of formalized information systems to the organization. This chapter surveys the MIS field in general, rather than aiming at specific hotel configurations that will be presented in depth in later chapters.

The MIS framework has become modelled around the overall corporate management structure and normally permits operating departments to pursue their own areas of interests. The management reporting system component of the MIS combines various departmental facts with company goals and objectives, and presents control, efficiency, and managerial effectiveness evaluations. Hence, the present design of the MIS is an integration of several interrelated subsystems that support managerial decision-making, assists in the planning and control of operations, and is responsive to the changing requirements of the organization.

Criticism of the MIS design concerns: a) the possible production of useless, irrelevant information, b) the threat of excessive costs from systems operation, and c) the dysfunctional impact the system may make on the overall organizational structure. Many of these factors are wholly dependent upon a proper design, which is both a management and a systems analyst's responsibility.

Definition of an MIS

There is no universally accepted or precisely stated definition of an MIS. Depending upon the expertise and perspective of the author, the need for timely information, the role of data transformation, the satisfaction of managerial functions, or the importance of a series of reports may be the focal point. Burch and Strater see the information system as revolving around data procedures and write, " . . . a systematic, formal assemblage of components that performs data processing operations to (a) meet legal and transactional data processing requirements, (b) provide information to management for support of planning, controlling, and decision making activities, and (c) provide a variety of reports, as required, to external constituents."[1]

Voich, Mottice, and Shode discuss the MIS as an integrative framework, and offer this definition: " . . . a group of information systems that are interconnected in their

---

1. Burch and Strater, *Information Systems: Theory and Practice,* Hamilton Publishing Co., Santa Barbara, CA, 1974, p. 71.

design, operation, and management to serve operations and facilitate the performance of the management process."[2] Acknowledging information as the most basic resource of the organization, Matthews makes this contribution: "The objective of the information system is to make available a broad base of comprehensive, accurate information. The concept of the management system is the provision of an orderly, systematic method of controlling and directing this vital management resource—information."[3]

An MIS will, herein, be defined as a collection of interrelated and interdependent subsystems dependent upon a data base that supports the managerial decision-making process, helps monitor and control operations, and is responsive to the dynamic needs of the firm. Much controversy has arisen due to the lack of standardization of definition of the MIS. Many experts agree that performance evaluations are difficult since nebulous, ambiguous, or arbitrary definitions do not lead to sound criteria for validation or review. The belief that a system that is difficult to control and evaluate may not enhance managerial effectiveness or improve the coordination of the firm has raised much concern. It should also be noted that the MIS references herein are to automated systems.

MIS Characteristics

Although the management information system design may vary from industry to industry, or within any industry, basic underlying principles can be isolated. The MIS:

1. provides a means by which to achieve organizational objectives.

2. treats information as an important resource and takes responsibility for its proper handling and flow.

3. has comprehensive informational product that enables the integration of functional operations, communications, and overall organizational coordination.

4. interfaces people and hardware (to some extent) in relationships designed to free personnel to fulfill jobs requiring the human capability (human engineering).

5. provides a collection of historical and/or transactional data to support corporate planning, decision-making, and evaluation.

Since an MIS possesses these basic characteristics, its design configuration must mirror the firm's organizational structure to assure that the objectives of the company will be met.

Task Application to the MIS

A task being considered for MIS involvement should be analyzed according to the following four criteria:

---

2. Voich, Mottice, and Shode, *Information Systems for Operations and Management,* South-Western Publishing Co., Cincinnati, OH, 1975, p. 31.

3. Don Q. Matthews, *The Design of the Management Information System,* Auerbach Publishers, Princeton, NJ, 1971, p. 8.

1. *Repetitive Nature of Task.* How often does the task need to be performed? Is it a routine procedure dependent upon objective evaluation and not subjective? (e.g., reservations vs. account adjustments).

2. *Urgency of Output.* Are results needed quickly for the task? How much speed is desired in obtaining the output? (e.g., guest statement at checkout).

3. *Availability of Input Data.* How easily can the support data be identified, collected, and coded? Is there sufficient input to generate desired output? (e.g., development of the guest folio from registration).

4. *Effect of Output.* What effect will the output have on managerial effectiveness? Will it improve customer service? Will it aid decision-making? (e.g., high-risk account listings).

After the preceding factors have been dealt with, a tentative decision of whether to add the task to the MIS network can be made. Final consideration must be given to how the manual procedures, presently employed, are going to be fitted to meet the requirements of the MIS design. The manual operations should be scrupulously analyzed with regard to: feasibility, necessity, achievement, and freedom from bias.

If an operation is performed in a long, drawn-out fashion requiring numerous intermediate processing procedures, it may not be feasible to automate this function; deletion may be wise. A manual procedure of several steps may contain unnecessary operations or numerous handlings of the same data and therefore can be simplified in the MIS process. The value gained from performing a given task must also be resolved, so that unnecessary procedures, which achieve very little, are not continued. The way a data operation is performed presently may be a result of the capabilities or preferences of the person doing the job, and MIS application may require the creation of a new procedure. Normally, the flow of an MIS procedure is different from the manual one it replaces because more symbolic logic leads to fewer complications.

Hence, the application of the MIS process, or the inclusion of presently performed manual tasks to an automated system, requires close attention and analysis. The preparation of a task for MIS inclusion may be of a major benefit to the firm. Often this evaluational benefit is overlooked or underestimated. The task-oriented characteristics stated above can also be applied to large-scale processes or operations.

MIS Configurations

The system design determines how much change will take place from the input data to the resultant output. The design also tends to be different than the manual procedure it replaces, and is usually a customized computer application. The overall management information system can serve the organization as an *integrated network* (monolithic), as a *distributed series* of independent systems (modular), or as some *combination* of these two. Since both the integrated and distributed forms of the MIS have strengths and weaknesses, there is no generally accepted determination as to which one is the most beneficial. Although the integrated or total system has become more fashionable, systems analysts continue to design each configuration so as to be most consistent with the organization it will serve.

The Integrated MIS

Initially, businesses employed an application-by-application approach to satisfy their informational needs, and it was not until the past decade that firms became interested in a complete system capable of serving many organizational functions. Administrative emphasis shifted away from well-structured tasks and reductions in clerical operations to improvements in the abstract areas of corporate planning and managerial decision-making. The development of advanced generation computing hardware and the increased acceptance of the computer as a managerial tool are credited for enabling participating management to gain potential economic and competitive advantages over nonusers. The total system approach revolves around the consolidation of all data processing and information generation functions, and may impose significant changes or demands on the organizational structure.

In order to gain insight into the design of the integrated MIS it is important to understand the system components. The general characteristics of an information system deal with the acquisition, processing, retention, transmission, and presentation of information useful to management. Radford[4] identifies specific subsystems and offers clarifying descriptions.

1. Administrative and Operational Systems. Those components created to support routine functions in the organization form the administrative and operational systems. Since a large number of these routine tasks are mechanized and computer-supported, these operational subsystems often are. In most firms these systems are the data processing centers. Although separate departments may have their own data systems, the information produced is transmitted to other functional areas and to the general management, where specified. There is a data base constructed for each divisional operation which provides for future use of the stored information. Examples of operational systems are: Sales, Production, Distribution, Financial and Personnel Management.

2. Management Reporting System. This system is designed to provide periodic reports to managers on matters relating to their decision-making tasks. Three categories of reports exist: a) those required for control, b) those relating to efficiency, and c) those dealing with effectiveness. Data for the first two types of reports come from the respective administrative and operational systems discussed above. Information for the third type of report results from a combination of the first two reports and the budgeting and operation goals of the organization (i.e., the allocation of available resources). Generally, the structure of the management reporting system follows the structure of the organization it serves. Reports are timely and are consistent in form to agreed-upon specifications and formats. The whole system of reports displays increasing summarization and corresponding absorption of uncertainty, the higher the level in the hierarchy of the firm. Personnel managers, for example, would concentrate mainly on the first two types of reports, while the executive vice-president would most likely require all three kinds.

3. Common Data Base. The data base is the component part of the MIS that acts as a storage compartment for data and information used by more than one department of the organization.

---

4. K. J. Radford, *Information Systems in Management,* Reston Publishing Co., Inc., Reston, VA, 1973, pp. 55–68.

The common data base is central to the whole information system and does not contain all the data and information treated by the administrative and operational support systems. Membership in the common data base is restricted to information common to two or more of the operational or management reporting systems. The data in the base therefore contains a wider range of activities than any one of the surrounding systems. Data passing between departments must be in a standard format in order to be acceptable and recognizable to each system it enters.

Standards are constructed which serve as the linkage between peripheral systems and the data base. As the data base continues to grow, conforming to standards and a continuous updating and editing are critical. Security must be maintained as information contained in the data base is vital to the organization.

4. Information Retrieval System. The process by which historic data and information may be drawn from the data base, for use in planning and decision-making, is called the retrieval system. The function of the retrieval system is similar to that of the management report system,

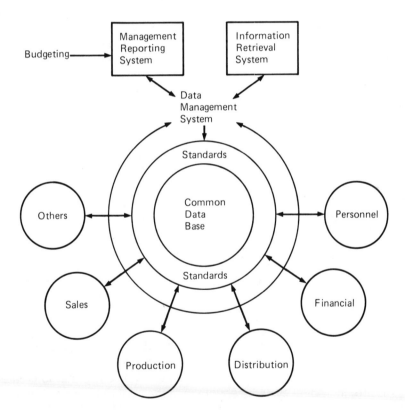

Figure 8.1. The MIS Integrated Configuration
(Redrawn with permission of Reston Publishing Company, Inc., a Prentice-Hall Company, 11480 Sunset Hills Road, Reston, VA 22090. Figure from *Information Systems in Management* by K. J. Radford.)

in that it provides information to all levels of management. Although similar in function to the management reports, the retrieved information is not as well structured or periodic. The information retrieval system provides information only upon demand, and usually provides management with relevant background for effective decision-making.

5. Data Management System. The data management system is responsible for arranging and controlling the flow of data and information between components of the information system. This subsystem serves as a communication link between the other components. The major tasks of this system are: a) supervising the capture and updating of data and information for the common data base, b) servicing the needs of the peripheral components of the system for information from the base, c) maintaining a system of cross indexing of data currently in the information system as a whole, d) generating reports in the formats required by the management reporting and information retrieval systems, and e) providing security for data in the base. Data management is usually insured by the use of complicated software.

Figure 8.1 depicts the five system components discussed above, and their interrelationships. Note that the functional systems provide information to the common data base only through a buffer of standards, and that both the management reporting system and the retrieval system are dependent upon the data base for their information.

Critics of this approach maintain that meeting all the informational requirements of an organization is technically impossible and economically infeasible. Others feel that unless management makes a total commitment to this system, only chaos will result, since it is dependent on all levels of the organization for support. Another criticism centers on the fact that although all the internal departments may be represented in the total system, the system fails to include the important external variables that may be nonroutine, yet still affect the firm. Also, the integrated system forces functional areas to become more dependent on one another than is normally the case, and this may result in disastrous outcomes for the firm.

In his book on management information system design, Matthews gives this viewpoint, "The advantage of the larger systems is not that several functional requirements have been brought together but rather that the larger systems meet the needs of the several functions more completely and more efficiently than the individual systems."[5] Since the integrated system is designed to service users throughout the entire organization, it is essential that management be committed to the system and that the system's advantages be realized.

The Distributed MIS

Unlike the integrated configuration, the distributed MIS is a series of systems, not one large system. Often, the total system concept is achieved by the implementation of *modular* systems that are eventually consolidated and linked together to create a large singular structure. Individual systems enable management to better comprehend each

---

5. Don Q. Matthews, *The Design of the Management Information System,* Auerbach Publishers, Inc., Princeton, NJ, 1971, p. 17.

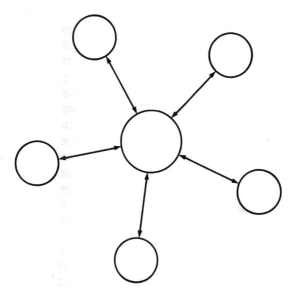

Figure 8.2. Integrated MIS Configuration

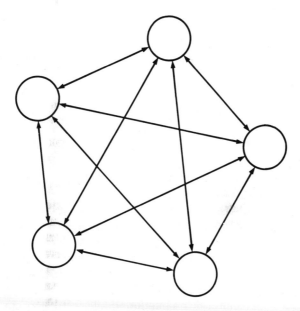

Figure 8.3. Distributed MIS Configuration

functional area and provide internal data and evaluation to each department. The distributed MIS network is interfaced for communications, but the subsystems are relatively independent. There is no artificial creation of dependencies that do not exist as natural operations of the firm.

Normally, it is possible to identify three basic conditions that differentiate subsystems found in distributed systems: (1) subsystems that will need to interact with other subsystems, (2) subsystems that will need to share files and data processing facilities, and (3) subsystems that will require very little interaction, that will be isolated, and for the most part, self-sufficient.

Systems analysts have argued that because some firms have operating departments that are so diverse, it does not make sense for all departmental data to flow into one common data base. A real advantage of the distributed system is that the data and output of the MIS are located closer to the functional area users, where it is most needed.

Figures 8.2 and 8.3 illustrate the basic integrated and distributed configurations the MIS may take on. Again, emphasis on the centralization and the interdependencies of subsystems are the outstanding characteristics of the *integrated network.* The distributed system is a series of subsystems informally linked and independent of one another (except for communication purposes).

Combined MIS Configurations

Most organizations that employ an MIS probably have both distributed and integrated system characteristics to some degree. Although it is possible to discuss and theoretically identify the *monolithic* and *modular* system networks, often the MIS configuration found within the firm is difficult to discriminate. Burch and Strater provide this explana-

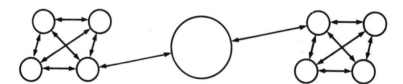

Figure 8.4. Integrated MIS with Distributed Subsystem Components

tion: "In reality, a distributed system is an information system with some degree of integration. Or looking at it another way, an integrated system is an information system with some degree of distribution. There is no absolute. Moreover, there are a number of functions which can be integrated in varying degrees and, in addition, combinations of functions can be integrated. As a result, there is an almost endless list of different varieties of integration."[6] Figures 8.4 and 8.5 depict some typical versions of the MIS configurations. Figure 8.4 illustrates the integrated MIS with integrated subsystem components, while Figure 8.5 is a representation of a distributed MIS with integrated sub-

---

6. Burch and Strater, *Information Systems,* p. 91.

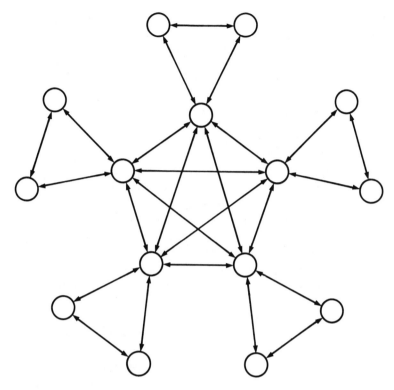

Figure 8.5. Distributed MIS with Integrated Subsystem Components

system components. The combined MIS offers the advantages of both systems while avoiding some of the possible shortcomings experienced by implementing either one structure or the other.

Early MIS Promises

During the preliminary development of formalized information systems, systems designers marketed the MIS by touting its potential capabilities to the firm. Some of these promises were unrealistic, which has caused much criticism of the MIS in general and has dissuaded some users from pursuit. The claim that the MIS can define the information needs of the firm surely has attracted the attention of business organizations eager to improve their decision-making. The MIS was also supposed to: 1) provide rapid answers at a low cost, 2) be the central communications link of the firm, 3) reduce clerical work and errors, and 4) improve the overall coordination and consistency of the operation. Since the MIS was to guarantee better management, it was also expected to provide a means for improved allocation of the company's resources. Small and Lee state,

The potential benefits of a successful MIS are indeed impressive. However, there is a general consensus that the reality has so far fallen short of expectations. The original enchantment with the possibility of quickly achieving a large-scale and all encompassing MIS has been replaced with a pragmatic acceptance by both management and designers of the long, hard road ahead. The literature confirms that the idealized concept of the total computer-based system has not been achieved by any company. In fact, some feel that this may be an impossible attainment.[7]

MIS Performance Evaluation

Due to the lack of a universlly accepted definition, the performance of a management information system has been difficult to evaluate. Although specific businesses have developed their own criteria, five basic evaluative approaches can be enumerated:

1. *Cost Justification*—also referred to as cost effectiveness; what does the MIS cost and what benefits are derived from it? If the benefits outweigh the costs then the system is believed to be performing well. This cost-benefit criterion loses much of its applicability when management tries to assign dollar values to intangible, informational output.

2. *Speed and Accuracy*—a measurement of the MIS mechanism, in terms of speed and accuracy, as compared to the procedures it replaced. Since the computer's major advantage lies in its quickness and attention to detail, this may not be an appropriate evaluation criterion.

3. *Reliability*—this criterion is a solid ground for evaluation. The reliability of a system surely will affect its performance, but a reliable system that is underemployed may not score well on an overall critique.

4. *Satisfaction of Demand*—the ability of the system to satisfy the user's requests for information. The biggest problem with this type of a standard is that the user's requests may in no way suit the user's needs. The system does not evaluate the legitimacy of the user's demands, it merely transmits information from its files, and therefore may not be performing well even though it is producing information.

5. *Operational Simplicity*—the ease of system operation, both in terms of hardware and software. Again, attention is usually given to the system's ability to meet user's requests, no matter how irrelevant the request may be.

The MIS deals with the transmission of messages and not with evaluating the meaningfulness of their content. It is for this reason that an MIS evaluation should be made along all five criteria, not just one, as has often been the case.

Criticism of the MIS Design

Although some limitations and shortcomings of the integrated and distributed configurations have been mentioned earlier, the overall MIS design has also received criticism. In his article entitled "Management Misinformation Systems," Russell L. Ackoff questions the fundamental assumptions upon which the MIS concept is built. He enumerates four

---

7. Small and Lee, "In Search of an MIS," *MSU Business Topics,* Autumn 1975, p. 51.

of these assumptions and proceeds to debate their truth; he also presents morals and an example to support his conclusions.[8]

Ackoff does not agree that management suffers from a lack of relevant information; instead he believes that management suffers more from an overabundance of irrelevant information. His focus on this information overload leads him to conclude that filtration and condensation of information should be the mechanics of a sound information system, not the generation of more information. In addition, he concludes that since decision variables are so complex and decision models are not well developed, management does not know what information it needs or is pertinent to decision-making.

The premise that management decisions will improve with more information is strongly challenged by Ackoff. Citing management's inability to comprehend the delicate relationships among decision variables, he claims that history actually proves the opposite. In his opinion, there are too many possibilities and too many complexities to clearly prove that better decisions are outcomes of having more information.

Turning to the assumption that better interdepartmental communications enable managers to coordinate their decisions more effectively and, hence, improve overall performance, Ackoff alludes to the competitive atmosphere that usually is found in most firms. He perceives the organizational units as being in competition for company resources and believes that information concerning what other departments are doing may only hurt the overall performance of the firm. He claims that there is a need to determine appropriate measures of performance, so that communications may help those units that are striving to achieve corporate goals.

The fourth weakness of the MIS scheme that Ackoff attacks is the commonly accepted assumption that management does not have to understand how an information system works, only how to use it. He claims that management may become unable to control the system or evaluate it, and therefore cannot justify it from a managerial viewpoint. Ackoff summarizes his feelings by stating that no MIS should ever be installed unless managers for whom the system is intended are trained to evaluate it and control it.

Some other experts have criticized the MIS concept on the basis of its development by computer-trained, technical personnel; not by management. The common argument centers around the fact that the systems specialist is not capable of appreciating the manager's dilemma nor the type of information management may require. Additionally, management's lack of participation in the construction, implementation, or operation of the system has been cited as the greatest factor leading to the potential failure of even the most expertly designed packages.

Hence, both management and system engineers can be held responsible for some of the failures that have taken place. The inadequate follow-up by both parties, the designer's lack of understanding of management's tasks, management's improper

8. Russell L. Ackoff, "Management Misinformation Systems," *Management Science,* December 1967, pp. B145–B156.

training and systems usage, and the fact that computer orientation has interfered with the overall corporate objectives, all combine to show the total weakness of the earliest MIS systems.

Things in the management information systems marketplace continue to improve and the future looks bright. The increased acceptance of computer-based systems and the awareness of technical computer operations by new, young management personnel combine to create a more favorable environment for the improved MIS configurations.

Summary

The concept of a management information system is not a new one. The recent advent of computers has, however, altered and extended the capabilities of MIS configurations. The information system is normally modelled around the organization it is designed to serve, and is constructed in such a manner as to allow departments to pursue their individual areas of interest.

Although there is no universally accepted definition of an MIS, a broad definition usually includes mention of: timely information, data transformation, assistance in management functions, and reporting formats. The MIS is a collection of interrelated and interdependent subsystems dependent upon a data base that: 1) supports the managerial decision-making process, 2) helps monitor and control operations, and 3) is responsive to the dynamic needs of the firm. The ambiguity of broad definitions has led to evaluative problems. Unless the MIS functions and responsibilities are specified for a particular application, it is almost impossible to construct performance objectives and to evaluate the benefits of the MIS.

Common MIS characteristics include such things as organizational goals, responsibilities for information handling, integration and coordination of the firm, human engineering, and a collection of transactional and historical data. The MIS is designed to serve the organization and to help it meet its objectives through efficient use of its most important resource—information.

The delineation of tasks for MIS application is dependent upon repetition, urgency, availability, and the effectiveness of the output. Additional characteristics include such factors as feasibility, necessity, achievement, and freedom from bias. All things considered, the MIS should only include those tasks that will enhance managerial effectiveness and further the goals of the organization.

System design determines how much change will take place between the input data and the resultant output. The design might be distributed, integrated, or some combination of these two. The distributed, or modular MIS, tends to be a series of small systems rather than the one large system found in the integrated design. Almost all MIS configurations have both some integrated and distributed system characteristics and in reality it is difficult to decipher where one system design begins and another ends.

Early MIS promises have caused criticism and dissatisfaction with loosely designed configurations and have dissuaded some organizations from pursuing their application. It is anticipated that there will be a rapid upsurge in MIS applications due to advancements in both systems science and computer technology.

Key Concepts

Combined network   Integrated network
Configuration   Management information system
Cost effective   Modular
Cost justified   Monolithic
Distributed series network   Reliability
Human engineering   Subsystem

Questions for Discussion

1. The conceptualization of a management information system is not a new approach to handling the firm's most important resource, information. Outline its developmental stages.

2. Define the MIS concept and relate some of its component parts to hotel areas of specialization.

3. What difficulties arise, with respect to evaluation procedures, when a concept is loosely or broadly defined?

4. What are the common, basic characteristics of all MIS configurations?

5. What task criteria should be applied prior to inclusion of the task into the MIS?

6. What is meant by an application-by-application system implementation versus total system overlay?

7. Discuss the relevancy of a common data base to an organization information system. What determines which information is stored?

8. Explain the importance of the information retrieval subsystem component of the integrated configuration. Why is it so important?

9. Sketch an integrated MIS configuration and assign some hotel functional areas to it.

10. Compare and contrast the distributed MIS framework to the integrated system. What are the advantages of each system? What are the disadvantages?

11. Sketch a distributed MIS configuration and assign some hotel functional areas to it.

12. What is the difference between the theoretical design of the basic MIS system configurations and the combined configuration encountered by the firm?

13. What are the basic criteria that have developed for the evaluation of an MIS design?

14. List the basic assumptions of the MIS model and present a critique of them.

Computer Operating Systems

Chapter Objectives:

1. To sketch the brief historical development of computer components and systems.

2. To present the common characteristics and components of a computer system.

3. To explain hardware and software concepts in a comprehensible manner.

4. To illustrate various options by which business firms can participate in computer-assisted systems.

ALTHOUGH the hospitality industry did not begin participating in computerized information systems until the late 1960s, some other businesses became involved in the early 1950s. The advent of the computer not only changed the field of data processing, but also affected the entire workings of the business organization. In order to develop an appreciation and understanding for the contributions and dynamic modifications and extensions made by computer technologists, a brief review of computer operating systems and their effect upon the business firm will be presented in this chapter. Since only a general knowledge of computers is required for their usage, the material presented herein is not limited to any one specific computer system.

Experts in the field of computer technology often refer to their continuous, ongoing progressions in terms of generations. The delineation of one computer generation from another is contingent upon three factors: 1) the level of computer hardware and software, 2) the type of task and systems application, and 3) the organizational effect created by computer operations.

The Five Computer Generations[1]

The First Generation
This generation has been dated, by Withington, from 1953 to 1958 and is termed the "Gee Whiz" era. During this period, most of the larger American business firms sought to acquire computer machinery only to appear progressive. Few firms could cost-justify their expenditure and the applications of the system were confined to the most formalized and hence, the easiest to program, organizational functions (for example, payroll processing). Since the applications centered primarily around accounting procedures, the company's controller or financial officer was usually assigned the system. The computers of this generation, limited to routine tasks, did not have much effect on the overall operations of the firm. They were bulky units, made up of heat-producing vacuum tubes, that occupied a large room in an obscure part of the building. There was not much interaction between the computer specialists and the organizational management.

The Second Generation
Although the application technology remained oriented at well-structured tasks, more rapid access to information was demanded. During this "Paper Pusher" period, 1958 to 1966, software became recognized as an important resource and the computers of this time could handle large volumes of input data and information output. The business organization began to support programmer groups and to develop internal computer centers. Managers benefited from the increased production of reports, the tighter

---

1. Adapted from Frederic G. Withington, "Five Generations of Computers," *Harvard Business Review,* July–August, 1974, p. 100.

monitoring and control over operations, and the company's increased ability to track and vary product lines. The first *on-line* systems appeared in the airline and stock trading industries during this generation, and the transistor replaced the vacuum tubes of the first generation. These inquiry systems resulted in a new approach to information handling and questions were raised about who should control the changing computer system and its operators.

The Third Generation

Advancements in integrated circuit technology, transistors, and related component parts made remote terminals feasible during the era of the "Communicators" (1966 to 1974). The centralized computer, and its satellite terminals, forced divisional managers and other organizational people to give up some control of their internal data processing. With the introduction of time-sharing, many users became capable of simultaneous interaction with the computer and this allowed for the distribution of more timely information to all levels of the firm. This increased level of communications was accompanied by a centralization of control, reduced system response times, and improvements in customer service.

The Fourth Generation

Begun in 1974 and expected to terminate around 1982, this generation introduced the concepts of data-base management, floppy disc and bubble memory units, and the development and implementation of inexpensive satellite minicomputers. The "Information Custodians" of this time are concerned with the capturing and storing of large volumes of information so that relevant data can be applied to more decisions, and in a more timely manner, than ever before. Increasingly, more raw data are being partially processed at their time of input and are being stored as finished bits of information, rather than as scattered pieces of alpha and numeric data. The application of remote terminals with intelligence has allowed for an increase in the decentralization of decision-making, and provides a more comprehensive knowledge of the overall business situation to personnel located out in the field. The computers of this generation are faster, less expensive, and more compact than ever before.

The Fifth Generation

Easy-to-use programming and file manipulation languages are expected to follow in the "Action Aids" era starting around 1982. Computer experts envision personalized information systems in which individual users have the ability to program and to have small summarized data files for independent analysis. Also, realistic decision-making models are expected due to more data and an increased understanding of the relationships among the data variables. The system will most likely be composed of minicomputers that can perform numerous local operations and that are tied into a central main frame for centralized filing and production applications. Hence, independent decision analyses, based upon a comprehensive awareness of the decision variables, will be a routine procedure.

Throughout the evolution of the generations, Withington identifies a single ultimate objective: " . . . the machine that can collect, organize, and store all existing data, then apply them (the data) both to conducting routine operations in an optimum way and to supporting management actions."[2] The information contained in Table 9.1 is a classic summary of the past, present, and future characteristics of the facets of the computer evolution. Special attention to the fourth and fifth generations is paramount for today's managers, as the state of the art proceeds to run its course. Table 9.2 summarizes the characteristics of the technological advances made during the first four generations. The fifth has yet to occur and, therefore, is not listed.

Advances in Computer Design

Although attention has been given to the outstanding achievements made by computer systems, it is interesting to note what advances in computer design specifications occurred between the early 1950s and the mid-1970s. Table 9.3 offers a quick comparison of some original computer design specifications with their twenty-five year seniors. The major areas of advancement are delineated into the following categories: 1) speed, 2) size, 3) cost, 4) operation, and 5) overall technology. These categories usually are the advantages cited for a computer system preference over a manual or mechanical system.

Basic Computer Functions

All computer systems are composed of three basic hardware components parts and five functional areas of operation (see Fig. 9.1). These components are: the *central processing unit* (CPU), the *memory unit,* and the *input* and *output units* (I/O). The functions are: input, output, memory, control and arithmetic and logical operations. The CPU is made up of the arithmetic and logical unit in which all calculations and manipulations of the data take place. A control unit in the CPU is responsible for directing the flow into and out of all peripheral devices. This makes the CPU the controlling unit of operation and the location for computational analysis.

The memory unit is made up of addressable storage locations. Information that is loaded (read from input to the memory unit) into the system is either program instructions or input data and is held in memory until the CPU demands it. Following massaging in the CPU, the processed information flows back to the memory unit until output or storage or both is determined. Storage formats include: a) random access or b) sequential filing.

The I/O units serve as the communication link between the user and the system. Programs and data are inputed through these components and sent to the memory unit. Here the programs are converted to a machine-readable language for execution. After CPU processing, the output is available through the output devices. Recently, there has

---

2. Ibid., page 105.

Table 9.1. Facets of Computer Evolution

Name	Period	New hardware	New software	New functions	Organizational location	Effect on organization
Gee whiz	1953–1958	Vacuum tubes, magnetic records	None	Initial experimental batch applications	Controller's department	First appearance of technicians (with salary, responsibility, and behavior problems); automation fears among employees
Paper pushers	1958–1966	Transistors, magnetic cores	Compilers, input/output control systems	Full range of applications, inquiry systems	Proliferation in operating departments	EDP group proliferation; some workers and supervisors alienated or displaced; introduction of new rigidity but also new opportunities
Communicators	1966–1974	Large-scale integrated circuits, interactive terminals	Multifunction operating systems, communications controllers	Network data collection, remote batch processing	Consolidation into centrally controlled regional or corporate centers with remote terminals	Centralization of EDP organization; division data visible to central management; some

	Date					
Information custodians	1974–c.1982	Very large file stores, satellite computers	General-purpose data manipulators, virtual machines	Integration of files, operational dispatching, full transaction processing	Versatile satellites instead of terminals, with control still centralized	Redistribution of management functions, with logistic decisions moving to headquarters and tactical decisions moving out; resulting reorganization; field personnel pleased / division managers alienated; response times shortened
Action aids	c.1982–?	Magnetic bubble and/or laser-holographic technology, distributed systems	Interactive languages, convenient simulators	Private information and simulation systems, inter-company linkages	Systems capabilities projected to all parts of organization; networks of different organizations	Semiautomatic operating decisions; plans initiated by many individuals, leading toward flickering

(cont. next page)

Table 9.1 Continued

Name	Period	New hardware	New software	New functions	Organizational location	Effect on organization
					interconnected	authority and management by consensus; greater involvement of people at all levels; central EDP group shrinkage

Credit line: Frederic G. Withington, "Five Generations of Computers," *Harvard Business Review*, July–August 1974, Copyright © 1974 by the President and Fellows of Harvard College; all rights reserved.

Computer Hardware Characteristics

FIRST GENERATION: VACUUM TUBES	• slow (1/1000 second) • bulky (required lots of space) • gave off lots of heat (required venting) • a millisecond operating system (10^{-3})
SECOND GENERATION: TRANSISTORS	• faster than predecessor (1/1,000,000 second) • improved amplification of system signals • development of the transistor chip • progress from miniaturization to subminiaturization to microminiaturization • a microsecond operating system (10^{-6})
THIRD GENERATION: INTEGRATED CIRCUITS	• silicon chip • very small (usually 1/1000 of sq. in.) • required very little power to operate • fast (1/1,000,000,000 second) • a nanosecond operating system (10^{-9})
FOURTH GENERATION: LASER BEAM (LSI)	• distributed information systems using beams • large scale integration (LSI) • combining voices, data, and graphics • output printing in pages, not lines • a picosecond operating system (10^{-12})

Table 9.2. Technological Generations of Computing

been a larger amount of emphasis placed upon the design and development of I/O hardware that is capable of inputing data and programs of variable formats. For example, both a deck of computer cards and a terminal connected to the CPU by an acoustic coupler can serve as inputing device formats to the same computer system. The output may also take various formats: line, printed, punched, sketched, taped, or be flashed on a screen. The details of computer hardware and software options are covered in detail in a later section.

The User
Automated systems can be thought of as extensions of previous manual or mechanical processes and the user's requirements should dictate the system's requirements. Generally, the user's needs can be classified as:

1. minimization of costs (economy)

2. ease of system access (availability)

	Original Unit	Recent Design
SPEED —of calculation/operation	1/1,000 second (millisecond)	1/1,000,000,000 second (nanosecond)
SIZE —of system hardware with same intelligence	thirty ton hulk, massive unit	hand-held 1/2 lb. calculator
COST —efficiencies to scale with same capabilities	$500,000.00	$600.00
OPERATION —meets user's requirements with same results	Required on-the-premises team	Requires high school education
TECHNOLOGY —of engineering design with same power source	Vacuum tubes (used large power supply)	Laser beam (with large scale integration)

Table 9.3. Advances in Computer Design

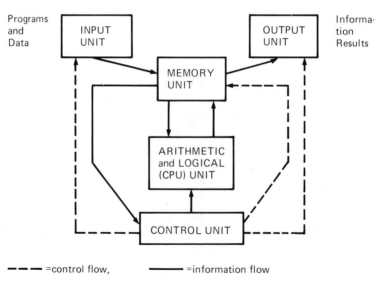

Figure 9.1. Information and Control Flow

3. reproducibility of results (predictability)

4. simplicity of system operation (practicality)

5. quality of system design (reliability)

6. optimization of output (intelligibility)

The computer system should be capable of satisfying the user's demands while still affording practical, technical, and feasible machine configurations. The user should specify any special demands so that the system can respond quickly and accurately. The question of legitimacy of future commands, expansions, and reports rests with management.

Hardware Concepts

Hardware Components

Although some of the basic hardware configurations will be discussed (in CPU options), there are many options available to a system user. The following section lists some of these options and Chapter 11 presents possible applicability to various aspects of the hospitality industry. It should be noted that although many of these options require additional peripheral computer hardware, mention of these devices has been held to a minimum.

Input Formats

The objective of the input function is to enter information as efficiently and as cheaply as possible. The following devices are presently used:

1. punch card

2. paper tape

3. magnetic tape

4. disc packs (cassette, flexible, floppy)

5. magnetic ink

6. cathode ray tube (CRT)

7. video display terminal (VDT)

8. graphic terminals

9. optical character recognition (OCR)

10. mark sense cards

11. key pad terminals

12. verbal recognition (VR)

13. touch-tone telephones

The punch card was the original input device and remains a common *input format.* Although cards are cheap and versatile, paper tapes, also inexpensive, are capable of being stored in small rolls. The use of tapes and discs has become popular with improved computer peripheral equipment, and the use of these mediums means that input can be accomplished at high speeds. Magnetic ink has the advantages of magnetic input speed and it can be read by the user. A bank check, for example, will usually have the customer's account number in magnetic ink for immediate inputing. The use of CRT, VDT, and graphic terminals has intensified interests in the field of soft-copy input and display and has been a significant factor leading toward a paperless, or partially paperless, computer environment. The OCR and mark sense formats are important developments in the area of computer identification of simplistic or partial input coding. The ability to recognize optical scanning formats, or printed input, by photoelectric cells within the hardware is of significant importance to future computer system efficiencies. Similarly, the electric relays of the touch-tone phone pad and the POS terminal key pad, have eliminated much of the complexity and time-consuming functions involved in developing alternate input codes. The recent experiments with verbal recognition, which requires a headset and makes use of a limited syntax (or vocabulary), may be the wave of future input formating. All in all, much of the research done in the input area has led to faster and simpler formats for more efficient loading of software and data.

CPU Options

The objective of CPU developments has revolved around increased speed in the arithmetic and control functions of the mainframe, or central processing unit. The CPU has undergone extensive technical revisions during the past two decades and, recently, alternative CPU formats were developed that further enhance the processing abilities of a computer system. A few of these options are:

1. *Mainframe.* A large central unit of older computer designs capable of handling several remote terminals and printers. This large unit usually contains the processor, the memory unit, and the system's power supply.

2. *Minicomputer.* Originally selling at costs of $11,000, the minicomputer has become very affordable at around the $2,000 price range. Many computer specialists have pointed out the economic advantages of having a series of minis for branch processing, as opposed to using one large computer. This is an example of the concept of distributed intelligence. In many branch processing systems, the minis communicate with each other and if one machine fails (goes down), then another one can be picked up for immediate access and use.

3. *Microprocessor.* Devices containing microprocessors (computers on a chip) are termed smart machines. Basically the microprocessor is a silicone chip with an integrated circuit pressed on it. The chip is inexpensive and comes preprogrammed. The microprocessor is typically used to control one specific function and generally cannot be user-programmed.

4. *Microcomputers.* Although initiated as a hobby for do-it-yourself computer enthusiasts, the microcomputer is becoming an important small business data processing device. The main advantages of the microsystem are in its simplicity of operation and programming and in its significant price/performance achievements over other systems. Although the microcomputer is not the equivalent of a minicomputer, it is beginning to receive some attention in the marketplace.

Memory Units

A lot of research and development has been aimed at improving the memory capabilities of the system, since more storage of larger volumes of information is desirable. Recent memory unit formats include:

1. paper and magnetic tape

2. mini and maxi discs (moving head discs)

3. flexible and floppy discs

4. digital cassettes and cartridges

5. bubble units

6. silicone chips

The movement toward mass storage with a minimization of moving parts, has produced storage on tapes, discs, and (most recently) chips. The portability of paper and magnetic tape storage has had many desirable cost benefits. The development of floppy discs and cassettes has further enhanced storage capabilities beyond previous expectations but the development of the bubble unit has set new standards. The bubble unit works magnetically and retains large amounts of stored information even when its power is turned off. The bubble memory is of solid state construction and is high in access speed and low in power consumption. The bubble memory should make a significant impact on system design in the near future.

Output Formats

The purpose of a systems output is to report processed information in the most effective format and at the most efficient speed. The options available are:

1. printed page (either high or low speed)

2. terminal copy (either hard or soft)

3. graphics output

4. punched card

5. magnetic tape

6. paper tape

7. disc packs

8. voice synthesizer

9. microfilm and microfiche

10. laser beam printing

The printed copy, or hard copy, has been the most popular format because it produces a written record of the output. Recent attempts at soft copy, information flashed on a screen, or verbal outputs (using a synthesizer) have made significant headway toward the paperless environment. Microfilm and microfiche output are basically photo-reduced and super-reduced films of output that can be stored with minimal space. The development and implementation of the laser beam as a line printer has revolutionized the format of the printed output page and has done so at remarkable printing speeds.

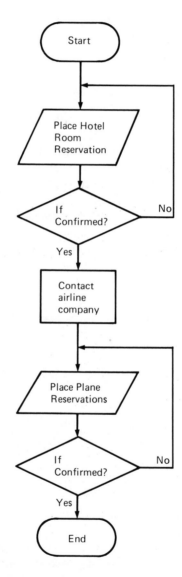

Figure 9.2. An Example of a Flowchart

Software Concepts

Algorithmic Design

An algorithm is composed of a set of unambiguous rules specifying a sequence of operations providing a solution to a problem. *Flowcharting* is a common technique of algorithmic design. A diagramming of the logic of the problem solution is defined as a flowchart (see Fig. 9.2). The flowchart not only depicts the solution to the problem, but also simplifies the development of the computer program.

Programming

A computer program is a set of instructions for system operation or data manipulation and handling. The program is written in a computer language, and the selection of the language is at the discretion of the programmer. Language selection may be dependent upon the characteristics of a solution technique, the formulation of the problem, and/or the system design. An algorithm is simply a series of steps leading to the solution of a problem (be it mathematical equations, or rank ordering a list of data). The design of the algorithm will facilitate effective programming. Depending on the requirements of the solution, a programmer may try to intelligently select that language needing the fewest programming statements (lines of code or instruction) and/or the language requiring the least amount of operating time to solve the problem.

Programming statements can be for direction during processing and control, for declaration, or input/output instruction. Many different languages, and versions of languages, exist and new languages are presently being developed for future implementation. Computer languages can be machine-oriented, procedure-oriented, or problem-oriented. Improvements in computer technology usually are accompanied by changes in programming languages. Languages may be referred to as "high" or "low," depending upon how similar they are to the spoken language and how simple the language is to use. Present technology is aimed at producing more high-level languages, as these are the farthest from machine language and approximate the spoken language, which is easier to relate to. Programming statements can be identified as being either:

1. processing statements (A + B = C)

2. control statements (Go Sub)

3. declaration statements (REM: this program calculates sales)

4. input/output statements (formats)

Operating Systems

An operating system is basically a program, or series of programs, designed to maintain the continuous operation of a computer system. If the computer system had to be monitored and controlled by a human operator, at all times, this would certainly decrease most of the speed and economic advantages attained through computerization.

Hence, the operating system is an automated collection of program components designed to control the use of system resources, track system usage and charges, and to maintain overall control of the system's operation.

Software Systems

The term software incorporates both computer programming and programming systems. Although a program has been defined as a set of instructions designed to make the computer perform certain operations in an indicated order, programming is not a simple task. The instructions must be in a code the computer can understand and this requires the use of a machine language. No two computers have the same machine language, and user programs are generally not written in this code. In fact, due to the complexity of machine languages, programs are written in either an assembly language or a translation language, to be converted to the machine format by an internal, computer-system device. Hence, a source program, written in a machine-readable language, is essential for computer processing.

An assembly system language is machine-oriented and is closely related to the machine language. Due to this machine orientation, this system language is thought of as being hardware-oriented, not problem- or people-oriented. Assembly programs are read into the computer system through a processor that converts the program instructions into the proper machine language. The machine language program is then operated upon. Hence, the assembly language is simply an abbreviated machine language that is less complicated and requires much less rigorous detail. These languages are referred to as "low" languages since they are most closely akin to machine language.

A translating system is one that is based primarily upon a problem application, rather than on the specifics of the computer hardware. The languages of a translating system are "high" languages in that they are located the farthest away from the eventual machine language code required by the computer system for execution. Since most of these languages closely resemble the spoken language (for example, BASIC, COBOL, FORTRAN, or APL), the computer system requires the use of a compiler for conversion. The compiler operates like the processor discussed in the assembly system. The source program leaves the compiler in an object format for execution. The main advantage of a translating system is that it is easier and quicker to learn, since it most closely parallels the spoken language. While the time involved with writing and editing programs is greatly reduced, the fact that the translation languages are basically machine independent allows for the possibility of writing programs that can be used with more than one computer system.

Additional software found within a computer system includes a series of utility programs (used to perform loading, printing, and other routine operations) and a set of diagnostic programs (used to assist the programmer in error detection). Most computer systems are designed in such a manner that their operating systems assist the programmer during program creation, loading, and execution.

Problem Solving

The computer is capable of handling problems which occur only once and those which occur frequently. The rate of occurrence will determine the precise approach and programming techniques for solution. The isolation and analysis of a problem area is a prior necessity for the identification of problem variables. In other terms, determination of the factual situation will point up the programming algorithm. Data gathering, coding, and inputing follow and are performed in a consistent format to the specifications of the program. Processing of the data will render information for output. Hence, problem solving is a function of both the algorithmic design and the programming.

Computer Processing Modes

There are three basic computer mode systems: *batch processing, real time,* and *time-sharing.* In addition to these, there may be a special purpose system designed for specific application. All operating systems: 1) handle all input and output operations, 2) handle the scheduling of the system's resources, 3) control the operation of the system's resources, and 4) chart the use of the system's components for accounting and analysis purposes.

Batch Processing

A batch-processing system is best for routine jobs that occur at regularly scheduled time intervals. The system groups programs and data together and then handles them sequentially. Keypunched cards, sorters, and readers are characteristics of this mode. The user has no interaction per se with the computer and must wait until the job is requested, loaded, and executed before getting any feedback. The time differential between program request or the beginning of a run and the availability of the output is called the turnaround time. This operating system has inherent time delays in its turnaround since jobs are processed in succession and on a systems priority scheduling basis. The decision of which job to mount, and when, is under the direct control of the systems operator, not the user. Hence, information does not flow directly into a computer device, but must await a request. Recent advances have created shorter turnarounds and allow for remote batch processing.

Real Time

A real-time system allows the user to interact directly with the computer. An outstanding characteristic of a real-time operation is that it generates information fast enough to affect the decision-making process involving the input data. Whenever information is available very shortly after inputting, the system is operating in a real-time mode. The real-time device need not be directly connected to the computer and usually does not allow the user to enter programs or alter existing cataloged or library programs. Only input data and outputs from cataloged programs can be found in a true real-time system. Such situations as changing status in inventory or availability, lend themselves to a real-time mode.

Time-Sharing

Time-sharing is distinguished from other forms of computing by its input/output devices, not by what happens at the computer. The I/O devices in a time-sharing system are directly connected to the computer and allow the user to interact directly. This enables programming and immediate feedback from the computer to the user and renders time-sharing unique, in that it allows several users to interact simultaneously with the computer without one having any knowledge of another's behavior.

Time-sharing is possible because of the extremely fast CPU hardware in the computer network. I/O devices are relatively slow and thereby allow simultaneous users to be hooked-up. Characteristics of the time-sharing system are:

1. allows many users simultaneous access

2. remote terminals located away from central unit

3. simplified software
   a. languages are usually a combination of words and elementary mathematics (high language)
   b. programs available from a library or can be quickly written

4. best suited to problems frequently occurring at irregular times

5. cost effectiveness

   a. may not require a computer team
   b. terminals may be rented
   c. may not require a capital commitment
   d. CPU, hook-up, and file storage costs are usually variable

Comparison of Modes

Although all operating systems have a number of common characteristics, each has specific operational capabilities. The batch-processing system has had inherent problems with its turnaround time since it employs rather complicated software. Since the system serves each user in sequence, an invalid program will not be detected immediately and even when it is, it must be debugged and reentered into the waiting sequence. An example of proper usage of a batch system is in the area of payroll. Payrolls come out at regularly scheduled time intervals and can be executed in a routine manner.

In real-time systems the emphasis is on maintaining a series of programs and data bases. No direct link may exist between the computer and user, but the user can get a relatively quick system response. This system has proven effective in the reservations field for the status of available spaces. Time-sharing, on the other hand, is a direct connection to the computer and the immediate response of the system makes it all the more attractive. It also may be cost-effective and can handle several users simultaneously. A time-sharing design has been applied in the development of point-of-sale terminals that are slowly replacing the cash register.

User's Manual

The written instructions that specify the system's operating procedures are called the *user's manual.* This manual usually includes the system's rules and policies, sample data entry forms and output reporting formats, detailed operating instructions, error correction procedures and a troubleshooting guide for emergency situations. The operating procedures will typically cover all the necessary functions required for normal computer usage, data handling, resource scheduling, and recovery procedures in case of system failures. Also accompanying the user's manual may be a set of training materials designed for employees who will operate the system and (possibly a separate set) for management who will interpret the output and use the system as part of their decision-making process.

Personnel in Computer Systems

In-house systems that require on-the-premises personnel may employ all, or some, of the following:

1. *Data Recorders*—keyboard operators and typists. In a hotel this could be the cashiers, front desk clerks, and secretarial staff that compile data for inputing.

2. *Computer Operator*—person in charge of the overall hardware operations. In most in-house hotel systems there is simply no need for a computer operator in this context. Rather, the personnel that provide systems maintenance and assume responsibility for systems continuity are closest to this job description.

3. *Programmer*—person that converts data and instructions into language for the computer's un-derstandability. Some hotel systems come with already written library routine programs for typical hotel functions (for example, reservations or night audit). However, oftentimes the hotel system does lend itself to customized programming by management personnel.

4. *Systems Analyst*—person responsible for the overall design of the computerized system. The hotel system is usually designed by both hotel people and computer systems people. Some of the prepackaged systems modules have been designed for general industry consumption.

Summary

The field of computer technology can be analyzed in terms of its computing generations. Experts delineate five distinct time frameworks and identify significant system charac-teristics for each. The first generation applied computer technology to routine, well-un-derstood tasks and although the systems were not cost justified, firms acquring this hardware were seen as progressive. The second generation dealt with the demand for more rapid access to information. During this generation software became an important resource and the first on-line systems were applied in the areas of airlines and stock market trading. The next generation benefited from advances in the electronics field and remote terminals, cabled to a central processor, became reality. Fourth generation technology is involved with satellite minicomputers and the development of enormous data bases. Decision-making is becoming more decentralized due to distributed intelligence and a better comprehension of the business environment. Prognostications of fifth generation systems include personalized information systems in which individual users have the ability to program and to maintain summary files. Even more realistic decision models are expected due to more data and an increased understanding of the relationships among decision variables.

Computer systems are composed of three component parts: the CPU, memory unit, and I/O devices. The user, through the input component, requests programs and data for execution. The input is received by the memory unit, which assigns it to a storage area. The CPU controls the flow of information and messages within the system and directs the program and data from the memory to the CPU for processing. Following the computational run, the CPU directs the program and output back to the memory unit for storage and/or outputting. The CPU then controls the movement from the memory unit to the output component. The user receives the output from a prespecified output device. The overall system requirements are essential for network continuity of the system controls.

The user's needs are essential for the design of a feasible computer system. Considerations of economy, availability, predictability, practicality, reliability, and intelligibility are important for a system that is capable of responding to the user's requests. The computer programmer normally will choose that language that requires either the fewest number of programming statements to execute or the language requiring the minimum operating time to generate a desired output. Similarly, the development of a flowchart, depicting the algorithm, can also facilitate the programming. The computer's approach to problem solving is a function of the algorithm and the programming technique.

There are basically three computer operating modes: batch processing, real time, and time-sharing. Each has special characteristics that make it more suitable to a given situation than either of the other two. Batch processing is best for routine problems that occur frequently. The inherent problem with the batch system is that only one program is executed at a time. Requested programs must wait in sequence until the operator calls for them. A real-time mode allows the user to employ a set of cataloged programs and to update the status of the data in the programs at almost any time. The real-time system may not afford the user direct interaction with the computer, but does permit a reasonably quick systems response. The time-sharing system is composed of satellite terminals directly linked to the central computer. The user has interactive dealings with the computer and can program or operate existing programs with instantaneous feedback. Time-sharing has been shown to be potentially cost-effective since a capital outlay may not be required and only variable rentals and operating expenses may be incurred.

Key Concepts

Algorithm	Minicomputer
Batch processing	Off-line
Central processing unit	On-line
Computer generations	Operating system

Computer system

Control flow

CPU options

Flowchart

Hardware system

Information flow

Input formats

Input unit

Memory unit

Microprocessor

Output formats

Output unit

Programmer

Programming language

Programming

Real-time

Software system

Time-sharing

User

User's manual

Questions for Discussion

1. What is meant by a computer generation?

2. What differentiates one computer generation from another?

3. List the five computer generations and the general characteristics associated with each. Refer specifically to the delineation criteria found for question 2 above.

4. What does Withington perceive to be the ultimate goal of the computer system generations?

5. Analyze the twenty-five year changes between the early 1950s and late 1970s computer capabilities.

6. Outline a basic computer system's information and control among its hardware components.

7. Explain the operation of the CPU with respect to input and output data moving through the system.

8. What factors are generally considered as the user's needs?

9. List the possible input formats available on computer systems.

10. What CPU options exist and what are their relative characteristics and costs?

11. What does the phrase algorithmic design mean? Relate it to programming.

12. What is a programming language and what factors determine which language is used?

13. What is a computer operating system and how does it work?

14. What types of problems can the computer handle?

15. What are the basic computer modes and what are their common characteristics?

PART

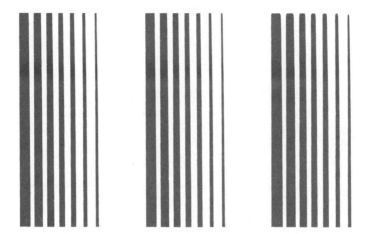

HOTEL COMPUTER
SYSTEMS

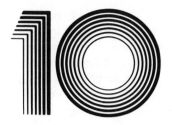

The Development of
Hotel Computer
Systems

Chapter Objectives:

1. To provide an overview of the development of front office computer systems.

2. To sketch the typical guest cycles of the 1950s, 1960s, and 1970s and the machinery used to monitor them.

3. To discuss the technological, analytical, and operational perspectives with regard to the industry's late start into computer assistance.

PRIOR to the late 1960s there were virtually no hotels involved in analyzing, designing, or implementing a computer-based information system. The lodging industry was growing at a rapid pace and although other industries had computerized at least their routine data processing tasks, innkeepers did not appear to be paying any attention. With the development of time-sharing technology and innovative designs for specific industry applications, system designers and hotel managers finally got acquainted. Today a significant portion of the hospitality industry has some dependence on computer processing, with about 15 to 20 percent of the industry employing a comprehensive management information system. It is anticipated that by the mid-1980s a majority of the industry will employ some sort of computer technology for monitoring most or all phases of its business. The following historical sketches are not intended to be complete, but serve as an overview to the development of front office computer systems. The later chapters will provide in-depth analyses of each of the major hotel systems modules.

Hotel Industry Factors

In trying to assess the apparent failure of hotels to become involved early in computer-oriented projects, it is important to remember some of the unique features of the industry:

1. There is perhaps no business where there are so many small transactions occurring with such rapidity.

2. Similarly, interim charges must be instantaneously posted to separate customer accounts to insure collection.

3. Internal control is difficult due to the number of remote point-of-sale outlets and the number of employees involved in handling transactions.

4. The customer is treated as a guest and stays in the establishment for a longer period of time than in almost any other business concern.

With these points in mind, simplified versions of the 1950s, 1960s, and 1970s guest cycles follow.

The 1950s Guest Cycle

During the early 1950s the general business community began experimenting with first generation computer hardware and software. Due to the large capital requirements, however, only the very biggest industrial concerns could afford computer installations, and most everyone was uncertain about the computer's future role in the business enterprise. At this time, the hospitality industry was preoccupied with a post-war growth period, the beginning of convention business, and the construction of international operations. The lodging industry was primarily composed of small, independent properties that could neither be bothered by unrelated technological advances nor afford to experiment in such luxuries. It was during this decade that front office equipment was manually operated and establishments were small enough to enable management sufficient control over the guest cycle and the hotel's books.

Just about all of the hotel's transactions were recorded manually and all records were kept in a notebook or index card file arrangement.

Reservations

Reservations were usually received by mail and arrived at the assistant manager's or manager's desk. From there the requests were forwarded to the reservations clerk (if there was such a person) or to the front desk. Reservations were entered into either a bound diary, a loose-leaf notebook, or onto a visible index file. Often the hotel maintained a reservation horizon of three to six months, and might not accept requests for space any further in the future.

Check In

Upon arrival the guest would approach the desk and fill in either a space on the register sheet or complete a registration card. Room assignments for guests with reservations were made on the day of arrival, using a card replacement scheme. As guests departed, the clerk would simply enter the reservation card into the vacant room rack slot, thereby insuring the guest, with a reservation, of a room. Once all reservation cards were transferred into the rack, walk-ins could be assigned from the remaining vacancies. The room rack was usually a metal piling of vertical card slots with symbols and color codings used to indicate room status. Some hotels employed carbonized registration cards and copies of the guest's personal data were distributed to the switchboard and the bellman; the completed original sometimes being used as the guest account record. An official rack slip was typed once the registration process and room assignment were completed.

Guest Accounting

The guest account may have been maintained on a typed account card, or the registration card, which was placed in a loose-leaf binder or index card file, according to the room numbers. All service or revenue departments were required to maintain a journal of charged sales and to forward, by runner or pneumatic tube, a voucher of the charge to the billing or desk clerk. Upon receipt, the clerk would time stamp the voucher and post it to the respective guest account. Room charges were posted by the night auditor from the transient ledger account record. Also, the hotel usually maintained an individual guest credit file as a means of monitoring the level of charge balances and cash pay-outs.

Night Audit

The night audit consisted of a manual procedure, or occasionally a posting machine, that began with the completion of unposted vouchers left over from the billing clerk's shift. The auditor also was responsible for posting all room charges and any additional late charge vouchers. All departed guest accounts had to be transcribed to a separate transcript sheet, and any unsettled accounts labelled for billing. The auditor then proceeded to verify all charge postings by comparing all account entries with the day's vouchers. A transcript was then prepared and all of its totals were proved against departmental sales records. If a posting machine was employed, its main advantage was its printing and accumulated totals capabilities. All account records had to be located, inserted into the machine, keyed, and refiled. This often led to erroneous filing procedures and inaccurate balances were commonly picked up. The night auditor typically cleared the machine of all of its accumulated totals upon completion of the night audit function.

Checkout

At checkout time the guest's bill was prepared and any late charges posted. Upon settlement of the account, the cashier notified the desk clerk that the guest had departed. The clerk changed the room's status in the rack to "on change" and, in turn, notified the housekeeping department. Registration cards, or rack slips, were marked to show the guest's departure, and the card was entered into the hotel's guest history file.

The 1960s Guest Cycle

As the computer scientists progressed into their second and third generations, the hotel industry began to experiment with off-the-premise (or contract) computing. Although only *back office functions* were tried this was the beginning of computer assistance for the innkeeper. Since most industries have similar back office functions (including accounts payable, inventory, purchasing, and payroll), the hotel merely had to collect its data and furnish the input to a computer service bureau. The computer manufacturers began to recognize the potential of the hospitality industry, but unwisely tried to apply hardware and software that had worked in other, less random entry, businesses. The inherent problems associated with complicated front office functions went unnoticed and the hotel computer systems fell flat. The computer designs were unrealistic and they eventually crumbled with analysts citing the enormous amount of hotel data collection and its coding as an impossible routine. These early systems were not planned jointly by hotel management and systems analysts and this led to a mutual lack of understanding and a minimization of acceptance by hotel personnel. Additionally, the variance between the theoretical modelling and reality (in the hotel environment) further puzzled computer specialists and led them to conclude that the attainment of a viable front office system was way off in the future. Innkeepers, fearful of losing the traditional face-to-face, personal contact with the hotel's guests through automation, were not terribly disturbed by the failure of these early in-house attempts.

The hotel in the 1960s was overrun by enormous volumes of paper; the recording and re-recording of transactions became intensified as larger hotels began to be constructed. The typical guest cycle of the 1960s was an improvement over the 1950s but most of the advances in hotel data processing were made in the back office areas, not the front office per se.

Reservations

With the advent of on-line inquiry systems (tested mainly by the airlines) the hotel attained computer-assisted reservation networks. Large chain operations developed central or regional computer installments and used a combination typewriter and telephone communication line, as peripheral devices, to investigate room availability. Advantages were gained in the speed of confirmation and the accuracy of documentation. Several independent reservation systems began to appear and these vehicles offered the independent operators a chance to subscribe to an automated network. Typically, the reservation terminals were capable of two-way communications and in the late 1960s the cathode ray tube (CRT) became available for video display of information.

Check In

Not very much was altered during the sixties. The registration card became the common record of registration and it was constructed in such a manner that carbonless copies could be made simultaneouly. Copies were distributed to the room rack and the switchboard operator with the original designed to serve as the guest's folio. Room assignments were still made based upon the status of the room rack and at the discretion of the desk clerk.

Guest Accounting

Major improvements were made in the area of guest account posting. The evolution from hand transcription to electromechanical machinery impacted upon the efficiency of the desk to chart the guest's transactions. Similar strides were also realized in the realm of internal communication devices. Telewriters, intercoms, pneumatic tubes, and telephone communications gave the hotel the constant flow of information it demanded, even though the deletion of some paper documents may have occasionally led to lost support documents and erroneous postings. Vouchers were still used to verify a charge sale that was recorded in the departmental sales journal; although vouchers were not the exclusive form of communication to the desk. Machine-prepared folios were held in a folio bucket and filed by room number. Credit limits were surveyed by the auditor and high risks were singled out for managerial action.

Night Audit

The night audit remained very much the same as it had been, with the exception of the machine audit technique. Accompanying the development and improvement in posting machine technology came the creation of the audit tape. Although the front office posting machine enabled the posting of individual entries to folios, it also, simultaneously, accumulated departmental totals and generated an audit tape. The audit tape provided for an *audit trail* or tracing of all the day's entries, at any point in time. The night auditor's work was simplified and accelerated because an initial trial balance of the audit totals would eliminate much of the research and physical sortings previously required. The auditor's work still consisted of verifying the bookkeeping recordings and proving the departmental account totals.

Checkout

The machinery at the front desk allowed for a quicker checkout procedure. The guest accounts were better maintained and fewer discrepancies arose due to fuller data explanations and supportive cross-referenced documentation. Checkout also was accompanied by improved internal communications that notified the housekeeping staff and operating departments (for the purpose of discontinuing charge privileges) of the guest's recent departure. The registration card, or its duplicate, was then filed in a guest history file as a base for future marketing strategies.

The 1970s Guest Cycle

Whereas the close of the third and the beginning of the fourth computer generations began to develop distributed intelligence, the hospitality industry remained reluctant to become involved with total system design. Before the mid-1970s, however, with the advent of the minicomputer and microprocessor units, price/performance became attractive to the lodging community. Large hotels renewed their interests in front office data processing and the computer vendors realized that the industry required customized programming applications for guest accounting, night audits, and rooms management.

The cash register, for example, evolved from a cardboard box, to a mechanical register, to an *electronic cash register* (ECR), to a *point-of-sale* (POS) *transaction terminal.* The manual posting procedures advanced to mechanical posting machines, to electronic processing procedures based on data relay. The room rack began to be replaced by the electronic folio array and registration was made faster through video techniques. The traditional guest room key underwent changes and became a perforated room key board that provides the front desk with the ability to alter room locks upon request. The control of the hotel's physical environment, especially with regard to energy consumption, became monitored by computerized energy sensor systems. And the night audit became a convenient push-button operation that actually allowed the auditor a chance to audit, not merely post, entries. All in all, the 1970s were the beginning of a firm commitment to computer-based hotel information systems with more progress being anticipated in the 1980s.

Although there was much fanfare given to computer-assisted hotel management systems, the fact remains that less than 20 percent of the industry employed an integrated system design by the mid-1970s. A large number of establishments had some computerized modules and the following cycle highlights are slanted toward this automated technology.

Reservations

The reservation package had advanced to the point of using fewer electronic switching devices and not requiring a person to receive, process, and confirm requests at the host inn. The customer could go to a chain affiliate, or any one of a number of agents, and get a relatively instantaneous confirmation at almost any hotel. The real progress of the 1970s reservation modules has been in their interaction with the total hotel system. Upon receipt of a reservation, the system automatically blocked the room on the date requested and generated a standardized letter of confirmation. The reservation confirmation led to the construction of a folio account in the computer's memory and any preregistration activities such as prepayments or advance deposits were accurately maintained in the system until the guest checked in. Also, the reservations forecast function could be used to display future expectations, actual bookings, and an arrival listing.

Check In

With the interlocking of the reservation and registration modules came a faster and more accurate check-in capability. The guest who held a reservation might not even be required to fill in a registration card, but merely asked to verify the personal data of the reservation file. Once the guest had approved the registration display, occupancy began, since the computer had already made the room assignment, according to a preprogrammed assignment format. The need for rack slips and telephone operation listings had been replaced by electronic visibility displays that could be used to identify who the guest is and where the guest is lodged. A list of room availabilities and status reports was accessible, upon demand, at several different points throughout the front office and housekeeping areas.

Guest Accounting

Improvement in the speed of recording and the accuracy of postings had been attained through computerized accounting packages. The interfacing of the remote POS terminals with the guest accounting module enabled instantaneous postings to guest accounts, simultaneous to the hotel's operating department's recording of the charge. This, of course, had led to the elimination or minimization of voucher transfers (except as a support function) and had enabled the hotel to perform an audit at any point in time. Late charges were also avoided as the POS was programmed to only accept charges to those rooms that were currently occupied. Hence, the need to fetch folios and thumb through piles of vouchers for the posting procedure had changed to an electronic transfer from the point-of-sale to the folio without additional documentation, runner, or folio hunting. The guest credit limits were no longer supervised by the desk clerk's review, but were automatically identified by the computer. The guest accounting module was usually programmed in such a manner that guest accounts that approach the house limit were not allowed any charges until management reset their limits or cleared their balance due.

Night Audit

The tedious job of the night audit had been reduced from bookkeeping, mathematics, and auditing to mostly just auditing. Similar to the simplification that the initial posting machine accumulation totals and audit tapes provided, the instantaneous postings, simultaneous account entries, and trial balances throughout the day combined to make the night audit a feasible task, even for the largest properties. Some hotels that previously experienced 11- to 12-hour night audit routines found the computerized audit to be performed in fifteen minutes or less. The auditor was freed to perform audit checks and prove account totals from cross-reference documents.

Checkout

The presentation of an orderly, itemized and well-documented guest statement reduced the number of guest discrepancies and assured the public of the hotel's honesty. The ability to present a video facsimile of the statement to the guest for approval prior to printing it, significantly sped up the checkout process and saved the establishment time and paper. A guest who provided a credit card (upon check in) for deferring payment of any bills would have already received authorization and would only need to sign the voucher (often this was not even mandatory for validity). Hence, the guest went to the desk, accepted the statement, settled the account, and left. Any nonzero account balances of departed guests were automatically transferred to the nonguest ledger account, and an itemized bill was simultaneously printed.

Analysis of Late Hotel Computer Participation

An analysis of hotel computer participation can be made along three perspectives: technological, in terms of computer system advances; analytical, in terms of the contributions attained; and operational, in terms of the guest cycle.

Technological Perspective

The fact that the lodging industry got off to a late start enabled it to reap the benefits of other industries' research and developments, with regard to computerized systems. While most businesses really became *computer-oriented* and *computer-dependent* during the 1960s, the hotel industry's lack of participation may have accidently been economically wise and scientifically sound.

The 1970s brought new technology of a significantly enhanced quality, more computer capabilities for less money, and easier to operate software packages. While most other industries struggled to alter their already existing computerized networks to accommodate the latest concepts of distributed intelligence, innkeepers were just beginning to get involved. Hence, the benefits to the hotel industry, from a technological perspective, derived from their late start were:

1. less complicated software required to operate system

2. fewer system errors due to technological refinements

3. smaller hardware configurations

4. development of customized industry programming

5. increased computer efficiencies at lower costs

6. presence of computer-trained hotel personnel

Analytical Perspective

The application of computer technology to the hotel industry was slow because management felt automation would: 1) depersonalize the business, 2) reduce guest contact by employees, 3) replace necessary personnel, 4) interfere with the growth trend of the industry, and 5) take control over the operational services of the hotel. Although similar concerns were initially held by other businesses, the lodging industry felt it was a special, service-oriented business that would lose its market if the computer were to become an integral part of the firm.

The actual experiences of many innkeepers has shown the computer-assisted hotel management system to:

1. minimize the amount of data rehandling.

2. reduce the required number of source documents.

3. provide instantaneous postings to guest accounts.

4. allow personnel more time to spend with guests.

5. add a desirable sense of professionalism to the hotel.

6. provide management with a better knowledge of the firm.

7. allow for tighter internal control of operations.

8. enable energy monitoring and conservation.

9. improve communications throughout facility.

10. simplify reservation, check-in and checkout procedures.

11. enhance the night audit function.

12. improve employee morale.

13. produce comprehensive management reports.

Operational Perspective

The operations of the hotel have been streamlined and more efficiently designed with the guest, as well as management, in mind. The improvement of guest services, that are directly attributable to automated applications, includes both tangibles and intangibles. A partial listing of advances made in the guest's interests are:

1. increased accuracy of hotel records.

2. faster check-in and checkout procedures.

3. quicker confirmation and processing of reservations.

4. better security of guest room and personal data.

5. production of intelligible, itemized statements.

6. improved communications among operating departments.

Guest Cycle:	FUNCTIONS: Reservation	Registration	Room Assignment	Folio
1950s	Held on: 1. Index card 2. Calendar Pad 3. Notebook	Registration Book	Based Upon: Physical Lists Delivered to Desk by Housekeeping	Guest Account Book
1960s	Held on: 1. Density Boards 2. Block Boards	Registration Card	Based Upon: Room Rack	File Card Account Record
1970s	Held on: Electronic Memory	Video Screen Verification	Based Upon: Predesignated Algorithm with System	Electronic Soft Copy
1980s (presented in later chapter)	Held on: Verbal Entry System	Self-registration	Based Upon: Algorithm in a Dispensing Machine	Self-Review Available in Guest's Room
Key Characteristics	Horizon Expanded by Increased Size of Holding File	Reduction in Check-in Time	Increased Speed and Accuracy Gained in Status Reporting	Relatively Paperless Approach to Record Maintenance

Table 10.1 Simplified Comparative Evolution of Guest Cycle

Entry Postings	Cash Collections	Night Audit	Checkout	Guest History File
Vouchers Run to Desk	Cardboard Box	Pencil and Paper (Manual)	Manual Production of Statement	Former Registration Book File
Vouchers Delivered by Runner, Telewriter, Pneumatic Tubes or Telephone	Mechanical Register	Posting Machine Assistance	Machine-Assisted Preparation of Bill	Former Registration Card File
Direct POS Entry	ECR and POS	Electronic Programming	Updated Electronic Preparation	Electronic Memory File, or Hard Copy File
FM Transmission, Light Wave Transmission, or from Key Pad	POS	Electronic, but done Continually	Electronic Funds Transfer Interface	Electronic Memory File
Improved Verification and Authorization Prior to Acceptance in System	Gains in Cashier Auditing and Balancing and Cash Control	Improved Audit Trail and Internal Controls	Improved Speed and Accuracy of Statement Preparation	Better and Faster Retention and Retrieval of Data

Summary

The hotel industry was late to start getting involved with computers and this ironically afforded the industry many advantages. A lot of computing power could be purchased at a reasonable price and the costs of most of the research and developments were borne by the early computer participants.

Table 10.1 is a simplified comparison of some essential guest cycle functions for the 1950s, 1960s, 1970s, and projections for the 1980s. The development of hotel computer systems greatly altered the traditional guest cycle in many ways. Technological advancements, analytical improvements, and operational benefits combine to render the hotel better able to relate to the guest and to handle the corresponding accounting transactions. All in all, things have and will continue to change rapidly.

Key Concepts

Audit trail   Energy sensor system
Back office functions   Peripheral devices
Computer-dependent   Point-of-sale (POS) terminal
Computer-oriented   Random entry
Computer service bureau   Room key board
Electronic cash register (ECR)

Questions for Discussion

1. What were some of the industry characteristics before computer experimentation in the early 1970s?

2. Explain the corresponding behaviors of general business and the hotel industry, with regards to computerization, during the 1950s, 1960s, and 1970s.

3. Compare and contrast the reservation procedures of the 1950s, 1960s, and 1970s. What were the major advancements?

4. Compare and contrast the check-in procedures of the 1950s, 1960s, and 1970s. What were the major achievements?

5. Compare and contrast the guest accounting procedures of the 1950s, 1960s, and 1970s. What were the major achievements?

6. Compare and contrast the night audit procedures of the 1950s, 1960s, and 1970s. What were the major achievements?

7. Compare and contrast the checkout procedures of the 1950s, 1960s and 1970s. What were the major achievements?

8. What beneficial factors to the hospitality industry were derived from their late participation in computer utilization?

Hotel Information Systems

Chapter Objectives:

1. To introduce the hotel information system (HIS) concept.

2. To enumerate HIS objectives and their potential impact upon the firm.

3. To present a basic listing of HIS-associated terminology.

4. To give an overview of HIS hardware and software concepts and designs.

5. To explain the consultant's role in the HIS decision-making and implementation process.

HOW MUCH do hotel managers need to know about computer science to use computers? About as much as they need to know about auto mechanics to operate a car. Too often, lodging management has allowed the gap between computer capabilities and computer applications to widen because of a lack of knowledge about automation. Another factor inhibiting the rapid acceptance of hotel information systems (HIS) is the fact that few firms have opted to use them. Fears of excessive investment and operating costs, possible retention of unnecessary information, potential loss of personalized guest services, and failures of early system attempts have rendered much of the industry without computer assistance. This chapter will focus attention on the HIS overview and Chapters 12 through 15 will deal with specific hotel modules. It is important to note that initially all hotel data handling and guest services were labor intensive (since all of these procedures were carried out manually). With the development of HIS applications has come a shift toward a more capital intensive environment.

The HIS Concept

The HIS concept deals with the enhancement of managerial effectiveness through the proper handling and flow of the hotel's most important resource: information. The hospitality industry has been involved with the manual charting of guest transactions and the production of volumes of paper documenting these activities. The development of an HIS is simply an attempt to simplify the data procedures of the hotel, at a cost savings, and with increased speed and improved accuracy.

Hotel information systems have the following primary objectives:

1. Present management with timely and comprehensive *reports.*

2. Eliminate or reduce the number of unnecessary *source documents* and/or *data handling procedures.*

3. Provide increased *operational control* and *immediate visibility* into operational status.

4. Enable management to better monitor and control the *guest cycle.*

5. Enable the hotel to provide improved and expanded *guest services.*

6. Provide cost *savings.*

One of the primary objectives of the HIS concept is to present management with timely and comprehensive information from a collection of raw, isolated facts. This is accomplished effectively through a reduction in clerical procedures and a minimization of data rehandling. In order to produce effective managerial reports, automated systems depend upon data entry and data base storage. The development of the data base operation is simplified through a reduction or elimination of source documents, except as required by law.

Managerial controls can be gained in such hospitality areas as: cash control, ticket control, inventory control, housekeeping, guest settlement, and the night audit. The instantaneous balancing of charges, cash receipts, and postings, for example, is certainly a desired and necessary procedure that the hospitality industry benefits from. In addition to its speed, an HIS is very accurate and oftentimes eliminates many of the typical posting, mathematical, and illogical filing problems prevalent throughout a traditional charting of the guest cycle.

Improved guest services have been offered by hotels that have implemented an HIS, with improved employee morale being an additional plus. The fact that the hotel data is processed quicker and more accurately has led to cost savings and cost justification of some system configurations in numerous operations.

HIS Terminology

The following systems terminology, although not limited to HIS applications, is common among hospitality vendors.

1. *Acoustic coupler*—permits use of a phoneset as a connection to the computer.
2. *Chip*—a silicone chip containing the intelligence of the operating system; also, referred to as chip hardware.
3. *Contract programming*—customized programming for a fee; programs specifically designed for the user.
4. *Cost effective*—or cost justified; a system of which the benefits far outweigh the costs.
5. *CRT terminal*—"cathode ray tube;" a terminal used to project information on a screen (soft copy); yields a reduction in paper usage.
6. *Data base*—a collection of information available to a computer system.
7. *Distributed processing*—a network where computer power is not centralized, but is distributed to the user.
8. *EDP*—"Electronic Data Processing;" an automated method for reducing the number of times data is handled; also, implies the processing of data by electronic means.
9. *FDP*—"Field Developed Program;" term used by vendors to connote the development of a system in the application's environment.
10. *Flexible system*—one in which the user can do some programming.
11. *Hard copy*—a printed output format.
12. *In-house system*—a flexibly programmed system, requiring an on-the-premises EDP staff, usually developed jointly by the hotel's management and the vendor; a long-term commitment requiring a large capital outlay.
13. *Integrated system*—or total system; a system that is an interfacing of modular components; may include both front and back office functions.
14. *Interactive programming*—requires an exchange of information and control between the user and the computer process (see lead-through programming).
15. *Interface*—a shared boundary of interconnection between system components.
16. *Lead-through programming*—a step-by-step interactive format requiring a user response to a system question prior to advancement through the system program (also called a drop-through technique).

17. *Line printer*—device capable of printing items on a statement, guest check, or report.

18. *Master-slave interface*—a series of input slave devices connected to a master mainframe for communication of input, output, and processing at a remote location (also called remote processing).

19. *Modular system*—applications programmed on a functional basis for independent systems application, or interfaced for the formation of an integrated system.

20. *Multiplex*—to simultaneously transmit two data streams on a single channel.

21. *Multitasking*—the processing of several computer jobs concurrently.

22. *OEM*—"Other Equipment Manufacturers;" more than one computer manufacturer's equipment used in a composite system.

23. *Off-line*—computer processing phase in which peripheral hardware operates without being under the control of the CPU.

24. *On-line*—peripheral equipment functions under the control of the CPU; also involves the user's ability to interact with the computer.

25. *Operating system*—responsible for the entire information systems functioning; communicates to and deals with file management; the part of the system that runs the programs.

26. *Order entry terminal*—see POS terminal.

27. *Parameter driven system*—the individual specifications of the user determine storage capacities, required system functions, number of I/O devices, and the overall system configuration.

28. *Point-of-Sale*—or POS; the application of systems technology at the point-of-purchase or transactional location.

29. *Post-sale*—the application of systems technology after the point-of-sale.

30. *POS terminal*—a communications device located at a remote point-of-sale and linked to the accounting records. An intelligent or nonintelligent, cash register-like device.

31. *Pre-sale*—the application of systems technology prior to the point-of-sale.

32. *Real time*—a method of computer processing in which the throughput is efficient enough to affect the user immediately; a very short interval between input and output.

33. *Soft copy*—a video displayed output format.

34. *Source document*—the original written recording of a transaction.

35. *Stand alone*—a piece of hardware containing a complete processing system (I/O, memory, and CPU).

36. *Text editing*—the alteration of inputted data to remove errors and provide for intelligible processing.

37. *Throughput*—a measure of system efficiency; the rate at which work can be handled by a system.

38. *Transactional system*—a system composed of a high volume of small transactions occurring at remote locations.

39. *Turnaround*—the amount of time from when input is submitted until the output is generated.

40. *Turnkey system*—a preprogrammed application package capable of performing only a limited number of functions; usually a minicomputer system; requires no EDP staff; available for usage shortly after installation.

41. *Vanilla system*—a one-computer vendor system; all components of a given system supplied by one computer manufacturer.

42. *Vendor-designed system*—system designed by vendor for a specific user (or group of users); normally a system that enables some in-house programming but does not require an EDP staff.

43. *Voice synthesizer*—a verbal system response generated by a computer from a limited verbal syntax (voice output).

HIS In-House Approaches

Three approaches that lodging management has taken toward in-house computer system implementation are the: 1) turnkey system, 2) vendor-designed system, and 3) customized system.

Turnkey System

The turnkey approach is favored by innkeepers since it is primarily a minicomputer-based, relatively low cost, and quickly installed automation. The turnkey package usually comes preprogrammed to perform a limited number of required functions and cannot be user programmed, which makes it an inflexible system. Although initial investments are inexpensive ($2500 to $6500), additional expenses are incurred if the vendor must be recruited to alter or upgrade existing programs. The cost of this system usually begins relatively low and increases over its life. Since the needs of the hotel are dynamic, system alterations may increase the system's cost while the output may decrease in value or appropriateness.

The operator who opts to enter the computerized HIS market through the turnkey system approach will usually gain computer usage within a two-week installation horizon. Also called an *off-the-shelf* approach to computing.

Vendor-Designed System

Although not normally a minicomputer-based system, some vendors are beginning to design total system packages built upon a series of minis. The concept is: the vendor custom designs a system for another user's specific operation and then the hotel purchases it, as is, for installation. The purchased system is then learned by the in-house personnel for implementation and operation. This approach saves programming time and significant development costs, yet provides customized applications and flexibility. The training of the new employees is usually included in the price of the systems package. The innkeeper who elects this option will normally have the HIS operational within six to twelve months. The vendor-designed system has an intermediate cost and has sufficient flexibility to extend its functional life.

Customized System

The customized in-house system involves an internal computer team, or contract personnel, and involves the highest capital expenditure of the three options cited. This in-house design is the most flexible and best understood system since management and systems analysts normally work jointly on the HIS development. Management's needs are usually satisfied and because the system is modelled around a specific property, it tends to be well-accepted by the operating personnel. The system's hardware and software are usually not simple, like they might be in a generally-marketed, limited applications package. The hotel must determine its own hardware, software, and personnel needs. Because, historically, hotel management knew little about these details, the customized system has not usually been the first system implemented. The long-range flexibility of this design and its specialized application are assumed to negate the additional expenditure required to build the system.

HIS Hardware

Most hotel systems employ the same basic components that any other computer-based industry system would, but certain specialty devices and common hotel components need to be given delineation. Instructions for using the system's hardware can usually be found in the user's manual that accompanies the system.

Processor Configurations

The most essential system component is the processing unit. In HIS configurations the processor may be either a mainframe or a minicomputer (microprocessors also are used, but not too much in the larger systems). The size of a mainframe can range from a small compact model to a very large structure, depending upon the needs of the system design. Typically, the mainframe houses the processor (CPU), the memory unit, and the system's power supply. The mainframe is designed to be located away from the point-of-sale and has slaves, or remote terminals, interfaced with it for communications. Figure 11.1 is a simplified sketch of a master-slave configuration depicting the use of I/O entry units in combination with the mainframe.

The minicomputer can be isolated similar to the mainframe or it can be contained in

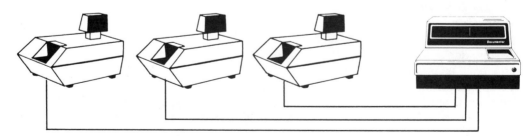

Figure 11.1. Master-Slave Configuration
(Courtesy of Addressograph Multigraph Documentor Division)

a terminal for either stand-alone or master terminal servicing to a series of satellite terminals. The stand-alone capability simply means that the unit contains all the components to function independent of any other device. It has a key pad or similar format for input entry, a display or print unit for output, contains the minicomputer CPU, and possesses its own memory capabilities. Usually stand-alone units are programmable and possess many report-producing options. The minicomputer has significantly lowered the price of in-house computing.

The minicomputer as a master terminal employs essentially the same concept as the use of a mainframe. The major difference lies in the fact that the CPU is located inside a terminal; it is not an independent systems component. The primary reason for cabling several terminals into a central mini is to gain economic advantages (in terms of only having to provide one CPU device) and to permit consolidated data and reporting functions. In Figure 11.2 a design of the master minicomputer configuration is provided to differentiate the mini from the mainframe design. The remote terminals usually transmit transactional and accounting data to the master terminal and each unit usually has control over its own cash drawer operation.

It is important to note that minicomputers generally cannot store as much data or process jobs as fast as a larger computer system can. Also, the mini is limited in the number of jobs it can perform at one time and is usually designed for a small number of applications. The reason for their huge success in HIS design is due to their appro-

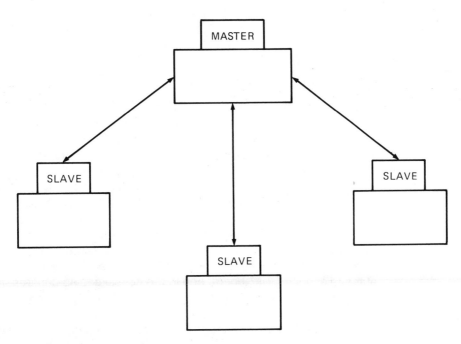

Figure 11.2. Minicomputer Master Design

priateness to the application and their cost advantages (they are cheaper systems and require no EDP staff). Although not as popular in its usage now, the microcomputer is anticipated to replace the mini within the next decade or so.

Memory Units

The HIS configuration usually is dependent upon a magnetic tape cassette or disc storage. Storage may be made in a random access or sequential filing mode, each of which has its capabilities and shortcomings. The random access filing mode is the fastest storage to retrieve because the search process will lead directly to the addressed data file regardless of where it is located. The sequential access is inherently slower because the search procedure requires that all the files be screened from the first through to the requested file. The size of storage areas varies greatly; while some slave terminals may possess storage, the master memory unit normally possesses significant file space. The memory capability of the HIS is surely one of the greatest limiting factors to its overall performance. Hence, the size and speed of storage are the central limiting features of the computerized system. It should be noted that all successful HIS applications to date have employed a disc storage due to its random access capabilities.

Terminals

The system's terminals can either be of an *intelligent* or *nonintelligent* design, the major differentiations being dependent upon memory capabilities and the performance of local functions. A terminal containing no memory in its individual unit is classified as a nonintelligent terminal and requires connection to an intelligent device for operation. The ability to gain cost advantages and to better optimize the system's processing capabilities has made nonintelligent terminals fairly popular in HIS configurations. The nonintelligent terminal functions as an input-output device only and is the slave unit in a master framework.

Intelligent terminals are capable of performing some local functions (adding, subtracting, applying taxes, or accumulating totals) and possess memory capabilities. The main advantage of an intelligent terminal is that it is capable of operating off-line, retaining its transactions, and allowing for text editing prior to its data being sent to the processor for manipulation. The minicomputer is an example of an intelligent terminal that operates on-line, but can also be constructed to do some functions off-line. Hence, the test of the intelligent terminal lies in its memory and functional capabilities.

The two most common types of terminals found in HIS schemes are: 1) display terminals and 2) POS terminals. Display terminals are either of the CRT or VDT variety and transmit data and information in soft copy on a television-like screen. The display terminals have a keyboard for data entry and information retrieval and are usually found in the front office, at the telephone switchboard, and in the housekeeping departments. Since hard copy is still critical to legal reporting and to the production of satisfactory support documents, most display units will have an optional printer attached to them. Should a displayed report, for example, be desired in hard copy, the printer can be used to reproduce it on paper. Display terminals (which may function as POS terminals) usually are designed to incorporate a lead-through format, requiring the operator to respond to system inquiries, and to enable text editing prior to advancing through a computer program routine. Some display units are also capable of producing graphics and flashing important messages on the screen.

The POS terminal has replaced the cash register at the revenue center location and is used to input transactional data, calculate the guest check, and to produce, in hard copy, the guest statement. The POS may also possess a small display unit, similar to a cash register's window, for verification of input prior to processing. Figure 11.3 depicts the basic types of terminals and highlights the major differences in construction.

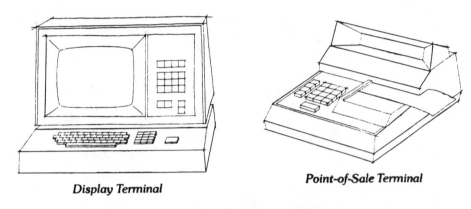

Display Terminal

Point-of-Sale Terminal

Figure 11.3 Types of Terminals (Courtesy of Motorola)

Terminals are a large share of the types of devices found in the hotel industry due to the number of points-of-sale and the essential communication links required. The terminals may be preprogrammed, specialized, and/or programmable. A preprogrammed terminal is usually installed with a lead-through, or drop-through, format. The instructions are found within the continuous operation of the terminals and there are some automatic calculations that may also be taking place simultaneously (for example, the automatic application of taxes to items being purchased). A specialized terminal is one that has been custom designed, either through its keyboard or its unique physical structure, to handle specific problems of the user. For example, several food outlets employ keyboards that are programmed, or coded, with the menu item names on the keys rather than prices. Other specialized terminals are *OCR* devices designed to read input from a character recognition code sheet inserted into a reader located on the terminal (see Fig. 11.4). Programmable terminals require the user to be knowledgeable in the basic workings of the hardware and software, but enable the user to develop customized reports and functions for the terminal.

The specialized and preprogrammed terminals are receiving significant attention in the hospitality industry because they are a cost-saving alternative to the designing of customized computers or computer-operating systems.

Figure 11.4. Documentor OCR System
(Courtesy of Addressograph Multigraph Documentor Division)

Security of stored information and/or confidential data may be assured through a key-lock, security-access system or through complicated user identification codes. In either case, management is protected against illegal access to sensitive files or parts of files.

Printers

HIS printing units can be of an *impact* or *nonimpact* design and of a high or slow speed character. The fact that a printing device works on an impact basis is reflective of its speed (slower) and cost (cheaper) than its nonimpact counterpart. High speed printers are usually located at the front desk for guest folio preparation upon demand and the slower printers are found in accounting areas or back office functions. The speed of the printer and the type of paper required are variables that affect the price of the unit. The printer may be an attached component (a display terminal) or self-contained (the POS). Regardless of the capabilities of the HIS printer (usually about 120 lines per minute), the

---

HOTEL INFORMATION SYSTEMS MODULAR OVERVIEW

RESERVATIONS
1. Formulation of the Reservation Inquiry
2. Equation of Inquiry and Availability
3. Recording of Transactional Data
4. Confirmation of Reservation
5. Maintenance of Reservation Record

GUEST ACCOUNTING
1. Creation of Account
2. Entry of the Transactional Charge
3. Posting Function
4. Auditing Procedures
5. Settlement of Account

ROOMS MANAGEMENT
1. Room Status Determination
2. Room Assignment
3. Guest Information
4. Automated Minor Services
5. Housekeeping

GENERAL MANAGEMENT
1. Revenue Analysis
2. Operating Statistics
3. Financial Analysis
4. Back Office Interface
5. Decision-Making

Table 11.1. HIS Modular Overview

hotel must concern itself with the speed required for its needs, as significant cost savings can be made in this area.

There are specialty printers that have been devised for the HIS configuration, such as journal printers, voucher printers, tab printers, guest check printers, reservation confirmation printers, and folio printers. All in all, the applicability of the printer is a function of the work requiring hard copy formatting.

HIS Software Modules

Most HIS systems are designed and implemented in phases. The following modular segmentations are in accordance with the most typical designations and are discussed in detail in later chapters (see Table 11.1).

1. *RESERVATIONS* (horizons from one day to two years)

2. *GUEST ACCOUNTING* (monitoring and control)

3. *ROOMS MANAGEMENT* (room status, availability, and housekeeping information)

4. *GENERAL MANAGEMENT* (reports upon demand or periodically)

The advantage of implementing one module at a time has been shown to be a good method for computerizing on a cost-justified, afford-it-as-you-go, basis. Additional benefits to computerization on an incremental basis enables greater acceptance and understanding by the operational staff, reduces fears of job loss, and allows for sufficient employee adjustment. The modular approach is advocated, especially for the existing property, as it enables economic and psychological advantages to be gained over the alternative of a total system implementation. Note that Figure 11.5 is a representation of an actual total real-time system.

HIS Specifications

Points of Application

Computer technology can be applied to the hospitality situation either on a pre-sale, point-of-sale, and/or post-sale basis. The processing of reservations, rooms forecasting, precosting of banquets, and scheduling of employees are examples of pre-sale applications common in the hotel business. Point-of-sale (POS) transactions, taking place at all the hotel's revenue centers, require an instantaneous recording of data and simultaneous transmission of charges to the front desk for posting. The production of cost and revenue reports, the development of operational statistics, the analysis of the productivity and efficiency of the housekeeping and sales personnel are examples of post-sale procedures. These are computations that take place after the fact. (What was our occupancy last night?)

It should be noted that there are some hotel information systems available that are limited in their applications and that must be applied at specific time intervals. The hotel that only invests in a reservation system, for instance, may experience tremendous difficulty in trying to convert or modify that system to produce post-sale information. The reason for this revolves around the system's hardware capabilities and the parameters of its software. Hence, the determination of when the computer application should be brought to bear is a very important consideration in the design of computer-assisted hotel management system.

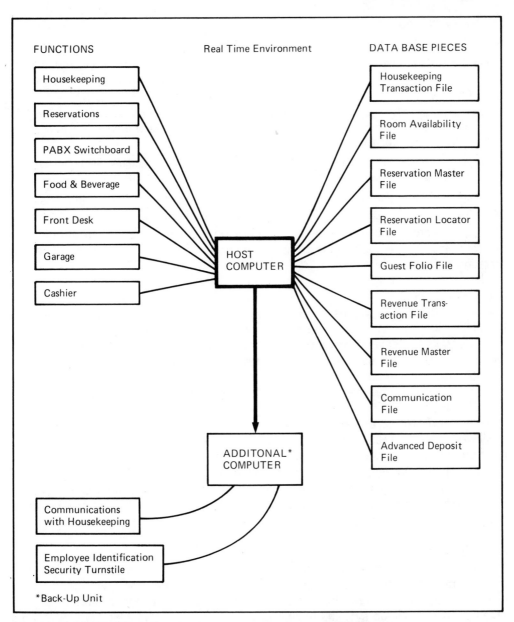

Figure 11.5. Representation of a Large Hotel HIS Configuration

Levels of HIS Operations

Hotel systems can exist in three general processing mode levels:

1. *Rapid Access/Inquiry Mode*—the ability to survey or search through an inventory to find a required piece of information (for example, checking room availability in response to a reservation request).

2. *Reporting/Output Format Mode*—the production of prespecified vouchers, forms, journals, and reports, outputted by the operating system from either a data base or from a local transaction (for example, the production of the daily report).

3. *Analytical/Deterministic Mode*—the ability of the software to search and operate upon data and information already entered into the system (for example, the night audit).

Typically, the HIS is capable of operating on all three levels and this certainly increases the capabilities of its output. Management must be careful to understand that there are different computer operating techniques, specified through the programming, that will instruct the computer through the appropriate search routine and reporting formats.

Computeritis

The belief that everything must be computerized is an overreaction to the implementation of the HIS. The fact that the feasibility and appropriateness of task application must still be carefully evaluated and that an inequitable computer orientation may interfere with the overall objectives of the hotel (with regard to changing the basis of the property to make it computer-compatible) must be kept in mind during implementation and operation. Computer orientation should be the objective, not computer dependence.

Preinstallation Requirements

The installation of an HIS is subject to many requirements. If the configuration involves a mainframe then much more site preparation is required as opposed to the employment of a minicomputer. Physical requirements of space, electrical supply, air conditioning, and the cabling must be given some consideration in the decision to automate. Upon completion of the necessary preparation of the site, an inspection and approval should be made prior to the equipment's installation.

Back-Up Systems

The fear of system malfunction or failure is a constant threat to hotels that have eliminated their room rack, discarded their out-of-date posting machine, and have opted for an electronic folio-filing system. In an attempt to maintain operations in case of system outages, many back-up systems have become popular in the lodging area. A manual back-up system may be maintained, but this is not very practical as the HIS is designed to replace this sort of a system. Disc packs can be used in a redundant manner so as to have identical data bases at two locations or more; should one fail the other would be accessible. Another approach is to have duplicate but separate back-up systems. Some HIS require two different-sized computers to handle various functions. Both computers may employ disc packs and these may both be recording the same information. Should one computer fail, all that needs to be done is that the other computer be operated until the original unit is restored. As long as one major switchboard is used for wiring all the peripheral devices to the CPU, the duplicate, separate system concept is very effective. Also available are distributed shared back-up systems in which a series of intelligent terminals all share the same information. In other words, as data is entered into one terminal it may also be entered simultaneously into all the terminals. Then, a failure of any one terminal would not necessarily lead to an inability to retrieve data or to a loss of data.

The development of solid state memory devices has led to the retention of stored information regardless of how long electrical power may be out. Most HIS are equipped with battery packs for emergency power sources, but these generally do not perform as well as is required in the case of long power failures.

HIS Maintenance

Perhaps one of the most critical concerns for the hospitality industry is systems maintenance. Since most HIS do not require an EDP staff and tend to make the operation computer-dependent, a vendor or contract maintenance program becomes critical. Although some computer vendors disclose the cost of their maintenance package as part of the system's expense, others may not make mention of postinstallation support. In the event of a system malfunction or failure (down time), some manufacturers provide an almost immediate service by a qualified field service representative. The user should try to adopt only those HIS packages that come with service programs that are available 24 hours a day, seven days a week. A hotel that experiences a systems failure and is unable to process guest transactions would be in a state of disorder. Local on-call service should be available and the system should have a built-in, back-up device to maintain its memory even during power losses. Also, it is not unusual for vendor contracts to guarantee the maximum time it will take for services to be rendered, on call.

HIS Expenditures

Other than the package cost being a function of the hardware configuration and specifications and the extent of the software modules, some additional financial considerations are:

1. *Shipping Costs*—usually a user expense.
2. *Insurance*—liability insurance on the system is usually carried by the vendor; additional insurance is at the user's expense.
3. *Environmental Consideration*—depending upon the HIS design, consideration may have to be given to air conditioning, electrical, and architectural alterations; all of which are at the customer's expense.
4. *In-House Communications*—the additional requirement of communications devices for system usage is a user's cost usually.

5. *License Fee*—some computer vendors may require a license fee for software usage and this is not always specifically included in the systems price quote.

6. *Taxes*—state and local taxes, where applicable, will need to be paid by the user.

7. *Maintenance*—vendor or contract maintenance may be an additional systems expense of significant magnitude, if not included in the HIS price.

HIS Investment Options

Investment options available to hospitality industry management include:

1. *Systems Ownership*—the outright purchase of system's hardware and software. Usually done only if management envisions lease costs increasing rapidly over time.

2. *Lease Arrangement*—vendors will lease systems to hotels for periods of 12, 24, or 36 months. Systems manufacturers usually encourage a one-year lease with renewal options, because this is mutually beneficial to the vendor and the user. On a one-year basis the user is not bound to a soon-to-be obsolete system, and the manufacturer is not committed to an existing installation for a long term. Monthly leases, for a minimum of three months, are possible but not very popular.

3. *Time- or Co-Op-Sharing*—the development of hotel user groups participating in shared systems applications is not very common now, but may offer significant cost benefits to smaller operators interested in computerization. The costs of systems operations are usually shared among all participants.

4. *Service Bureaus*—off-the-premise utilization of service bureaus, or computer centers, who sell services on a prorated basis. Hotels desiring to have a few limited applications automated may elect to furnish input data to private bureaus for inputting and processing. The outputted information is turned back to the user for application.

Determination of systems costs require a thorough analysis and feasibility study and management should be able to cost-justify the expense of the HIS. The design and implementation of modular application subsystems have provided for some cost economies and allow hotels to add modules one at a time, so long as they can bear the additional expenditures.

HIS Implementation Cycle

The decision to implement an HIS may begin with a collection of available information concerning vendor packages, vendor reputations, and the availability of professional consultants. Information on systems may be derived from trade journals, system vendors, consultants, or other users. Normally, the hospitality establishment will contact a group of vendors and request a proposal from each. The request for proposal (RFP) brings the vendors to the site for a site survey, which provides the vendor with opportunity to witness any unique characteristics that may pose special problems on the design and implementation of the HIS.

The site survey specifically is concerned with the: 1) parameters of the facility (size, statistics, and communication links), 2) design of an equipment configuration, 3) design of the software, 4) analysis of site preparation and associated costs, 5) development of

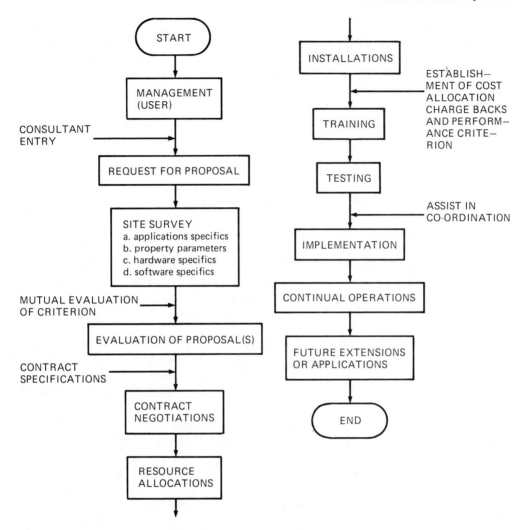

Figure 11.6. HIS Implementation Cycle

training programs, 6) analysis and stipulation of direct, indirect, and optional cost considerations, 7) system's security, and 8) back-up system design.

Since most hotel operations are concerned with getting data into the system, more so than gaining output, the HIS is often called a "front loaded" system. The vendor's proposal will focus attention on the number of terminals required, the capabilities of the CPU, the size of required memory, and the interfacing of various modules. Maintenance programs, upgrading software, and the availability of supplies and peripherals are not usually noted, but should be.

Following the site survey and the submission of proposals, management must evaluate the documents and select the system that best satisfies all of the hotel's demands. The user may elect to employ a consultant's assistance and the technical and legal dimensions of the proposal usually necessitate a lawyer and a systems analyst. Contract negotiations usually follow the selection of a vendor and the hotel begins to evaluate its resource allocations and determines how to best finance a system.

Once a system is selected and its financing determined, the installation, training, testing, and implementation follow. Figure 11.6 illustrates a simplistic overview of the HIS implementation cycle and highlights stages in which consultant participation might best be applied.

HIS Evaluation

Much of the dissatisfaction with early HIS applications to the hospitality industry revolved around the unfulfilled promise for cost effectiveness. The pioneering systems were not well-defined, or conceived, and management's lack of operational participation served only to further compound the problem and has made the documentation of cost savings difficult. Now, following improvements in the computer technology and better under-standing and increased acceptance of the computer as a management tool, many hotels are striving to operate on a cost-justified basis. Since modern systems are more efficient, more compact, and have fewer operating problems, some hotels have sound price/performance ratios.

The modular segmentation of total systems has also led to cost economies. Hotels unable to afford an integrated system can opt to implement only those subsystems that can be cost-justified. The introduction of the minicomputer, microprocessor, and cost-sharing arrangements has further enabled the expansion of the HIS installation to even the small, independent establishments.

Questions that the lodging industry wants to find answers to are: Do the costs of the system justify the expenditures? How can the intangible value of the derived informa-tional output be measured? A somewhat reliable index of HIS efficiency can be found by the use of throughput evaluations. Throughput refers to the rate at which jobs can be handled by the system, and this surely is an adequate basis for comparative operating systems. Also, since most operating systems are designed with, or can be converted to have, a diagnostic software package, this program can be used to evaluate the efficient use of the HIS resources by each of the systems functions. This method also provides dependable feedback on computer operations.

Management should not only try and evaluate the internal system's operations but must also reflect on: 1) return on investment, 2) cost justification of operational ex-penses, and 3) price/performance ratio of the system's functions.

HIS Potential Problem Areas

The application of HIS technology has yielded significant benefits to the lodging industry. The following, however, are several potential problem areas that management must be aware of. These problems can be summarized as:

1. *Lack of Adequate Terminals.* Terminals must be adequate both in number and capabilities.

2. *Limited or Insufficient Storage Capabilities.* The system should be bound by the individual hotel parameters.

3. *Improper Systems Usage.* An imbalance, or violation, in systems usage will be costly and inefficient to the overall system operation.

4. *Limited Applications Hardware.* Hardware that is not capable of generating desired output or accommodating essential input can lead to severe system problems.

5. *Lack of Operational Support.* The improper training of operating personnel or the lack of managerial participation can be viewed as mismanagement, which could be dysfunctional to the system's success.

6. *Bottlenecks in Interfacing.* The type of wiring scheme (hard- or soft-wired) and the electrical relay configuration may inhibit simultaneous system access and/or render some I/O devices inoperable.

7. *Inadequate Follow-Up.* The system manufacturer's failure to provide sufficient testing to insure accuracy and reliability has led to some unsuccessful implementations. Similarly, the maintenance of system packages is a critical area, requiring strict attention at the time of application and vendor selection.

8. *Lack of Awareness of Capabilities.* Management's failure to know the capabilities of the system's hardware and software may lead to the hotel incurring significant additional costs and render the hotel without access to information already available within the present system's configuration.

Summary

The HIS is concerned with the enhancement of managerial effectiveness through the proper handling and flow of the hotel's information. The primary objectives of the HIS revolve around: 1) reports, 2) data handling, 3) operational control, 4) monitoring and control of the guest cycle, 5) guest services, and 6) cost savings. Innkeepers interested in computer assistance should be familiar with the basic terminology surrounding system applications.

In-house computer systems can be adopted in one of three ways. The turnkey approach is the least expensive and fastest way to computerization. A vendor-designed system is an approach that is custom-designed for another user. Often there are commonalities among establishments that enable at least partial adoption. This approach saves programming time and development costs yet provides some flexibility. The third option available is a customized system. This system is the most expensive and takes the longest to develop. It is usually the best understood system since it is specifically designed for a particular establishment. This system also requires relatively complex hardware and software since it can be user programmed.

HIS hardware configurations involve options in: 1) processors, 2) memory units, 3) terminals, and 4) printers. The HIS software can be implemented in a modular segmentation according to these four areas: reservations, guest accounting, room management, and general management. The modular approach has begun a cost justification on an "afford-it-as-you-go" basis. Incremental computerization provides for greater acceptance and a better understanding of individual functions.

The HIS can be applied according to a pre-sale, POS, or post-sale time frame. Regardless of when applied, the HIS general can operate in three processing modes: rapid access/inquiry mode, reporting/outputting format mode, and an analytical/deterministic mode. The goal of HIS implementation is to lead management to a computer-oriented environment, not a computer-dependent one.

A consultant can be a valuable asset in the HIS implementation cycle. The identification of vendors, requests for proposals, site surveys, evaluation of proposals, allocation of resources, training, and implementation are areas in which consultants can be helpful. All in all, the HIS decision involves a large amount of capital and requires a rigorous evaluation procedure.

Key Concepts

Computeritis	Multitasking
Contract programming	OEM
CRT	Order entry terminal
Display terminal	Parameter driven system
Distributed intelligence	Preprogrammed
EDP	Random access
FDP	Sequential filing
Hard copy	Soft copy
HIS	Stand alone
In-house system	Throughput
Intelligent terminal	Turnaround time
Interactive programming	Turnkey
Interface	Vanilla system
Lead-through programming	

Questions for Discussion

1. How much do hotel managers need to know about computer science to operate the HIS?

2. List at least four reasons for the innkeepers slow adoption of computer-based information systems.

3. Explain the basic HIS concept and relate it to the objectives of the firm. What are the primary HIS objectives?

4. Discuss each of the in-house approaches with regard to their costs, operational capabilities, and implementation cycles.

5. How does a mainframe differ from a minicomputer? Describe each with respect to a master-slave arrangement.

6. What are the benefits of computerization by increments or modules?

7. What back-up system options exist for hotels and how do they work?

8. Why is maintenance an important HIS consideration? How can it be accomplished? Why is it often not included with the cost of the system?

9. What investment options are open to the hospitality establishment interested in computerization?

10. Discuss the HIS implementation cycle with respect to the role of an outside consultant and lawyer.

11. Why has it been so difficult to evaluate the HIS and what factors might contribute to simplification in the future?

12. Describe the potential problem areas of the HIS in conjunction with the guest cycle.

HIS Reservations
Module

Chapter Objectives:

1. To introduce the concept of an inquiry system specifically designed for reservations.

2. To explain the purpose of the HIS reservations module and its algorithmic design.

3. To identify the reservation functions available to management through computer assistance.

4. To point up the benefits that might be derived through the use of an on-line reservation module.

RESERVATIONS can be made for groups, tours, conventions, or individuals and each request for accommodation creates a need for an accurate room and rate availability listing. The hotel's ability to equate the guest's inquiry with availability is the essential linkage of the reservation process. Once the reservation is confirmed, the transaction must be accurately recorded to insure correct arrival and departure dates, number in party, number and types of rooms required, guest's personal data (name and address), and the quoted rate. As additional protection, the guest is also furnished with a written letter of confirmation.

The hotel must maintain the reservation record until cancellation or registration; any alterations the guest wishes to make (to the original request) must be entered into the reservation file. The purpose of the HIS reservations module is to collect, store, and provide visibility into areas requiring immediate responses to reservation horizon inquiries. Most vendor modules enable blocking of rooms, automatic registration procedures, confirmation, overbooking options, and automatic room selection and assignment. This chapter discusses the reservation networks and their working relationships to the hotel.

Reservation Networks

During the 1970s the hospitality industry witnessed many independent reservation networks enter and leave the marketplace. The failure rate has been higher for reservation systems than for any other external computer-hotel application. The reasons for many of these failures are:

1. *High Overhead.* The fact that the memory device, communication links, speed, and accuracy are critical to the reservation system has led to the installation of expensive, sophisticated computer equipment. It is this high overhead, coupled with extensive operating costs, that has left many reservation networks unprofitable.

2. *Consumer Contact.* Dealing directly with the consumer has been repeatedly cited as the major breaking point of the reservation business. The amount of time, personnel, and equipment that is invested simply does not guarantee bookings. Also, as people change their plans or desires, projected revenues dwindle while operating costs increase.

3. *Competition.* Other segments of the travel business have cluttered the hotel reservations market. Airlines, car rentals, and hotel chains have offered competition to many reservation systems and have left an insufficient volume of transactional business for the networks to share.

Today, the innkeeper desiring to automate the reservation function has four alternatives to select from. The first option is the development of an in-house system. This involves direct dealings with the public, an investment in equipment, and the presence of a reservation-system staff. All the costs of operations must be borne by the property and the system is limited, usually, to bookings only within that one hotel. A second route is to subscribe to a private reservation network that deals directly with the public. The network will handle the room requests, furnish its own equipment, and, typically, charges the hotel on a fixed cost plus a transactional use basis.

Chain systems, owned by chain hotels, link their operations in such a way that oftentimes additional subscribers can join the network, although they may only be support overrun facilities for the chain's operations. A nonaffiliate who joins a chain satellite system normally will not have to deal with the public a great deal since the chain will advertise a central number or individual property phone numbers for customer service. The fourth option open to the hotelier, which is not mutually exclusive of the other three options, is to enter into an *intersell agreement* with other firms. A reservation network that handles more than one product is an intersell system. A single call to an airline that can result in plane, car, and hotel reservations is an example of an intersell system. This reservation option allows the hotel a broader base of exposure and reduces contact with the public. This approach is clearly a low overhead approach.

Charges

Most independent reservation systems charge the hotel on a fixed rate and/or reservation-activity basis. The fixed rate normally is a function of the number of rooms the hotel has and is usually rated on a monthly basis, for example, $3 per room per month. Additionally, the reservation network may also, or instead, charge a fee as a percent of reservation activity. This cost-per-reservation-accepted may be a declining scale based on the guest's intended length of stay (e.g., $1.50 for the first night and $.50 for each night thereafter) or it may be a flat fee per use scale (e.g., $2.00 per reservation accepted).

In either or both cases, the cost of the reservation alone usually is not justified to the hotel unless the volume of reservations is sufficiently high or else the reservation system has additional benefits.

Many reservation systems have become popular as: 1) administrative communication networks for interproperty relay, 2) accounting transfer systems, and 3) as referral and promotional communication devices for local weather reports or special hotel features.

Reservation Systems

Reservations can be produced through national networks (estimated at 200 million per year) but the real concern is over whether to maintain them manually or electronically once they are received. Since the reservation initiates the guest cycle, and therefore management's ability to monitor and control its operations, the question of electronic assistance usually begins with the topic of reservations. Manual reservation systems require a series of entries on calendars, records, and files and a set of physical files for proper auditing and supervision of the process. Tedious clerical procedures are encountered in the preparation of letters of confirmation, filing of reservation changes, and recording of prepayments. Room availabilities are more difficult to chart in a manual system because either several source documents must be consulted or charts must be interpolated to yield accurate inventories. Also, the construction, development, and maintenance of the manual reservation record is usually of little or no purpose once the guest completes the registration process. For all these reasons hotels will adopt the

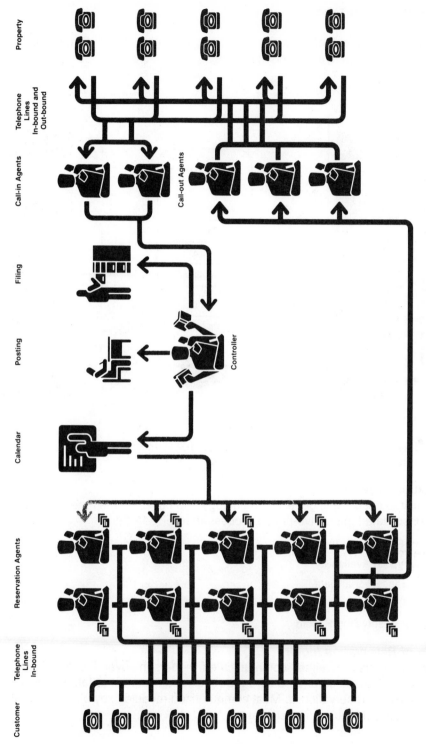

Figure 12.1. Representation of a Manual System (Courtesy of Compass Computer Services)

reservation module of the HIS. Figures 12.1 and 12.2 give visual comparisons of the manual and automated systems components.

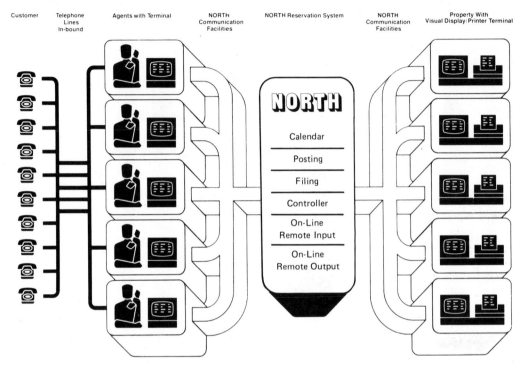

Figure 12.2. Representation of an Automated System (Courtesy of Compass Computer Services)

The Reservation Process

Although difficult to describe in general terminology, the basic on-line reservation module can be consolidated into a five-phase process (see Fig. 12.3):

1. Formulation of Reservation Inquiry

2. Equating Inquiry with Availability

3. Recording of Transactional Data

4. Confirmation of Reservation

5. Maintenance of Reservation Record

Formulation of Reservation Inquiry

The reservation request is either communicated in person, over the telephone, or through the mail. Regardless of its origin, the reservation request is formulated into a system inquiry by the reservationist. Most computerized modules key off some or all of the following essential inquiry data elements:

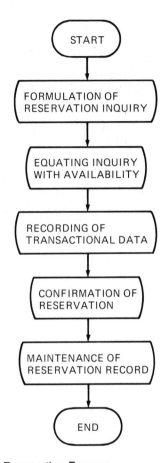

Figure 12.3. The Reservation Process

1. guest's arrival date

2. type of room desired

3. number of rooms requested

4. length of stay

5. number of persons

6. room rate range

This data is usually entered into a display terminal in less than 45 seconds (see Fig. 12.4). The system's response to the inquiry may be: 1) simultaneously processed, 2) intermediately massaged and then processed, 3) called-out and then processed, or 4) transmitted, reloaded, and then processed.

Simultaneous processing involves a fully on-line, real-time capability in which the

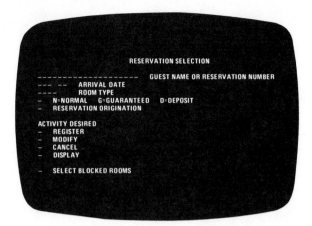

Figure 12.4. Reservation Inquiry Display (Courtesy of Motorola)

reservationist's response to the system's lead-through cues, on a terminal, are entered directly into the reservation-center computer. This capability is not common because it is: 1) very expensive and 2) error-prone because there is little time for text editing, or review, prior to system processing. Intermediate massaging is an efficient and popular reservation module design. In this mode the inquiry is entered by the reservationist on a display terminal and sent to a data center prior to being transmitted to the reservation center, or destination property, computer. This intermediate holding allows the operator the ability to edit and/or alter the inquiry prior to processing. Although not quite as quick a relay as simultaneous processing, it has many more advantages. Call-outs require that the reservationist telephone the reservation center, and that the inquiry be entered and processed at the computer site. The fourth possibility involves the transmittal of the inquiry from its point of origin to the reservation center, or destination property. At this point the inquiry is printed and loaded into another computer for processing and output. This method is neither common nor practical.

Equating Inquiry with Availability
Once the inquiry reaches the reservation center computer, the system's algorithm will seek to match the request with room availability. Keying off the inquiry data, the system can respond in a number of preprogrammed formats, which might include:

1. acceptance of the inquiry.

2. rejection of the inquiry due to nonavailability.

3. offering of alternate, available room types.

4. announcement of alternate, available room rates.

5. suggestion of an alternate hotel property.

It is important to note that the speed of the on-line system response is fast enough (usually less than 90 seconds) to enable the reservationist to alter the inquiry, while the customer may still be available for input. Once the inquiry is equated with room availability the computer will assign a specific room or group of rooms, block out the rooms (remove them from the availability inventory), and request the remaining transactional data to complete the file.

Recording of Transactional Data

Although this procedure may vary, the reservation system may be designed to only request guest data once the inquiry has been satisfactorily filled. Although the guest's name, address, and telephone number may be captured as the first part of a reservation call or visit, the system may elect not to clutter the inquiry with this data in case of a rejection or a guest's casual interest in availability. The following information is usually placed into the electronic record of the reservation transaction:

1. Guest's name

2. Guest's address and telephone number

3. Room type

4. Number of rooms

5. Quoted room rate (or range)

6. Number in party

7. Date of arrival

8. Date of departure

9. Reservation classification (for example, guaranteed)

10. Special requirements or services

The creation of this record, and its subsequent filing, enables the hotel to better service the guest and provides visibility into who the guest is, prior to the guest cycle.

Confirmation of Reservation

In the evening the system will produce letters of confirmation for reservations taken on that day. The reservation information is usually printed on a specially designed hotel form and a number of format options are available. The types of acknowledgements may be representative of letters of confirmation, requests for advance deposits or prepayments, or reflect changes in the original reservation (either a confirmation or cancellation). Figure 12.5 is an illustration of a machine-prepared letter of change in reservation confirmation.

Maintenance of Reservation Record

The reservation is maintained in an electronic file as a means of furnishing an instant recall, at-the-fingertips record of the transaction. Should the guest request changes in the confirmation, or even cancellation, the reservationist merely instructs the terminal to access the proper file and to make the corresponding changes to modify or cancel. The

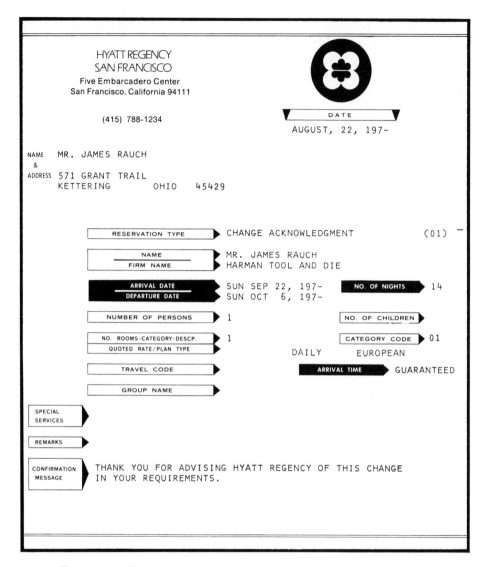

Figure 12.5. Sample Letter of Change in Requirements
(Courtesy of NCR Corporation)

maintenance of this file also provides for a guest account record for transactions that may occur prior to occupancy. The receipt of prepayments, advance deposits, or cash pay-outs, are pre-guest cycle activities that can be posted to the reservation record and be carried forward onto the guest's folio. Additionally, the reservation record can be formatted into a registration card (hard copy) or its video equivalent (soft copy) and will be automatically transformed into the electronic guest folio after the guest has completed the hotel's registration procedure.

The cost justification of the reservation module of the HIS would be next to impossible, claim many computer vendors, if it was not for its ability to interface with other front office functions: it moves the file from the reservation record through the guest history file. Figure 12.6 depicts the flow of the reservation record through the guest cycle.

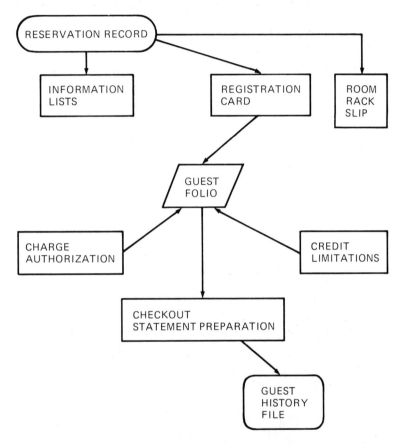

Figure 12.6. Flow of the Electronic Reservation Record

Reservation Module Functions
The following list is representative, but not exhaustive, of HIS reservation module functions:

1. Guest information collection
2. Preparation of a guest or master folio

3. Generation of registration cards

4. Initialization of room rack slips

5. Production of arrival and departure lists

6. Room availability reports

7. Ability to block out groups of rooms

8. Automatic room assignments

9. Printed letters of confirmation

10. Establishment of a guest account and record of prepayments

11. Generation of forecasted occupancy reports

12. Additional information for guest planning (weather, special events, transportation, and so on)

The hotel industry has made tremendous progress in the processing of reservations and in the construction of a reservation record. The establishment of this record saves time in registration verification, continual indentification of the guest's status, and in the generation of an electronic folio that can later be filed in the guest history memory. The expansion of the reservation horizon to as much as two years extends the manual system capability almost four-fold. Room availability status provides management with an accurate appraisal of operations and allows for forecasted occupancy reports. A listing of expected arrivals and departures also has carry-over significance to the house-keeping department, in addition to aiding the front desk with check ins. Some computer

Exclusive Hotel-Motel Software

Figure 12.7. Room Availability Selection Display
(Courtesy of Motorola)

systems are so efficient that they can even track turnaway statistics and produce analytical no-show reports.

Module Reports

The following reports are a representative sample of the information available through a reservations module.

1. *Room Availability Report* (Figs. 12.7 and 12.8)—lists daily room availability inventories by room type, that is, lists net remaining rooms in each category.

2. *Expected Arrivals and/or Departures Report* (Fig. 12.9)—lists the number of rooms expected to arrive at occupancy, the number expected to be departed, and sometimes also lists the number of stayovers (the difference between arrivals and departures).

3. *Reservation Transaction Record* (Fig. 12.10)—lists all guest reservations that had transactional activity, (either added, altered, or cancelled) on any given day.

DATE	#G	#R	%	GTD	BRIDAL 1	DOUBLES 122	KINGS 25	QUEENS 19	SUITES 6	THERMASOL 12	WATERBED 1
5/17/77	142	124	67%	102		110 90%	6 24%	7 37%		1 8%	
5/18/77	127	113	61%	96		102 84%	5 20%	3 16%		3 25%	
5/19/77	111	98	53%	76		90 74%	4 16%	3 16%		1 8%	
5/20/77	131	113	61%	57	1 100%	108 89%	1 4%	3 16%			
5/21/77	100	82	44%	42		80 66%		2 11%			
5/22/77	92	77	41%	35		75 61%		2 11%			
5/23/77	134	120	65%	57		117 96%	1 4%	2 11%			
5/24/77	131	117	63%	57		113 93%	1 4%	3 16%			
5/25/77	71	65	35%	57		62 51%	1 4%	2 11%			
5/26/77	100	64	34%	47		60 49%		3 16%		1 8%	
5/27/77	111	65	35%	42		61 50%		2 11%	1 17%	1 8%	
5/28/77	125	69	37%	43		65 53%		2 11%	2 33%		
5/29/77	83	40	22%	23		37 30%		1 5%	2 33%		
5/31/77	67	31	17%	23		28 23%	1 4%	1 5%		1 8%	
6/01/77	83	38	20%	23		35 29%	1 4%	1 5%		1 8%	
6/02/77	114	54	29%	31		47 39%	2 8%	1 5%	3 50%	1 8%	
6/03/77	300	151	81%	74	1 100%	116 95%	12 48%	12 63%	3 50%	7 58%	
6/04/77	345	165	89%	95	1 100%	122 100%	15 64%	12 63%	5 83%	9 75%	
6/05/77	334	157	90%	93	1 100%	116 95%	23 92%	12 63%	5 83%	9 75%	1 100%
6/06/77	156	88	47%	40		71 58%	8 32%	5 26%	1 17%	2 17%	1 100%
6/07/77	105	62	33%	26		52 43%	7 28%	1 5%		1 8%	1 100%
6/08/77	113	75	40%	25		66 54%	6 24%	1 5%		1 8%	1 100%
6/09/77	107	69	37%	17		59 48%	6 24%	2 11%		1 6%	1 100%
6/10/77	100	61	33%	35		37 30%	6 24%	17 89%			1 100%
6/11/77	104	59	32%	28		36 30%	6 24%	17 89%			
6/12/77	99	67	36%	27		61 50%	5 20%	1 5%			
6/13/77	93	62	33%	35		56 46%	5 20%	1 5%			
6/14/77	154	123	66%	96		117 96%	5 20%	1 5%			
6/15/77	93	55	30%	29		44 40%	5 20%	1 5%			
6/16/77	103	57	31%	33		51 42%	5 20%	1 5%			
6/18/77	61	24	13%	10		17 14%	6 24%	1 5%			
6/19/77	60	29	16%	13		24 20%	4 16%	1 5%			
6/20/77	59	40	22%	17		35 29%	4 16%	1 5%			
6/21/77	91	60	32%	17		55 45%	4 16%	1 5%			
6/22/77	84	55	30%	15		50 41%	4 16%	1 5%			
6/23/77	97	53	28%	16		32 26%	19 76%	2 11%			
6/24/77	297	124	67%	9		101 83%	20 80%	1 5%	2 33%		
6/25/77	277	113	61%	12	1 100%	104 85%	4 16%	1 5%	3 50%		
6/26/77	92	57	31%	10		51 42%	4 16%	1 5%	1 17%		
6/27/77	67	38	20%	5		33 27%	4 16%	1 5%			
6/28/77	68	39	21%	6		34 28%	4 16%	1 5%			
6/29/77	67	38	20%	5		33 27%	4 16%	1 5%			
6/30/77	83	47	25%	14		42 34%	4 16%	1 5%			
7/08/77	51	50	27%	45		45 37%	4 16%	1 5%			
7/09/77	53	51	27%	45		45 37%	4 16%	1 5%	1 17%		
7/15/77	83	36	19%	1		13 11%	4 16%	19 100%			
7/16/77	79	32	17%	1		13 11%		19 100%			
7/27/77	85	55	30%	2		53 43%	1 4%	1 5%			
7/28/77	85	55	30%	2		53 43%	1 4%	1 5%			

DATE 5/17/77   THE IBM HOTEL   FUTURE RESERVATION LIST (H07)   PAGE   1

The listing shows the date,(1) total number of rooms reserved,(2) number of guests,(3) total occupancy percentage,(4) the number of guaranteed rooms,(5) and rooms reserved by room type.(6) Stay-overs from previous days as well as arrivals for that date are taken into account on all totals shown.

Figure 12.8. Future Reservation List
(Courtesy of Griswold's Inn, Claremont, California and IBM)

4. *Cancellation Report*—a daily listing of cancellation by guest's name.

5. *Blocked Room Report*—identifies rooms that are committed by room number or type, guest's name, and the date that they are blocked for.

6. *Forecasted Occupancy Report*—provides a projection of future room revenues, availability, and occupancy loads.

7. *Refusal Report*—so long as the overbooking function is not violated and a reservation must be refused, the system tracks the nonavailability of rooms.

```
EXPECTED ARRIVALS 06/01/78 "YOUR HOTEL NAME"
12/21/77
PAGE     1


  RN#  NAME                  CONVEN    R   T        D $   P TIME    SPCL SERV
                                                    ADD RES

   432 BAILEY, MR D G                  1 DB50      1 G   2  9:00P 00
       BAKER, FAM EMILE S              1 DB44      4 N   3  7:55A A1 00 HF
  1046 BROTHERS, JAN        FFARE2     0 TH55      2 G   1 A034
                                                  LEFEBV PANDOL
       CARPENTER, M/M W L              1 TH80      5 C   2  7:00P
   338 COPELAND, M/M R BRUCE INSUR     1 DB60      3 D   2  5:00P
       EHAM, M/M/F M.                  1 DB44      2 G   4 E034
   803 GREEN, JENNIFER      INSUR      1 HS60      4 G   1  4:55P
  1046 LEFEBVRE, ANNETTE    FFARE2     0 TH55      2 G   1 A034
                                                  BROTHE PANDOL
   501 LORENZ, HILDA        FFARE2     1 TH55      2 N   1 E341
                                                  PFLUG, WILSON
       MARTINERI, JOAN                 1 DD38      1 N   1  3:00A
  1046 PANDOLFI, CARMEN     FFARE2     1 TH55      2 G   1 A034
                                                  BROTHE LEFEBV
   501 PFLUG, ANNA          FFARE2     0 TH55      2 N   1 E341
                                                  LORENZ WILSON
   330 RIVERA, MS GLORIA    INSUR      1 SB60      4 G   1  4:55P
       RUBICON, MR X                   2 DD80      2 G   1
       RUSSELL, D/M ALLEN              1 DD43      1 G   2 U341    00
   409 WARFIELD, JAMES      INSUR      1 DB70      4 G   1  4:55P
                                                  ZAHRA
   501 WILSON, DONNA        FFARE2     0 TH55      2 N   1 E341
                                                  LORENZ PFLUG,
   409 ZAHRA III, JOHN S    INSUR      0 DB70      4 G   1  4:55P
                                                  WARFIE
TOTALS                                14                  27

CREDIT INFO    D=    1  G=    9  C=    1  N=    3
```

Figure 12.9. Expected Arrivals Report
(Courtesy of EECO Hotel Systems)

Benefits of On-Line Reservations

The following benefits have been credited to electronic reservation modules:

1. Provides quicker and more accurate response to the customer.

2. Enables reliable forecasting of revenues and occupancies.

```
RESERVATION TRANSACTION REGISTER - "YOUR HOTEL NAME"
12/21/77
TR-PAGE    1
```

① ARV DATE	② NAME	③ DAYS	④ RMS	⑤ GUESTS	⑥ QNAME	⑦ RATE	⑧ TB	⑨ ST	⑩ CLK
12/21/77	DARNETT, MS GAIL	1	1	2		150.00	N	N	88
12/21/77	PANZA, SANCHO	7	1	3	PFLUG	350.00	N	R	88
06/01/78	BAILEY, MR D G	1	1	2		50.00	Y	N	88
06/01/78	BAKER, FAM EMILE S	4	1	3		44.00	Y	N	88
06/01/78	BROTHERS, JAN	2	0	1	FFARE2	55.00	Y	N	88
06/01/78	CARPENTER, M/M W L	5	1	2		80.00	N	N	88
06/01/78	COPELAND, M/M R BRUCE	3	1	2	INSUR	60.00	Y	N	88
06/01/78	EMAM, M/M/F M.	2	1	4		44.00	Y	N	88
06/01/78	GREEN, JENNIFER	4	1	1	INSUR	60.00	Y	N	88
06/01/78	LEFEBVRE, ANNETTE	2	0	1	FFARE2	55.00	Y	N	88
06/01/78	LORENZ, HILDA	2	1	1	FFARE2	55.00	Y	N	88
06/01/78	MARTINERI, JOAN	1	1	1		38.50	Y	N	88
06/01/78	PANDOLFI, CARMEN	2	1	1	FFARE2	55.00	Y	N	88
06/01/78	PFLUG, ANNA	2	0	1	FFARE2	55.00	Y	N	88
06/01/78	RIVERA, MS GLORIA	4	1	1	INSUR	60.00	Y	N	88
06/01/78	RUBICON, MR X	2	2	1		80.00	N	N	8
06/01/78	RUSSELL, D/M ALLEN	1	1	2		43.50	Y	N	88
06/01/78	WARFIELD, JAMES	4	1	1	INSUR	70.00	Y	N	88
06/01/78	WILSON, DONNA	2	0	1	FFARE2	55.00	Y	N	88
06/01/78	ZAHRA III, JOHN S	4	0	1	INSUR	70.00	Y	N	88

```
                                              TOTALS
⑪ CANCELLED TODAY                                  0
   CANCEL/MODIFY TODAY ⑫                            0
⑬ NEW TRANSACTIONS                                19
   REFILED MODIFICATIONS ⑭                          1
```

Item No.	Description
④	Number of rooms reserved
⑤	Number of guests in party
⑥	Associated Qname, if any
⑦	Room rate
⑧	Travel bureau indicator
⑨	Status of reservation:
	R = reservation was modified, excluding change of guest name or arrival date
	N = new reservation made today
	C = reservation cancelled today
	M = change was made on a reservation in the name or arrival date field
⑩	Clerk number assigned to person booking reservation
⑪	Total number of reservations cancelled today
⑫	Total number of reservations cancelled or modified today
⑬	Total new reservations made today
⑭	Total number of reservations modified today in the name or arrival date field

Figure 12.10. Reservation Transaction Register
(Courtesy of EECO Hotel Systems)

3. Reduces reservationist's clerical procedures thereby enabling more time to concentrate on marketing and promotion.

4. Eliminates paperwork and physical filing.

5. Facilitates changes that must be made to the reservation record, including cancellation.

6. Provides immediate visibility into who the guest is and what the guest's needs are, and at a time prior to registration.

7. Enhances the speed of registration by permitting a transference of data from the registration record to a registration card or its equivalent.

8. Provides for a pre-occupancy guest account to which prepayments, advance deposits, and cash pay-outs can be accurately posted and carried forward.

9. Establishes an initial record that accompanies the guest through the guest cycle thereby giving management tighter control over guest transactions.

New Developments

The reservation area was the first hotel module developed and therefore has received much of the vendor's research and development attention. Additionally, the airlines have spent millions of dollars developing their reservations technique, all of which can be applied or modified to the hotel market. The two most interesting recent developments in the reservation area are: self-reservation packages and voice output systems.

Self-Reservations

During the late 1960s, experimentation began on self-reservation systems. There are both interactive and noninteractive models being tested and by the mid-1980s consumers may be capable of using their television sets and telephones to reserve airline flights and hotel rooms and rent automobiles. The interactive systems allow the user to dial-up computer stored reservation packages and to display them on their own television screens. The computer then proceeds with a drop-through format requiring user responses to system cues. The user enters responses and data through a key pad (or touch-tone phones possibly), which leads to a booking.

Noninteractive program broadcasting is similar to that of a public television station. It is basically a continuous series of displays of tourist offerings and does not allow the viewer to participate in the display selection or request reservation space. The viewer must seek out traditional reservation methods but the exposure to hospitality packages is definitely increased.

Voice Output

Experimentation with talking computers (in the area of airline reservations) may make significant impact on the hotel's reservation module within the next decade. Presently, the research being conducted requires the user to possess a touch-tone phone and a headset. The computer offers a multiple choice listing of options, to which the reservationist responds by pushing designated buttons on the phone. The computer uses a limited vocabulary of words, put into digital code, from actual recordings of human voices. The future applications of voice input and output may replace the present system of personal identification numbers (social security, college ID, or driver's license) and personal signature with voice identification by computer. This would insure the hotel of a legitimate call for a reservation and would enable the hotel to establish accountability for reservation requests.

Summary

The trend away from manual reservation systems and toward on-line capabilities is due to the automated system's ability to store, search, and retrieve large amounts of data quickly and accurately. The list of on-line benefits is extensive and it is anticipated that self-reservations and voice output may be realities soon. All in all, the reservation function has received an enormous amount of research and development and has been the best received of all modular designs.

Key Concepts

Blocked room report	Refusal report
Cancellation report	Reservation activity fee
Interactive program broadcasting	Reservation inquiry
Noninteractive program	Reservation network
broadcasting	Reservation record

Questions for Discussion

1. What is meant by a "reservation horizon?"

2. What is the main purpose of the reservation module of the HIS?

3. Why have reservation networks been such failures? What corrective action would alleviate many of these shortcomings?

4. List the four entry modes to a reservation system. What are the pros and cons of each method?

5. What are some of the charge-back schemes (charges for services) used by firms within the reservations area?

6. Are the costs from reservation systems usually justified to the hotel? If no, what could make the network more attractive?

7. Compare and contrast the basic computerized reservation functions, and how they are performed within the hotel framework.

8. What are the major benefits of the on-line reservation system application?

9. What impact will the new developments in the reservation area have upon the guest cycle?

HIS Guest Accounting Module

Chapter Objectives:

1. To introduce the basic concept of the guest accounting module of the HIS.

2. To identify the purpose of the accounting module and its algorithmic design.

3. To point up benefits that have been experienced through the use of an on-line accounting system.

THE MOST central and critical part of a computer-assisted hotel system is the guest accounting module. This module enables management to gain considerable internal control over many important functions and provides a solid basis for improved monitoring of the guest cycle. The accounting module is primarily responsible for instantaneous guest charge postings, automated night auditing, and electronic guest statement display and printing. The construction of electronic folios provides for remote point-of-sale postings and simultaneous audit trial balances to be conducted throughout the day. Managerial controls in such areas as folio filing, account auditing, visibility into account status, cashier reconciliation, ticket control, and accounts receivable can be gotten from this module's application.

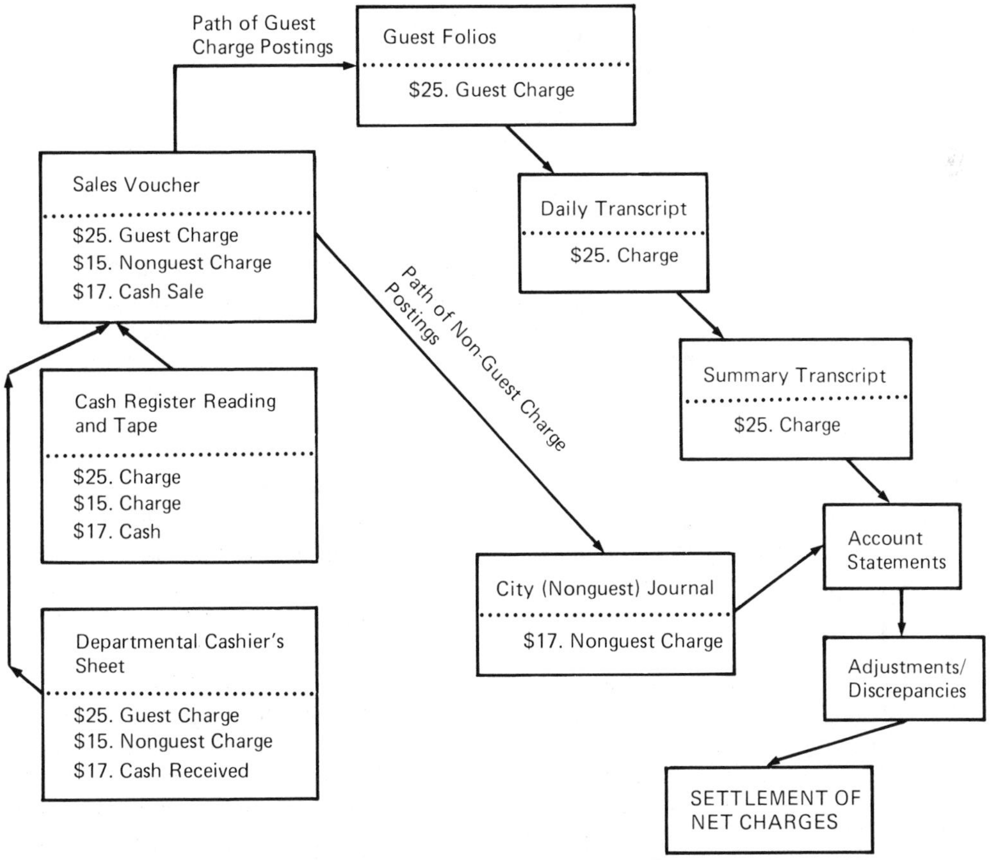

NOTE: Guest Charge - appears in eight (8) different locations
Nonguest Charge - found in six (6) different locations

Figure 13.1. Flow of Manual Charge Postings

The HIS accounting module has significantly reduced the volume of documentation required in guest charge transactions and has simplified the auditing procedures. A comparison of manual and automated guest charge postings is offered in Figures 13.1 and 13.2. Note the number of times the same data is entered into the various stages of the manual process. This transcription of numbers can lead to errors in postings and/or omissions. The computerized flow does not, of course, require vouchers, departmental support ledgers, or additional communication links like the manual process does.

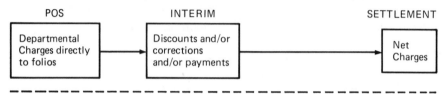

NOTE: The recording of the charge (only once) in the operating department creates a simultaneous entry into the electronic folio.

Figure 13.2. Flow of Automated Charge Postings

The On-Line Accounting Process

The guest accounting module embodies all the front office accounting functions and can best be analyzed through an identification of its component parts, which are: creation of account, entry of the charge, posting function, auditing procedure, and settlement of account. Figure 13.3 presents a flowchart of the accounting system components.

Creation of Account

Guests who hold reservations may have an electronic folio created from their reservation record in the reservation module. Others will have the requisite data entered into the module at the front desk upon check in. The front office display terminal will lead the clerk through an interactive account creation routine, and a transactions folio will be constructed. Most HIS packages allow the hotel to maintain:

1. one folio for each room.

2. a folio for each guest.

3. *master folios* for more than one room (group or convention accounts).

4. nonguest account records.

5. employee account records.

6. *control folios* for operating departments.

The use of room or guest folios is to provide the clientele with individual billings and records for their personal needs. The master folio provides groups with an aggregation of their collective transactions, whereas nonguest accounts are for persons with in-house charge privileges, who are not registered guests. Instead of posting charges to

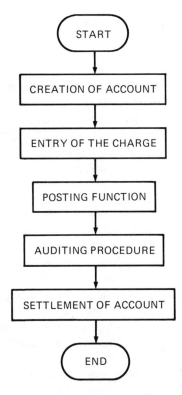

Figure 13.3. Flowchart of Guest Accounting Process

their guest rooms, nonguests are assigned account numbers, as employees may be. Some HIS packages enable the creation of employee accounts and also recreational or club accounts.

Important to the overall detailing of the guest accounting module, with particular relevance to the audit procedure, is the ability to construct control folios. Control folios are for examination of departmental activities and are primarily responsible for tracking all tickets or guest checks. A control folio for each revenue center enables a complete sorting and identification of missing or incorrectly posted tickets. Control folios serve as powerful internal control documents and greatly simplify the audit function.

Entry of Charge
An entry of charges can be made from a remote point-of-sale or at a local position at the front desk. Although the informational requirements for postings vary, most HIS accounting modules usually need the following minimum data to initiate the posting routine:

1. Room or account number (code number)

2. Name or partial name of customer (identification code)

3. Ticket number being posted (reference code)

4. Amount of charge (charge total)

Room or account numbers are assigned by the desk and hotel guests possessing room keys and nonguests holding account cards will have to furnish this data to the cashier. Upon entry into the POS terminal, a verification sequence is triggered and the system will seek internal authorization. Should the guest hold a key for an unoccupied room or for a room that has settled its account, the system will not allow the cashier to post the charge due to an invalid account code number.

The introduction of the customer's name or partial name is to further verify that the person making the charge is actually occupying a specific room or has been assigned a particular account number. Some vendor-design systems only require inputting of the first two letters of the last name, which appears to be a sufficient screening technique. The successful verification of both the room number and identification code will usually lead to a credit limit authorization. The credit check is internally performed by comparing total charges outstanding with the line of credit authorized by management. Although most modules allow management to only set an across-the-board house limit, some provide an optional leveling based upon the status of the guest (for example, repeat customer or known business associate) or the limit of the credit card the guest has designated for final settlement of the account. If the account is not of a high-risk nature or close to its credit limit then the system will proceed to the ticket sequence code.

For internal department accounting purposes, all guest tickets are usually numbered. The numbering scheme provides for an investigative search, and/or an analysis of business activity. By entering the ticket number or reference code to the posting data set, management is provided with a cross-reference document for auditing purposes. The entry of the charged sale total will again bring a status check against the account's credit limit and will enable the cashier a chance to verify the computation of the ticket's total. The cashier completes the typical entry procedure when the data is sent to the guest accounting module for posting.

Posting Function

The posting function deals with the immediate entering of charged sale data to an electronic file. The file is addressed by the code number and the corresponding identification code, while the reference code is used to trail the posting of the revenue total.

Room rate and tax are automatically posted to each guest folio for every occupied room merely by pressing a button. Additionally, the module usually is responsible for automatically balancing departmental accounts by cashier shifts and this further facilitates the audit by producing a trial balance equivalent. Although the posting within this module is performed electronically, and in some instances automatically, management usually has the option of attaching a voucher printer to the POS terminal as a physical cross-reference (hard copy documentation) to the posting.

Some modules also provide for text editing of previously entered erroneous data and automatic transference of charges between two folios, when required. Simultaneous to an editing or transfer correction being completed, the system maintains a complete audit trail for later, supportive analysis.

Auditing Procedure

Whereas the night auditor had been previously required to post all remaining departmental charges, room rates and taxes, and total all guest, nonguest, and departmental accounts, all the auditor need do in this module is audit. The lead-through structure of the audit program normally requires the auditor to respond to certain system instructions and then run the mathematical computations of the audit. Hotels no longer have to perform a tedious audit in the slow hours of early morning; the audit routine can theoretically be initiated any time, upon demand. This module provides for:

1. POS terminal auditing

2. Revenue auditing

3. Credit card auditing

4. Audit trail analysis

5. Cashier reconciliation

The audit trail may consist of cross-references from ticket numbers, work shifts, cashiers, POS terminals, and departmental accounts. All these available supportive facts have led to a simplification of the audit and have enabled hotels to perform computerized auditing in the ratio of one automated minute for every manual hour. Hence, a large hotel having a one-person, eleven-hour audit would take approximately eleven minutes in an HIS guest accounting module. This frees the auditor to balance accounts, not merely perform bookkeeping functions for long hours prior to the start of the audit procedure.

Settlement of Account

Some modules employ a display terminal to provide guest inspection of their statement prior to its printing. Most modules provide a preprinted folio for guests expected to depart on any given day. This preprinting has enabled a significantly faster checkout procedure and the itemized statements, containing abbreviated point-of-purchase information, have almost eliminated guest discrepancies. The system, with its instant posting capabilities, has eliminated late charges due to the ability to close out an account (an electronic posting file) upon guest checkout. Folios of departed guests with nonzero balances are automatically transferred to the nonguest ledger file and a bill is prepared for mailing. Should an account be closed out by accident, it can easily be reinstated. The checkout function triggers a communication to housekeeping and internally notifies all points-of-sale by closing the room number and name code out. The fact that this module is capable of being interfaced with the rooms and management modules has enabled better communications and more comprehensive reports for the entire hotel. Typically, most active guest folios remain in the memory for 24 hours following checkout.

Guest Accounting Module Functions

The following list is representative, but not exhaustive, of HIS guest accounting module functions:

1. Construction of electronic folios.
2. Capability to assign more than one folio per room.
3. Immediate departmental posting automatically.
4. Instant access to any guest folio without physical handling.
5. Assignment of guest credit limits to each folio.
6. Required credit and guest verification prior to accepting charges for posting.
7. Production of itemized guest statements.
8. Automated night audit (trial balances of all accounts).
9. Late charges automatically transferred to the city ledger for billing.
10. General ledger accounting.

Instantaneous posting of all charges following credit verification, which is performed internally by the system, leads to a major victory in the combatting of late charges and charges made by persons under false pretexts. The ability to look into a limited version of any guest's record, at any point in time, enables the switchboard, mail, desk clerk, and other departmental personnel to easily locate the guest and to properly provide accurate information regarding the guest's status. The production of itemized guest statements has provided management with a supervisory capability over high-risk accounts, while also affording the guest an accurate analysis of expenditures. A significant reduction in guest discrepancies and a high degree of system generated statement acceptance combine to shorten checkout time and tighten control over reconciliation of accounts. The guest cycle is better monitored and controlled and this can lead to competitive advantages in the hotel marketplace.

Module Reports

The guest accounting module is the heart of the HIS and enables management to review a myriad of formatted reports from specific operating department activities, such as ticket control, individual cashier analysis, and revenue summaries right through to line postings in the individual accounts. The analytical capacities of this module have greatly simplified the night audit and have provided the hotel control over its front office accounting cycle. Some system vendors can even provide microfilm reproductions of reports for a maximized retention of essential information in a minimum of file space. A small sample of representative reports follows:

1. *Account Folios* (see Figure 13.4). The guest or nonguest folio can be displayed in hard or soft

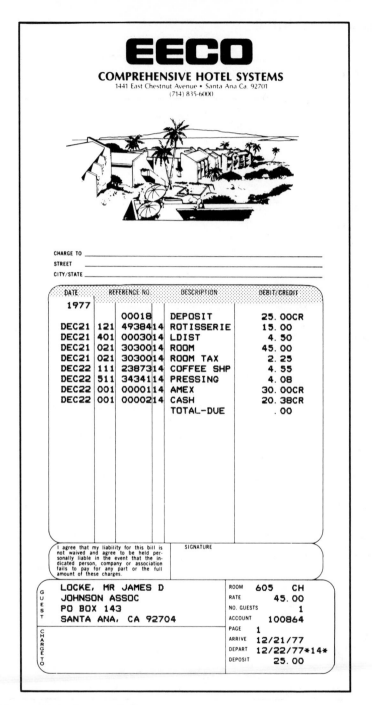

EECO
COMPREHENSIVE HOTEL SYSTEMS
1441 East Chestnut Avenue • Santa Ana Ca. 92701
(714) 835-6000

CHARGE TO _____

STREET _____

CITY/STATE _____

DATE	REFERENCE NO.			DESCRIPTION	DEBIT/CREDIT
1977					
		00018		DEPOSIT	25.00CR
DEC21	121	49384	14	ROTISSERIE	15.00
DEC21	401	00030	14	LDIST	4.50
DEC21	021	30300	14	ROOM	45.00
DEC21	021	30300	14	ROOM TAX	2.25
DEC22	111	23873	14	COFFEE SHP	4.55
DEC22	511	34341	14	PRESSING	4.08
DEC22	001	00001	14	AMEX	30.00CR
DEC22	001	00002	14	CASH	20.38CR
				TOTAL-DUE	.00

I agree that my liability for this bill is not waived and agree to be held personally liable in the event that the indicated person, company or association fails to pay for any part or the full amount of these charges.

SIGNATURE

GUEST

LOCKE, MR JAMES D
JOHNSON ASSOC
PO BOX 143
SANTA ANA, CA 92704

CHARGE TO

ROOM	605 CH
RATE	45.00
NO. GUESTS	1
ACCOUNT	100864
PAGE	1
ARRIVE	12/21/77
DEPART	12/22/77*14*
DEPOSIT	25.00

Figure 13.4. Account Folio
(Courtesy of EECO Hotel Systems)

copy at any time during the guest cycle. The status of the account provides both customers and management with important information.

```
NIGHT AUDITORS REVENUE REPORT - "YOUR HOTEL NAME"
12/12/77



R O O M    S T A T I S T I C S


HOUSE ROOMS              644
HOUSE USE                  2
AVAILABLE ROOMS                     642

OUT-OF-ORDER               3
VACANT                   209
COMPLIMENTARY             12
PERMANENT                  2
TRANSIENT                416

TOTAL AVAILABLE ROOMS               642


% OF OCCUPANCY        65.10
AVERAGE RATE          44.14

DOUBLE OCCUPANCY ROOMS     196
% OF DOUBLE OCCUPANCY    46.88

                    R E V E N U E    S U M M A R Y


              REGULAR      SPORTS       GROUP      PACKAGE       TOTAL

NUMBER OF ROOMS    286          0         121           11         418
NUMBER OF GUESTS   418          0         176           20         614
ROOM REVENUE   13,722.50       00    4,160.00      570.00   18,452.50


TOTAL MAP FOOD               .00
TOTAL FAP FOOD               .00
TOTAL SPORTS FEE             .00      TOTAL ROOM RATE    18,452.50
TOTAL SPORTS ROOM TAX        .00      STANDARD HOUSE     19,422.50
TOTAL SPORTS FOOD GRATUITY   .00                        ------------
TOTAL ROOM RATE        18,452.50      DIFFERENCE          -970.00
                       ------------
TOTAL                  18,452.50

TOTAL RECORD RATE      18,452.50


TOTAL FOOD GRATUITY          .00
TOTAL CONFERENCE GRATUITY    .00
```

Figure 13.5. Room Revenue Report
(Courtesy of EECO Hotel Systems)

2. *Room Statistics (and Revenue) Report* (see Figure 13.5). This report details the occupancy and revenues generated by sold rooms and may also present the average rate and other relevant room statistics.

3. *Ledger Summary Reports* (see Figures 13.6 and 13.7). City ledgers showing nonguest activity (and possibly national credit card activity) are typical system reports. Guest ledgers tracing all guest accounts by beginning balances, cumulative charges, and credits.

4. *Revenue Center Reports.* This report shows the cash, charge, and paid-out totals by department and serves as a macroanalysis of all department transactions.

5. *Ticket Control Report* (see Figure 13.8). This report charts all tickets and identifies missing or erroneous postings.

6. *Late Charge Billings* (see Figure 13.9). Letters and/or reports of nonzero accounts for departed guests are automatically transferred to the city ledger and bills prepared.

```
DATE  5/17/77      THE IBM HOTEL        SHIFT 2 AUDIT (H13)                                       PAGE   1
-----------------------------------------------------------------------------------------------------------

      SUSAN                                                            103.95CR
      BOB                                                              625.00CR
      ANN                                                              220.16CR
      CARL                                                             128.10CR
      ROOM                                                                 .00
      TAX                                                                  .00
ooooo LOCAL PHONE CALLS
      MILLER, RHONDA            104411    202                  2 B         .54
      KENNEDY, RON              102518    469                  2 H         .36
      WINSTON, MR. O.           102604    454                  2 H         .90
      MURRAY, BOB               104528    460                  2 H         .54

                               OPERATOR TOTAL                            5.75
                               COMPUTER TOTAL                            2.34
                               DIFFERENCE                                3.41

ooooo LONG DISTANCE CALLS
      MILLER, RHONDA            104411    202   (213) 777-5931  2 B       4.40
      WALTER, MRS CINCY         104215    451   (707) 315-7820  2 H       3.41
      HALLOWAY, GEORGE          104454    479   (405) 899-2315  2 H       5.21
      BEEDON, CARIL             104520    467   (714) 888-5672  2 H       2.35
      BRONSTON, KEITH           104566    452   (415) 293-8991  2 H       7.83
      BRONSTON, KEITH           104566    452   (714) 622-8991  2 H       2.50

                               OPERATOR TOTAL                           21.35
                               COMPUTER TOTAL                           25.70
                               DIFFERENCE                                4.35

      LAUNDRY                                                              .00
      MISCELLANEOUS                                                       .00
      TRANSFER                                                            .00
      SMORGASBORD                                                     158.66
      INDIAN HILL                                                     135.05
      CATERING                                                            .00
      BAKERY / GIFTS                                                   48.20
      CASA RAMON                                                          .00
      FANNY'S                                                             .00
      PREPAID COMMISSION                                              5.00CR
      PACKAGE PLAN                                                     22.00
```

Figure 13.6. Shift/Night Audit Report
(Courtesy of Griswold's Inn, Claremont, California and IBM)

```
DATE  5/17/77      THE IBM HOTEL        GROUP BUSINESS REPORT (H61)                          PAGE   1
--------------------------------------------------------------------------------------------------
     DATE   GROUP #  ACCT #  GROUP / INDIVIDUAL NAME       ROOMS  GUESTS   DEPOSIT    DEPART

   5/17/77  101977  101977  ALLEN & KLEIN, INC.              3      6        .00      5/18/77
                                        TOTAL GROUP          3      6        .00

   5/17/77  102592  104396  THEOLOGICAL ASSOCIATION          1      1        .00      5/18/77
                    104397     SHELBY, MR. D.                1      1      22.00      5/18/77
                    104456     RATHERS, MR. D.               1      1      22.00      5/18/77
                                        TOTAL GROUP          3      3      44.00

   5/20/77   90984   90984  LITERARY ASSOCIATION            17     17        .00      5/22/77
                    104544     HAYLEY, DR. D.                1      1        .00      5/29/77
                    104547     SWANSON, PROF. G. L.          1      1        .00      5/22/77
                    104546     O'FLATERY, DR. L.             1      1        .00      5/22/77
                    104545     LAUM, DR. HANS                1      1        .00      5/22/77
                    104548     SARTUR, MISS LOUISE           1      1        .00      5/22/77
                    104551     BERG, RONALD                  1      1        .00      5/23/77
                    104550     SALVINI, TONY                 1      1        .00      5/23/77
                    104549     PIERSON, MR. TOM              1      1        .00      5/22/77
                    104552     KELSEY, MR. L.                1      1        .00      5/23/77
                                        TOTAL GROUP         26     26        .00

   5/22/77  101517  101517  INDUSTRIAL ELECTRONICS          18     18        .00      5/23/77
                                        TOTAL GROUP         18     18        .00

   5/26/77   90984  104555  LITERARY ASSOCIATION             1      1        .00      5/29/77
                    104554     SUMMERS, MISS SHIRLEY         1      1      20.00      5/29/77
                    104553     KEARNEY, GERALD               1      1      20.00      5/29/77
                    104556     PEARL, MR. DOUG               1      1      20.00      5/29/77
                                        TOTAL GROUP          4      4      60.00

   5/26/77   90985   90985  CITY COLLEGE                     8      8        .00      5/29/77
                                        TOTAL GROUP          8      8        .00

   6/08/77  102267  102267  ALEXA PAINT COMPANY             12     12        .00      6/10/77
                    103683     ROBLIN, MR. R.                1      1        .00      6/10/77
                    103684     HENDRICKS, MR. JACK           1      1        .00      6/10/77
                    103686     ELLIS, MR. RON                1      1        .00      6/11/77
                    103685     JALLINS, MR. TOM              1      1        .00      6/10/77
                    104164     WILKINS, MR. W.               1      1        .00      6/10/77
                    104407     BETT, MR. ED                  1      2        .00      6/10/77
                    104406     HENNISON, MR. TOM             1      1        .00      6/10/77
                    104408     RYMAN, MR & MRS               1      1        .00      6/11/77
                                        TOTAL GROUP         20     21        .00
```

Figure 13.7. Group Business Report
(Courtesy of Griswold's Inn, Claremont, California and IBM)

Benefits of On-Line Accounting

1. Instantaneous posting has produced a significant reduction in transcription and communication errors.

2. Internal verification of charges, prior to system acceptance for posting, has reduced the number of unauthorized charges and the number of high risk accounts.

3. Automatic posting of room rates and tax.

4. Elimination of late charges.

5. Production of legible, itemized guest statements that minimize guest discrepancies and provide for an accurate documentation of account expenditures.

6. Faster checkout as a result of quicker statement preparation and reconciliation.

7. Enables visibility into the in-house credit status of any account.

8. Provides management with improved internal control over the accounting phase of the guest cycle.

```
TICKET NUMBER CONTROL - "YOUR HOTEL NAME"
12/21/77
TN-PAGE    1

LOC.  021 - GROUP ROOMS
            59998  THRU   59999   TURNED IN.

LOC.  101 - ROTISSERIE
            32526  THRU   32526   TURNED IN.
            32527  THRU   34342   MISSING.
            34343  THRU   34343   TURNED IN.

LOC.  121 - COFFEE SHOP
            23456  THRU   23457   TURNED IN.
            23458  THRU   55554   MISSING.
            55555  THRU   55555   TURNED IN.
            55556  THRU   56554   MISSING.
            56555  THRU   56555   TURNED IN.
            56556  THRU   59999   MISSING.
            60000  THRU   60000   TURNED IN.

LOC.  131 - ROOM SERVICE
            23423  THRU   23423   TURNED IN.
            23424  THRU   33494   MISSING.
            33495  THRU   33495   TURNED IN.
            33496  THRU   45324   MISSING.
            45325  THRU   45325   TURNED IN.

LOC.  141 - BILLY'S PUB
            43526  THRU   43526   TURNED IN.

LOC.  151 - BANQUET MISC
            23452  THRU   23452   TURNED IN.

LOC.  161 - GUEST LAUNDRY
            23432  THRU   23432   TURNED IN.

LOC.  921 - ALLOWANCE
            32345  THRU   32345   TURNED IN.
            32346  THRU   59998   MISSING.
            59999  THRU   59999   TURNED IN.

LOC.  931 - SUNDRY
            59998  THRU   59998   TURNED IN.

LOC.  941 - PAID OUT
            59999  THRU   59999   TURNED IN.
```

Figure 13.8. Ticket Control Report
(Courtesy of EECO Hotel Systems)

New Developments

Although most of the automation of the guest accounting process is fairly recent, two related advances may impact upon this module in the near future: 1) the application of an on-line credit card authorization terminal and 2) the implementation of electronic fund transfer cards.

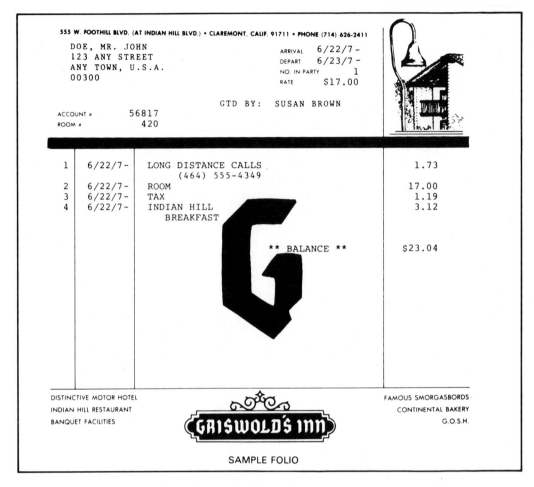

Figure 13.9. Guest Accounting/Check Out
(Courtesy of Griswold's Inn, Claremont, California and IBM)

Credit Authorization

National credit cards are shifting their dependence away from hotels securing member approval codes through telephone calls and surveys of bad credit lists and toward on-line authorization terminals. The authorization terminal can be located at the front desk and has instant access to the credit card company's national files. The desk agent inserts the guest's credit card into the terminal and the magnetic strip on the card's back communicates necessary data to the card company's central computer. A verification and authorization of credit are quickly relayed back to the hotel, thereby alleviating the hotel's concerns and labor in securing authorization. The on-line authorization terminals are not yet in wide use, but could be soon. The Express III terminal of American Express is shown in Figure 13.10.

Electronic Fund Transfer Cards

The success of electronic banking has led from guaranteed check cashing terminals, to cash dispensing terminals, to the development of *EFT* terminals. The EFT terminal is receiving exceptional resistance because of its threat to governmental control over the money supply. Questions dealing with who will control transfers (from guest accounts directly into business accounts at the point-of-sale) and what security steps must be taken to protect the consumer are now being raised. The ability of the hotel to collect revenues from its clientele's bank accounts and to have those monies immediately available to the hotel's account is the epitome of instant cash flow. This particular design may never exist but some variation of the EFT concept is inevitable.

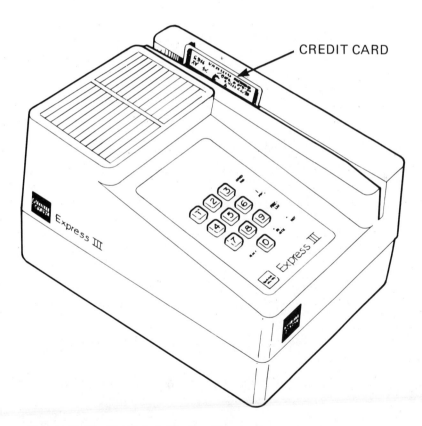

CREDIT CARD

Figure 13.10. Credit Authorization Terminal
(Courtesy of American Express)

Summary

The guest accounting module surely is a central and critical link within the hotel information system. This module, more so than any other component and system, enables management to gain controls and monitoring capabilities over the guest cycle. This module is primarily responsible for charge postings, auditing, and statement preparation. It has significantly reduced the required number of hotel documents and has greatly simplified auditing procedures.

The preference toward on-line accounting is directly related to the desirable benefits this module can provide. The variety of reports, the increase in controls, the enhancement of credit and charge verification and authorization procedures combine to yield a much needed strengthening of management's front office functions. All in all, the guest accounting module performs an extensive list of critical functions necessary for the hotel's success.

Key Concepts

Cash dispensing terminals	Electronic fund transfer (EFT)
Cashier reconciliation	Master folio
Control folio	Ticket control
Electronic folio	

Questions for Discussion

1. Why is the guest accounting module referred to as the most critical and central of the HIS?

2. What are the primary responsibilities of the guest accounting module to management?

3. Compare and contrast the traditional, manual guest accounting methodology with its on-line counterpart.

4. Outline the flow of information within the guest accounting module. If this module were interfaced with the reservation module what benefits and/or shortcomings would be derived?

5. Discuss the benefits of this module with specific reference toward managerial control over front office functions.

6. Which reports, available through this module, are the most essential to management, and why?

7. Discuss the impact of the new developments on the HIS and the hotel's functions in general.

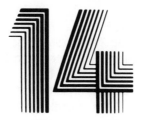

HIS Rooms Management
Module

Chapter Objectives:

1. To introduce the basic concept of the rooms management module of the HIS.

2. To explain the purpose of the module and its algorithmic design.

3. To enumerate the functions available through this computer-assisted HIS module.

4. To isolate the benefits that can be derived from implementation of a rooms management system.

THE ROOMS management module is critical to the maintenance of room status reports, coordination of the housekeeping function, and the elimination of the room rack. The ability to have up-to-the-minute knowledge concerning the availability of guest accommodations has enabled the hotel to maximize its occupancy and to better schedule its personnel. One of the major advantages gained through computer application has been the tightening of the communication link between the front office and the housekeeping department. A better interface has provided the hotel with a faster cycling of its rooms and a reliable means of cross-referencing room status information. Additionally, the housekeeping requirements, as a function of the occupancy load, can be translated into personnel schedules and productivity indices.

The ability to display limited guest data at the desk and switchboard has led to the elimination of the room rack and the preparation of guest information lists. Video terminals that bring the user a capsule of room rack equivalent information can be accessed by inputting either the guest's room number or name. This visibility into the guest list has enhanced the hotel's ability to better serve the guest and has begun the trend toward a paperless front desk operation.

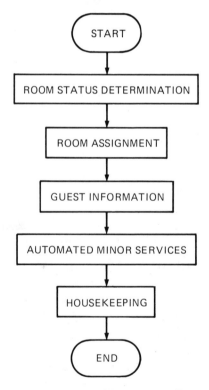

Figure 14.1. Flowchart of Rooms Management Process

The On-Line Rooms Management Process

The rooms management module is an important information and communications branch of the HIS package. This module, however, can be segmented into a five-phase process. The component parts of this process are room status determination, room assignment, guest information, automated minor services, and housekeeping. Figure 14.1 depicts the rooms management process.

Room Status Determination

Whether the guest is a walk-in or a call comes for a reservation six months hence, the ability of the hotel clerk to sell a room is primarily contingent upon accurate, up-to-date room status information. Status determination is basically an occupancy reporting of a room's:

1. housekeeping description

2. future availability

3. discrepancy with records

The housekeeping description is important for the immediate, or short-run (within one day) selling position of a guest accommodation. Some traditional housekeeping statuses are: "on-change," "out-of-order," "requires inspection," and "ready." All but the ready status inform the rooms clerk that an accommodation is not available for occupancy, at this time. The application of computer technology provides an instantaneous housekeeping status update that enables the hotel to determine immediate room assignments (as rooms become available).

The concept of future availability status is aimed at a longer than the same-day level of reporting (mainly with advance reservations). As discussed earlier in Chapter 12, a request for future accommodations leads to a system inquiry of room availability status. Visibility into long-run availability horizons has given the hotel more reliable status information and enhanced its ability to maximize occupancy.

Discrepancy evaluation reports identify those rooms whose status is not in agreement with the housekeeping department and the front desk. This type of documentation has served to reduce the number of sleeper accounts and has provided a cross-referencing of room status.

Room Assignment

Room modules may be programmed to automatically assign rooms, present an abbreviated availability list for clerk selection, or require the rooms clerk to survey all available accommodations. Automatic room assignment algorithms are constructed according to parameters specified by the hotel. Rooms are usually electronically determined based upon specified zones of the hotel (like guest seating in a dining room) or else along a sophisticated index of room usage. Although not widely available, some modules are capable of tracking room histories (frequency of sales) and of rank ordering these loads into usage factors. The algorithm then assigns rooms so as to distribute occupancy loads more evenly over the rooms inventory. The rooms clerk always maintains the prerogative to override the system.

The interactive room assignment formats are more common and furnish the clerk direct control over assignments. The abbreviated listing of rooms, by types and rates, shortens the clerk's decision time and allows for a faster check-in procedure. The review of all rooms available may be quite involved in a fifteen hundred room property and therefore the abbreviated listing was devised. The room clerk's selection of a room may be along the same parameters designated for the automated approach and the clerk's inspection of room status may allow for the assignment of a guest to a room whose status is other than "ready."

Guest Information

The HIS room module has enabled visibility into the guest's data to the point where information racks, room racks, and telephone lists are being eliminated. This module is designed to provide capsuled, or limited, reviewing of only basic personal data concerning the guest. This information, however, is sufficient to enable a switchboard operator or desk clerk, using a display terminal, to conveniently and quickly identify who the guest is and to what room the guest is assigned. This limited access to room rack equivalent information has begun a paperless approach to front office management and has extended the hotel's ability to provide better guest services.

Automated Minor Services

The application of automated technology has also simplified many minor hotel guest services and allowed the hotel to perform them even more effectively, such as wake-up calls, message notifications, and do not disturb systems. This allows the hotel to concentrate on many of its more important objectives. An automated wake-up system permits the front desk to input the guest's room number and requested wake-up time into the terminal. At the specified time the system will automatically ring the room and continuously call back every ten or fifteen minutes until the phone is answered. If there is no response for the third or fourth ring, the system stops calling and makes note of the guest's failure to answer. Should the guest answer, a prerecorded morning greeting is played and upon its completion the system will disconnect. Some sophisticated wake-up devices require the guest to speak into the phone to establish a wake-up confirmation. A notation of the answered call is usually retained for the day within the system.

The electronic message-waiting functions vary in their design from a flashing on the television screen to an automatic telephone call pattern. The basic idea for repeatedly trying to get the guest's attention is to make mention of a message at the desk. The system's ability to keep calling back is more economical, efficient, and productive than an operator's persistance could be. A function like the "do not disturb" system is basically a relay system that can be interfaced with the desk and the housekeeping department. This serves to eliminate the traditional hang-up signs the guest placed outside the room (to announce make-up or a desire for privacy). The advantages of this service lie in the assumption of room security (a passerby is no longer able to determine the presence or absence of the occupant) and gives the housekeeping department an early message regarding the guest's desires.

Housekeeping

There has been a large amount of technological development aimed at the hotel's housekeeping function. Vendor modules are normally capable of: 1) scheduling house-keeping personnel, 2) determining their productivity, and 3) presenting the housekeeping status of any room upon request. Personnel are scheduled based upon the house count and the expected number of arrivals for the following day. The volume of rooms requiring attention will lead directly to a determination of the number of housekeeping employees required. Additionally, most modules assign specific rooms to each person and are capable of determining their productivity by measuring their average length of time in a room, and the number of rooms attended in any given shift. A sample display of a system-generated schedule appears in Figure 14.2. Note that the specific room as-

TYPICAL DISPLAY OF AN INDIVIDUAL MAID-ROOM SCHEDULE PROVIDED BY MOTOROLA'S INN-SCAN 400 COMPUTERIZED MANAGEMENT SYSTEM.

Figure 14.2. Housekeeping Personnel Schedule (Courtesy of Motorola)

signments, the recordings of times in and out and the present statuses of the rooms assigned are listed. The times in and out are captured through the employee's usage of a telephone dial-up to the computer. Most systems require the housekeeper's code number, room number (although not always necessary), and the present room status code. When the room is ready for inspection and/or sale, follow-up calls to the computer initiate a time recording for each change in status. This enables the determination of a productivity rate for each housekeeper. Changes in room status simultaneously update the room status listing even though they are phoned to the computer under the guise of a housekeeping code. The interrelationship of room status and housekeeping has revolutionized intrahotel communications and has enabled the hotel to better cycle its rooms.

Rooms Management Module Functions

The following list is representative, but not exhaustive, of HIS rooms management functions:

1. Summarized guest information listings.

2. Production of room status reports.

3. Sales forecasting/marketing reports.

4. Occupancy reports (analyzed by type).

5. General housekeeping reports.

6. Evaluation of housekeeper's productivity.

7. Overall maintenance analysis.

8. Engineering department reporting.

9. Assorted, automated minor guest services.

The development of accurate room status reports is a much needed managerial index to operations. Similarly, the production of analytical occupancy reports can provide management with a better understanding of its market and improve success in sales. A new consideration has come in the area of maid scheduling and productivity reporting. There are some systems that are so sophisticated that they can analyze the present occupancy, schedule the required number of maids for the following day, assign rooms to specific personnel, and conduct an ongoing evaluation of the housekeeping personnel as they perform their tasks. These productivity reports both inform management of inefficiencies and provide information on the exact location of all housekeeping personnel during their shift. Recent system attempts to tie in the engineering department have been designed with energy management and conservation in mind. Although not very widely publicized, there is testing taking place to determine better ways of controlling the guest's total environment at lower costs. The rooms management phase of hotel systems is an important concern to the industry and one that is now beginning to receive considerable attention.

Module Reports

Because the rooms management module overlaps several key areas, such as rooms, housekeeping, and minor services, there are a large number of reports that can be produced. Reports that deal only with rooms, those that link rooms and housekeeping, and those that forecast activities are usually all offered in a vendor-designed rooms package. A small sample of representative reports follows:

1. *Room Discrepancy Report*—identifies those rooms having discrepancies in status between the front desk and housekeeping reports; a form of exception reporting.

```
ACTUAL DEPARTURE GUEST LIST BY NAME - "YOUR HOTEL NAME"
12/21/77
PAGE   1

ROOM#   QNAME   ARV DATE  NAME                        CITY,STATE                    #GUEST

  628            12/19    ACHARD, M/M                 PARIS 75001 FRANCE               2
  942            12/19    ANGELINI, MR A M            ROMA, ITALY                      1
  332    PAPER   12/19    ATCHISON. M/M RICHARD       LEXINGTON, VA 24450              2
  432            12/19    BAILEY, MR D G              NAPANEE, ONT, CN                 2
  118            12/21    BAKER, FAM EMILE S          PHILA, PA 19131                  3
  724            12/19    BALLANTYNE, MR WILLIAM      LONDON, U. K.                    1
  127            12/21    BIXBY, SALLY                                                 1
  145            12/21    BLOUNT, HUGO                HOUSE USE                        1
 1046    FFARE2  12/21    BROTHERS, JAN               WEST HARTFORD, CT 06107          1
  338    INSUR   12/21    COPELAND, M/M R BRUCE       BLOOMFIELD, CT 06139             2
  144            12/21    DEHN, ALMA                                                   1
  709            12/19    DORSEY, DR/MRS R            CINCINNATI,OHIO 45243,USA        2
  142            12/21    EMAM, M/M/F M.              WINDSOR, CT 06220                4
 1046    FFARE2  12/21    LEFEBVRE, ANNETTE           WEST HARTFORD, CT 06107          1
  605            12/21    LOCKE, MR JAMES D           SANTA ANA, CA 92704              1
  501    FFARE2  12/21    LORENZ, HILDA               SANTA ANA, CA 92702              1
  143            12/17    MARTINERI, JOAN             COSTA MESA, CA 92304             1
 1046    FFARE2  12/21    PANDOLFI, CARMEN            WEST HARTFORD, CT 06107          1
  501    FFARE2  12/21    PFLUG, ANNA                 SANTA ANA, CA 92702              1
  330    INSUR   12/21    RIVERA, MS GLORIA           NEW YORK, NY 10003               1
  608            12/20    RUSSELL, D/M ALLEN          PINE BLUFF, AR                   2
  124            12/21    SOOTER, MELVIN                                               1
 1032    PAPER   12/20    STEWART, MR DOUGLAS         HOUSTON, TX 49287                2
  441    PAPER   12/19    WALDTEUFEL, MYRON           SCHWARTZWALD, FRG                2
  409    INSUR   12/21    WARFIELD, JAMES             MONTPELIER, VT 24041             1
  501    FFARE2  12/21    WILSON, DONNA               SANTA ANA, CA 92702              1
 1043    PAPER   12/20    ZAHRA, JOHN S               MONPELIER, VT 24041              1

TOTAL NUMBER OF ROOMS       23            TOTAL NUMBER OF GUESTS          40
```

Figure 14.3. Actual Departure Report
(Courtesy of EECO Hotel Systems)

2. *Expected Checkout Report*—enables more efficiency in the scheduling of housekeeping personnel; also, advises the rooms clerk of rooms that will become available for sale soon.

3. *Actual Departure Report* (See Fig. 14.3)—details who checked out, their room number, billing address, and folio number; some systems also display the remaining balance of guest accounts if any.

4. *Housekeeping Assignment Report* (see Fig. 14.4)—a system-produced listing of room numbers, their statuses, and messages, if any, for any housekeeper.

5. *Housekeeper Productivity Report*—contains a time in and out and an index of relative productivity for each housekeeper.

6. *Room Productivity Report* (see Fig. 14.5)—usually produced at the end of month, quarter, and year and provides a ranking of rooms by type based upon occupancy or revenue or both.

7. *Room Activity Forecast Report*—provides anticipated check ins and checkouts by expected

```
HOUSEKEEPING ASSIGNMENT LIST - "YOUR HOTEL NAME"
09/01/77
M4-PAGE     1



MAID:       1


ROOM     TIME     NBR BED                                 NOTES
NUMBER   CLEANED  GST TYPE

2321              4

2806              2

2902              2

3123              2

3421              4

3608              3

3821              3

4002              2

4410              4

4412              4

4414              3

4505              4












SPECIAL MESSAGE TO MAIDS: MEETING AT 4PM IN REVERE ROOM FOR ALL
HOUSEKEEPERS.

TODAYS MESSAGE: PLEASE CLEAN EMERGENCY EXIT STAIRWELLS TODAY.
```

Figure 14.4. Housekeeping Assignment Report
(Courtesy of EECO Hotel Systems)

```
HYATT REGENCY SAN FRAN.                    31 DAY ROOM PRODUCTIVITY-BY CATEGORY- 1 01 7- THRU  7 31 7-

           O C C U P A N C Y - R O O M   D A Y S                                     R E V E N U E
                                                                                                                    AVER.   AVER.
  CT   DAY   TOTAL         HSE                          TOTAL      %  NUMBER                          DAY USE        *PER    PER
  NO   USE   AVAIL  COMP   USE  000 VACANT  TRANS  PERM   OCC  DESC OCC GUESTS    TRANSIENT PERMANENT & OTHER       GUEST  OCC-RM

  11    0   1,456     8     0    0    76   1,372    0   1,372 SKING 94.2 2,297    55,034.38    .00       .00       23.96   40.11
  12    0   1,829    20     0    0   225   1,584    0   1,584 SKING 86.6 2,541    65,647.25    .00       .00       25.84   41.44
  13    0   1,891    93     0    0   261   1,537    0   1,537 SKING 81.3 2,666    68,763.02    .00       .00       25.79   44.74
  14    0   2,511   105     0    0   360   2,046    0   2,046 DKING 81.5 3,462    97,758.50    .00     25.00       28.25   47.79


  **     2  24,975   423     0    0 3,268  21,262    0  21,262 TOTAL 80.4 34,627  873,565.40    .00    208.00       25.88   43.31


           JULY 01 197-                        PERIOD ENDING            JULY 31 197-
           PERIOD THIS YEAR                                            PERIOD-LAST YEAR
              24,975                          TOTAL AVAILABLE ROOMS        24,176
                                   MULTIPLE                                                     MULTIPLE
        %        REVENUE           OCC RMS   OCCUPIED AND VACANT ROOMS    %       REVENUE        OCC RMS
       78.2     873,565.40           205        TRANSIENT OCC          65.1    596,532.10          93
        .0          .00                0        PERMANENT OCC           .0         .00              0
       78.2    $873,565.40           205     TOTAL ROOMS OCC           65.1    596,532.10          93

        2.1                                     COMPLIMENTARY           1.9
         .0                                     HOUSE USE                .0
         .0                                     OUT OF ORDER             .9
       19.7                                     VACANT                 32.1
      100.0        208.00                       DAY USE & OTHER                    50.00
                                             TOTAL                    100.0    596,582.10
```

Figure 14.5. Room Productivity Report
(Courtesy of NCR Corporation)

arrivals, departures, stayovers, and vacancies and assists in planning front desk and house-keeping requirements.

8. *Room Allotment Report* (see Fig. 14.6)—summary of date and rooms committed (or blocked) in the future.

9. *Room History Report* (see Fig. 14.7)—provides the revenue history and room usage index of guest accommodations by room number and type.

10. *Current House Information Summary* (see Fig. 14.8)—gives a summation of the current occupancy load by total number of rooms; and, also, may show room revenues, average rates, and rooms profile by status.

Benefits of On-Line Rooms Management

1. Instant room status updating

2. Elimination of the room rack and guest information lists

3. Automatic room assignments

4. Maximization of occupancy through improved housekeeping and front desk communications

5. Automated wake-up service

6. Automated message-waiting service

7. Automated housekeeping scheduling and productivity analysis

8. Better knowledge of room productivity and usage loads

```
ALLOTMENT SUMMARY - "YOUR HOTEL NAME"
PAGE  1
12/21/77

                    GROUP ROOMS     INDIVIDUAL ROOMS
    DATE       BLOCKED     SOLD      BOOKED    UNSOLD

  06/01/78        55         6          14       420
  06/02/78        55         6          11       423
  06/03/78        55         4           7       427
  06/04/78        15         3           7       467
  06/05/78        15         0           6       468
  06/06/78         0         0           5       484
  06/07/78         0         0           4       485
  06/08/78         0         0           4       485
  06/09/78         0         0           4       485
  06/10/78         0         0           4       485
  06/11/78         0         0           4       485
  06/12/78         0         0           5       484
  06/13/78        10         0           5       474
  06/14/78        10         0           6       473
  06/15/78        10         0          14       465
  06/16/78        10         0          14       465
  06/17/78        10         0          14       465
  06/18/78        10         0          15       464
  06/19/78        10         0          15       464
  06/20/78        10         0          14       465
  06/21/78        10         0          12       467
  06/22/78        10         0           4       475
  06/23/78         0         0           4       485
  06/24/78         0         0           4       485
  06/25/78         0         0           4       485
  06/26/78         0         0           4       485
  06/27/78         0         0           4       485
  06/28/78         0         0           4       485
  06/29/78         0         0           4       485
  06/30/78         0         0           4       485
  07/01/78         0         0           5       484
  07/02/78         0         0           5       484
  07/03/78         0         0         132       357
  07/04/78        95        37         399        -5
  07/05/78        95        29         133       261
```

Figure 14.6. Room Allotment Summary
(Courtesy of EECO Hotel Systems)

New Developments

Perhaps the most outstanding contribution to the hotel, generally, and the rooms department, specifically, has been the development of energy monitoring systems. The objective of these systems is to monitor the hotel's energy consumption and thereby reduce its energy costs. The most important feature of these systems is their ability to minimize the building's energy loads while not significantly affecting the hotel's comfort systems. Heating, lighting, ventilation, and air conditioning equipment are essential to the hotel's existence and therefore the more efficiently they are operated, the better off the property will be. Energy management systems vary in their design but basically they

HISTORICAL DATA

The system quickly provides accurate data on the income-producing history of any single room.

It also provides precise historical data on any group of rooms by a specified type in summary form.

It also provides accurate historical data on any group of rooms in a specified location such as a particular floor.

Figure 14.7. Room History Report
(Courtesy of Motorola)

are capable of monitoring both the facility's internal energy demands and regulating the external utility's supply.

Energy Monitoring Processes

An extensive concern over energy cost and consumption has led to the development of efficient energy monitoring systems. A computer-based system can produce savings of about 30 percent (in energy costs) and therefore has an anticipated payback period of about three years for a hotel of 200 rooms. A general overview of a monitoring system consists of five processes:

1. Construction of expected consumption rates for events (room occupancy) or devices (refrigeration equipment or lighting).

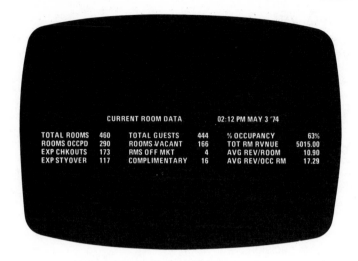

Figure 14.8. Current In-House Summary
(Courtesy of Motorola)

2. Continuous measurement of energy consumption for strategic locations and mechanical systems.

3. Processing of demands by equipment and location.

4. Analysis of energy demands based upon the variance between expected consumption and actual rates.

5. Adjustment in event or equipment requirements according to expectations (see Fig. 14.9).

The monitoring system operates continually and is efficient in reducing consumption and demands through analysis of expected usage requirements and actual rates. The automatic nature of the system enables a relay of corrective action (back to the problem location or device) and frees engineering and maintenance personnel to concentrate their efforts elsewhere.

Energy Monitoring Designs

There are two broad types of energy monitoring systems: noncomputing systems and computing systems.

A noncomputing system basically is a master switchboard of device timers. This type of system functions according to preestablished time sequences and simply turns devices on or off. Often noncomputing systems are compatible with a firm's present computer system and can be added.

A computing system is event-driven, using enthalpy-sensing meters for analyzing energy consumption and providing energy efficiency ratios (EER). These systems are capable of altering building demands by measuring variances in consumption rates. The computation of system adjustment and the ability to isolate malfunctioning devices are

Figure 14.9. The Energy Monitoring Process

the outstanding characteristics of an energy computing system. This type of system generally cannot be connected to present computer systems because it is sensor based.

Investment Criterion
Vendors claim that the decision to implement an energy-monitoring system should be a function of the monthly energy bill. A rule-of-thumb value of $5,000 is generally stated but older buildings or buildings with special problems or needs may have to override this rule-of-thumb estimate for decision-making.

Benefits
The benefits of an energy monitoring system are:

1. reduction of energy costs

2. work without interruption or interrupting other equipment

3. frees maintenance and engineering personnel to other areas

4. presents no additional safety hazards

5. has a fairly rapid payback period

Summary
The rooms management module performs an important coordination of several guest service centers, such as front desk, housekeeping, and switchboard, and enables the hotel to optimize its room sales through better information. An up-to-the-minute room status system assures the property of complete availability and advises the various service departments of guest loads, vacancies, and statuses. The rooms module has been instrumental in the elimination of the room rack and in the development of an improved communication network throughout the facility.

The rooms module, which has the ability to interface with other modules, is essential to the enhancement of management's visibility into who the guest is and into the hotel's status. Recently, room status systems were expanded to incorporate energy monitoring systems and employee scheduling/productivity systems. These innovations have rendered the rooms module a more complete package capable of significantly enhancing management's ability to operate the hotel.

Key Concepts

Energy efficiency ratio (EER)
Energy monitoring system
Event driven
Housekeeper productivity analysis
Housekeeping assignment report
Occupancy load
Room discrepancy report

Questions for Discussion

1. Why is the rooms module considered an important factor in the optimization of hotel occupancy?

2. In what way does this module assist management in the coordination of guest services?

3. Explain the process by which employee productivity is analyzed. Give your opinion as to the value and merit of this procedure.

4. How does the rooms management module determine discrepancies in room status? Of what value are these variance reports?

5. Are automated minor services practical? What impact will a large degree of automated services have on the guest? On the hotel's ability to cost-justify its computer-based operations?

6. Of all the reports available through this module, which one do you consider most essential or most powerful and why?

7. List five benefits that can be derived through the implementation of this module. What additional benefits can be derived through modular interfacing with the reservation and/or guest accounting systems?

8. What are the advantages and disadvantages of an energy monitoring system?

9. Explain the various types of energy monitoring processes and how they work to conserve the consumption of energy in the hotel.

HIS General
Management Module

Chapter Objectives:

1. To introduce the basic general management module of the HIS.

2. To explain the configuration, interface capabilities, and algorithmic design of the management module.

3. To enumerate the modular functions available through computer assistance in this area.

4. To present the derived benefits associated with the general management module.

THE GENERAL management component of the HIS is responsible for the determination and dissemination of information throughout the hotel. The types of reports, who receives them, and how often they are generated are the kinds of executive parameters that management needs to delineate. Managerial controls on the microlevel include internal control of guest cycle accounting, improved departmental communications, and a better capability for monitoring operating revenues. On the macrolevel, managerial concerns are oriented toward financial analysis, operational statistics, and the formulation of decisions based upon variance reports and similar documents. The management module differs from any of the other three (reservations, accounting, and rooms) in that it cannot be applied independently; at least, not without requiring an enormous summarization and coding of operating data. The development of analytical, statistical, and financial calculations requires departmental and back-office data, and if only this module were implemented, then all the required data would have to be independently captured and entered into the program. The expense involved in this data collection, and the amount of time and integrity required would make this singular module approach both irrelevant and infeasible.

Although most hotel vendor systems appear to be front-office oriented only, many provide back-office capability. These particular software packages usually interface with the HIS at the management module level. The only manner by which to get an accurate appraisal of overall operations is through an incorporation of back-office information, since all the front-office modules are primarily concerned with POS revenue transactions not with production-cost data.

The shortcomings of manually-produced documents have centered around the inability of the front office to secure timely and accurate back-office data. This has led to management reporting on an after-the-fact basis. Overhead expenses, general ledger status, payroll costs, inventory levels, and other costs-of-goods sold can be integrated with revenue information to yield an accurate and current base of control for the entire operation.

Additionally, the management module also provides for a charting of employee entry and exit times and for system security measures. Many vendor systems require employees to pass inspection points, using identification cards or badges, in order to record each employee arrival and departure to and from work. This provides a tighter security for the premises and can even be used to restrict employees from certain unrelated job areas. With regard to computer security protection, management must specify who is allowed access to what information and must devise a method for eliminating unauthorized systems access and/or usage.

The On-Line General Management Process

The general management module combines all departmental data into an overview of the information stream. The process can be discussed in terms of five phases: revenue analysis, operating statistics, financial analysis, back-office interface, and decision-making. Figure 15.1 is a simplified flowchart of the management module process.

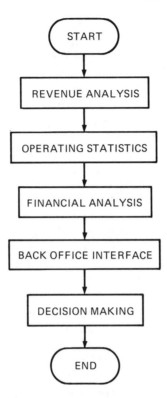

Figure 15.1. Flowchart of Management Process

Revenue Analysis

All revenue centers have POS capabilities and will continuously relay sales data to the front office. Regardless of whether the revenues are generated by cash or charge, all transactions should be entered. This provides management with revenue controls with regard to:

1. Cashier reconciliation. Since all cash and charges are entered, management should know how much cash should be in each terminal cash drawer.

2. Charge posting. The charge sales are instantaneously posted and folio balances will reflect outstanding balances.

3. Ticket auditing. Since the POS terminal will accept ticket control numbers, management can trace all transactions (cash and charge), so long as the cashier is instructed to post these numbers.

Revenue tracking and analysis is usually done according to the hotel's chart of accounts and presents management with timely feedback on the hotel's volume of business.

Operating Statistics

A request for the current status of the hotel, in most systems, will automatically generate an occupancy summary, an average rate (by room and by guest) review, and a rate variance analysis. The occupancy statistics are usually by room types and some vendors offer an average number of guests per room calculation. The calculation of the average rates are accurate and give management an instant index of performance for the rooms department. The rate variance analysis is not generally performed in all management modules, but does offer management an index of the number of rooms that were sold either above or below their normal rate. Additional statistics can be obtained in a multitude of formats, most of which deal only with front-office appraisals.

Unless this module is interfaced with some back-office information, management will be limited to the amount of value the system's statistics will provide. Often several management report options contain identical or overlapping data, but in different formats. The system software should be developed to produce those indices management needs and wants most. Another factor to be considered in using statistical outputs in vendor-designed packages is that there be a standardization of terminology.

Financial Analysis

Analysis of revenues, receivables, and expenditures combine to yield a statement of financial position for management. The primary concern, and one which a computer-based HIS can provide, is an analysis of each flow. The time that elapses from the point-of-sale until the hotel receives cash for its goods and services can be accurately charted by the management module. Although cash flow is one of management's main concerns, additional analysis can be performed in such areas as revenue forecasting, statement of financial position, and statement of income and expenses. The revenue forecasting procedure is performed for advanced reservations and accurately projects a sales volume for the hotel for some future accounting period. The statement of financial position is for any point in time and is basically a balance sheet consisting of the hotel's assets, liabilities, and equity. The statement of income and expenses combines sales with costs-of-goods sold (both direct and indirect) to produce an index of profitability. All in all, the financial reporting facet of the management module is essential to its influence on the managerial process.

Back-Office Interface

Without a connection to back-office information the management module is limited primarily to revenue analysis. The software packages required to interface with the front-office modules are designed with commonality and standardization of input formats. The advantage in using a single vendor for both front- and back-office hardware is the avoidance of interface and separate system expenditures.

Common back-office interfaces are general ledger accounting, accounts payable, and payroll expenditures. The general ledger accounting mode centers around the hotel's chart of accounts and is responsible for producing all account balances, a statement of financial position (a balance sheet), and an income statement. The accounts payable branch is used to track purchases, creditor positions, and the bank position of the firm. Payroll, of course, is aimed at tracking labor costs via calculations of gross and net pay. Most vendor systems maintain extensive payroll documentation and can provide year-end analysis and tax reporting for employees.

Decision-Making

One of the major reasons for the management module is the consolidation of all departmental information into a data base to support managerial decision-making. On-line systems, by definition, react fast enough to a systems inquiry to affect the decision-making process. Hence, the speed and accuracy gained in computerized hotel information systems is optimized through the general management module. The production of intelligible and comprehensive reports of a timely nature far surpasses earlier manual or mechanical procedures.

Management Module Functions

The following list is representative, but not exhaustive, of HIS general management module functions:

1. Generation of analytical reports (occupancy, room status, budgets, etc.)

2. Cost center reports (labor, food, etc.)

3. Construction of sales reports (room, food, etc.)

4. Control reports (inventory, housekeeping, etc.)

5. Corporate/financial/accounting reports and statements.

6. Security systems provisions.

It is the combination of all data, and comparisons with the goals of the organization, that culminate in managerial reports. These consolidated, analytical evaluations and projections support the managerial decision-making process, help control operations, and highlight situations requiring corrective action. Standard accounting statements for

```
UNION SQUARE                          GUEST ACCOUNTS OVER CREDIT LIMIT        8 22 7-

            NAME              F  M
ROOM GST ADDRESS             I  I        CURRENT    AMT. OVER    EXP      STATUS OR REMARKS
   NO    ID  CITY STATE ZIP              BALANCE    CR. LIMIT    DEP

   225  790 STACY             L           203.96       53.96     8/23
            2652 EDWINA
            LOS ANGELES      CA  90027

   235  630 JACOBS           H  J         181.52       31.52     8/25
            516 OTIS AVE
```

Figure 15.2. Credit Limit Report
(Courtesy of NCR Corporation)

```
TRAVEL AGENT REPORT - "YOUR HOTEL NAME"
12/21/77
TA-PAGE    5

        TRAVEL AGENT                     GUEST NAME
LOUISE                          ZAHRA, JOHN S              ROOM#  1043
SARATOGA TRAVEL BUREAU          GRANITE INS CO             RATE      38.00M
50 BROAD ST                     50 E 12TH ST               QNAME PAPER
TICONDEROGA, NY 10229           MONPELIER, VT 24041        ARRIVAL    12/20/77
                                SETTLEMENT AX              DEPARTURE 12/21/77
DEPOSIT#     17                 ROOM REVENUE       38.00   ROOM NIGHTS    1
DEP CREDIT      70.00              FOOD PLAN          .00   FOLIO#  100857 #G-01
DEP CASH        63.00                 OTHER           .00   SALES TYPE  14
COMM HELD        7.00              TOTAL          38.00     SS: HF, A1
GUEST MESSAGE: VIP

-------------------------------------------------------------------------------

        TRAVEL AGENT                     GUEST NAME
MIDDLER, ELIZ                   BAILEY, MR D G             ROOM#    432
TRAVEL TIME TOURS               BRIGHTON LABS              RATE      50.00C
3492 DUNDAS ST                  PO BOX 75                  QNAME
TORONTO, ONT, CN M4G 3B8        NAPANEE, ONT, CN           ARRIVAL    12/19/77
                                SETTLEMENT AX              DEPARTURE 12/21/77
DEPOSIT#                        ROOM REVENUE      100.00   ROOM NIGHTS    2
DEP CREDIT                        FOOD PLAN          .00   FOLIO#  100842 #G-02
DEP CASH                              OTHER           .00   SALES TYPE  14
COMM HELD                         TOTAL         100.00     SS: 00
GUEST MESSAGE:

-------------------------------------------------------------------------------

        TRAVEL AGENT                     GUEST NAME
LORI                            MARTINERI, JOAN            ROOM#    143
TRIPS & TOURS INC               300 W GRAND AVE, APT E4    RATE      38.50
305 AVENIDA ASHFORD             COSTA MESA, CA 92304       QNAME
HUMACAO, PR 00661                                          ARRIVAL    12/17/77
                                SETTLEMENT CA              DEPARTURE 12/21/77
DEPOSIT#                        ROOM REVENUE      154.00   ROOM NIGHTS    4
DEP CREDIT                        FOOD PLAN          .00   FOLIO#  100850 #G-01
DEP CASH                              OTHER           .00   SALES TYPE  00
COMM HELD                         TOTAL         154.00     SS:
GUEST MESSAGE:

-------------------------------------------------------------------------------

        TRAVEL AGENT                     GUEST NAME
HENRY, DONNA                    RUSSELL, D/M ALLEN         ROOM#    608
WILSON TRAVEL                   12 WILLOW LANE             RATE      43.50
3941 MAIN ST                    PINE BLUFF, AR             QNAME
DENVER, CO                                                 ARRIVAL    12/20/77
                                SETTLEMENT VI              DEPARTURE 12/21/77
DEPOSIT#                        ROOM REVENUE       43.50   ROOM NIGHTS    1
DEP CREDIT                        FOOD PLAN          .00   FOLIO#  100851 #G-02
DEP CASH                              OTHER           .00   SALES TYPE  02
COMM HELD                         TOTAL          43.50     SS: 00
GUEST MESSAGE:

-------------------------------------------------------------------------------
```

Figure 15.3. Commissions Report
(Courtesy of EECO Hotel Systems)

both internal and external reporting and corporate-required documents are some of the typical outputs of an effective management information system in the hospitality industry.

Module Reports

Since the general management module overlaps with the other three modules, many of its reports are similar to those cited elsewhere. Some of the reports available are:

1. *End-of-Day Report*—basically an end-of-day rooms analysis that deals with gains and losses in room revenues due to variance flows in the average rate by room type.

2. *Credit Limit Report* (See Fig. 15.2)—identifies those guests who have exceeded their house limits or credit card authorized limits.

3. *Commissions Report* (see Fig. 15.3)—indicates all guests who were booked through an agency; commissions are either automatically computed by agency, or can be computed from the system display.

4. *Daily Report* (see Figs. 15.4 a–c)—details departmental revenues and expenses according to the hotel's chart of accounts; gives an estimated profit based on day's operation; gives statistics on current operations.

5. *Departmental Account Report*—based upon the interfacing of front and back office information by operating department.

6. *City Ledger Aging*—shows outstanding balances owed the hotel and for how many periods they have gone uncollected.

Benefits of On-Line Management

1. Improved cash flow due to better financial information.

2. Increased control over revenues, receivables, and payables.

3. More timely and accurate reports.

4. Standardization of terminology and techniques of analysis throughout the hotel.

5. Integration between front- and back-office information for a more complete reporting function.

6. Consolidation of other module inputs to yield comprehensive, intelligible outputs.

Summary

The management module is primarily responsible for satisfying managerial informational needs, identified through both a *micro* and *macro* appraisal of the firm. The general management module cannot be applied independently, at least not feasibly or practically, and therefore must interface with at least one other module. The aggregation of a wide range of data makes the management module a powerful tool in the analysis of hotel operations. This module is the critical linkage often needed between front- and back-office computer-based hotel information systems.

```
DATE  2/17/76      THE IBM HOTEL        MANAGER'S DAILY REPORT - PART 1 (H23)                           PAGE    1

                                    ROOM STATISTICS - TODAY

                     BRIDAL     DOUBLES    KINGS     QUEENS     SUITES    THERMASOL  WATERBED
                       1          122        25        19         6          12        1

ROOMS OCCUPIED      1 100%     110  90%   23  92%   19 100%    5  83%    11  92%    1 100%
ROOMS VACANT           %        10   8%    2   8%       %          %         %         %
ROOMS ON CHANGE        %         2   2%       %          %      1  17%    1   8%       %

# GSTS / DBL OCC FAC  2  2.0   134 1.2    28 1.2    21 1.1     5 1.0    13 1.1     1 1.0
AVERAGE SALES / ROOM 66.38         25.85      22.20     23.12    19.66     22.40     18.19
AVERAGE SALES / GUEST 33.19         21.22      18.23     20.92    19.66     18.95     18.19
AVERAGE RATE / ROOM  30.00         17.10      18.13     17.63    16.20     16.54     17.00
AVERAGE RATE / GUEST 15.00         14.04      14.89     15.95    16.20     14.00     17.00

                                    ROOM STATISTICS - MONTH-TO-DATE

ROOMS OCCUPIED      20  57%   3283  77%  714  82%  479  72%  125  60%  257  61%   17  49%
ROOMS VACANT       15  43%    901  21%  144  16%  173  26%   79  38%  156  37%   17  49%
ROOMS ON CHANGE        %       86   2%   17   2%   13   2%    6   3%    7   2%    1   3%

# GSTS / DBL OCC FAC 25 1.2   4465 1.3  1212 1.6   659 1.3  146 1.1  429 1.6    22 1.2
AVERAGE SALES / ROOM 31.67         22.95      24.74     23.72    54.92     23.40     20.60
AVERAGE SALES / GUEST 25.34        16.88      14.57     16.98    47.02     14.02     15.91
AVERAGE RATE / ROOM  23.50         17.60      17.87     17.70    22.04     20.69     17.82
AVERAGE RATE / GUEST 18.80         12.94      10.53     12.67    18.87     12.39     13.77

                                    ROOM STATISTICS - YEAR-TO-DATE

ROOMS OCCUPIED      60  46% 12130  76% 2743  84% 1810  73%  465  59%  943  60%   75  57%
ROOMS VACANT       65  50%  3541  22%  458  14%  621  25%  283  36%  582  37%   53  40%
ROOMS ON CHANGE     6   5%   311   2%   74   2%   58   2%   38   5%   47   3%    3   2%

# GSTS / DBL OCC FAC 93 1.5  19142 1.5 3901 1.4  2466 1.3  609 1.3 1503 1.5   105 1.4
AVERAGE SALES / ROOM 29.29         22.82      24.38     36.79    47.83     21.38     23.89
AVERAGE SALES / GUEST 13.90        14.46      16.93     27.00    36.52     13.41     17.06
AVERAGE RATE / ROOM  21.18         17.42      13.29     26.29    20.41     16.92     19.54
AVERAGE RATE / GUEST 13.66         11.04      12.86     19.29    15.58     10.62     13.96

      ROOM STATISTICS SUMMARY                                              ADV. DEP.      IN-HOUSE       A/R

                     2/17/76            M-T-D            Y-T-D
TOTAL ROOMS OCCUPIED 170  91.3%    4895  75.1%   18226  74.8%   OLD BALANCE    5,222.54CR     9,262.44     3,133.60
TOTAL ROOMS VACANT    12   6.4%    1485  22.8%    5603  22.9%   DIFFERENCE          .00          .00           .00
TOTAL ROOMS ON CHANGE  4   2.1%     130   1.9%     537   2.2%   NEW BALANCE    5,222.54CR     9,262.44     3,133.60

# GSTS / DBL OCC FAC 204  1.2     6968  1.4     27819  1.5
AVERAGE SALES / ROOM  24.84             24.16            24.98
AVERAGE SALES / GUEST 20.70             16.97            16.37
AVERAGE RATE / ROOM   17.31             17.95            18.50
AVERAGE RATE / GUEST  14.42             12.61            12.12
```

Figure 15.4.a Manager's Daily Report
(Courtesy of Griswold's Inn, Claremont, California and IBM)

The various functions and reports available through this module combine to provide a broad base of feedback to management. Derived benefits in the areas of finance, internal control, timely reporting, and travel agent accounting are an enhancement to earlier manual procedures. The general management module tops a hierarchy of computer functions and provides the broadest amount of information to the administration of the hotel enterprise.

Key Concepts

City ledger aging
Commissions report

Macrolevel analysis
Microlevel analysis

```
DATE  2/17/76      THE IBM HOTEL       MANAGER'S DAILY REPORT - PART 1 (H23)                    PAGE   2
--------------------------------------------------------------------------------------------------------
                               TRANSACTION TOTALS
                       2/17/76            M-T-D              Y-T-D            PROJ. MONTH

ON ACCOUNT           3,079.60CR        117,851.13CR       442,420.86CR       207,972.47CR

ROOM                 2,961.50           89,630.55         339,953.60         158,171.47

TAX                    207.18            6,259.81          23,767.80          11,046.71

LOCAL PHONE CALLS         .00               13.05              31.35              23.02

LONG DISTANCE CALLS    203.01            4,526.08          16,930.76           7,987.19

LAUNDRY                 35.75            1,260.35           4,391.70           2,224.14

MISCELLANEOUS            .00               55.23              97.05              97.46

TRANSFER                .00                 .00                .00                .00

SMORGASBORD            140.16            2,675.60           7,611.04           4,721.64

INDIAN HILL           507.78           13,053.71          40,490.06          23,035.94

CATERING               78.75            2,179.82          10,225.13           3,846.73

BAKERY / GIFTS          .00               45.37              96.66              80.06

CASA RAMON              .00              436.53            1,150.95             770.34

FANNY'S                 .00                 .00                .00                .00

PREPAID COMMISSION      .00                 .00                .00                .00

PACKAGE PLAN            .00                 .00                .00                .00

PAID-OUT                .00                 .00                .00                .00
```

Figure 15.4.b Manager's Daily Report

Questions for Discussion

1. Why is the general management module dependent on other HIS modules?

2. Explain the concepts of microlevel and macrolevel analyses in terms of informational needs.

3. What operational functions would be treated in a back-office system that are not treated in a front-office package?

4. What value does revenue analysis serve with respect to the internal controls of the property?

5. Discuss the concept of back-office interfacing and list the advantages and disadvantages of the complete HIS.

```
DATE  5/17/77      THE IBM HOTEL      MANAGER'S DAILY REPORT - PART 2 (H21)                    PAGE
-----------------------------------------------------------------------------------------------------
                                        RATE VARIANCES

   ROOM   ACCT 1  ACCT 2  ACCT 3  ACCT 4  ACCT 5  ACCT 6  GUESTS    RATE    MINIMUM    VARIANCE

    436   103790                                             1      23.00    22.00       1.00
    437   103791                                             1      23.00    22.00       1.00
    439   103789  103803                                     2      45.00    25.00      20.00
    441   103659                                             1      20.00    22.00       2.00-
    442   102435                                             1      23.00    22.00       1.00
    445   102922                                             1      20.00    22.00       2.00-
    447   10                                                 1      20.00    22.00       2.00-
    449   1      6                                           1      20.00    22.00       2.00-
          104398  104457                                            45.00    25.00      20.00
     51   104215  104281                                            23.00    63.00      20.00
    452   106566  106                                               28.00    20.00
DATE  5/17/77      THE IBM HOTEL      MANAGER'S DAILY REPORT - PAR                              PAGE
-----------------------------------------------------------------------------------------------------
                                        CREDIT CHECK

  ACCOUNT  ROOM  NAME                COMPANY                 LIMIT   BALANCE    METHOD OF PAYMENT

   101866  316  LANDEN, DICK         CONWEL, INC             50.00    158.81   CASH      5/17/77
   102367  356  MATT, MR & MRS D.                            50.00     80.25   CASH      5/17/77
   102922  445  TRANDEL, MR. D.      LUMBER DEALERS          50.00    195.48   CASH      6/04/77
   103380  435  MILTON, EARL         VICTORY VARSITY SHOPS  200.00    438.33   A/R       5/20/77
   104215  451  WALTER, MRS          Y                      200.00  1,218.86   A/R       5/19/77
   104240  46                                               100.00    161.73   CREDIT    5/16/77
   104270                                                    50.00    164.78   CASH      5/20/77
   10            MITH, JOHN                                         RT - PART 2 (H21)             PAGE
       777       THE IBM HOTEL       MANAGER'S DAILY
-----------------------------------------------------------------------------------------------------
                                        NO-SHOWS

  ACCOUNT  NAME                COMPANY

   103241  PEARL, MR & MRS                                    .00
   103772  LOWELLAND, MR. C.                                  .00
   103795  BUELLER, M          HUNTINGTON PLASTICS            .00
   103858                                                     .00
   10388   MILLER, RHONDA                                     .00
   10       777     THE IBM HOTEL    MANAGER'S D             24.00CR              PAGE
-----------------------------------------------------------------------------------------------------
                                        ACCOUNTS RECEIVABLE

  ACCOUNT  NAME                COMPANY                  DEPART   BALANCE

    99837  NILSON, MR. & MRS TOM   WESTERN EMPLOYMENT, INC.  5/17/77    56.26
   101551  BRUBAK, MR & MRS        ANDERSON COMPANY          5/17/77    26.75
   101867  WILSON, DICK            BABY CLOTHIERS            5/17/77   104.96
   103592                              & YOUNGSTON           5/17/77   199.94
   103655                              JONES                 5/17/77    22.00
   104                                                       5/17/77    23.54
                                                       PART 2 (H21)
```

Figure 15.4.c Managers Daily Report

6. Of the reports mentioned in this chapter, which appears to be the most valuable? What report is not cited in Chapter 15 that may be of value to management?

7. Explain the consolidation of information within this module and give your opinion of its merit.

Toward the Paperless Hotel

Chapter Objectives:

1. To highlight the future computer orientation of the hotel industry.

2. To point out the application of new and already existing hotel devices in an attempt to provide more self-oriented guest services.

3. To introduce the possibility of a paperless hotel environment during the 1980s.

COMPUTER-assisted hotel management modules have extended automated applications to almost every aspect of the hotel business. Although the objectives of the information system are numerous, there is some consensus that the HIS should increase productivity, profitability, and quality of service. In establishments where computers have been installed, employees have found more time to spend with guests and have gained a greater sense of professionalism in their jobs. Many aspects of customer service have been improved and the attainment of more efficient data-handling procedures has led to the elimination of disputed charges and late charge billings. Timely management reports have served to identify credit risks and to signal areas involving improper operational controls.

Hotels have experienced cost effectiveness depending upon the appropriateness of their system to their needs. A hotel employing numerous modules, which may not all be necessary, will find cost justification more difficult than a firm that has established its information demands and has implemented a system that conforms to financial constraints.

Because computers replace labor and the hospitality industry is traditionally labor intensive, the automated HIS configurations were expected to sweep the industry and revolutionize its ways of doing business. Early system failures, lack of vendor and managerial support, and poorly conceived initial systems have given computer applications a stigma that is only recently being overcome. As the union between the computer vendors and the hotel business grows stronger it becomes more important for management to comprehend computers and their software packages. The criteria for system implementation revolve around profitability, ease of operation, and reliability. Management must be able to define informational needs, specify system parameters, select an appropriate system configuration, determine system flexibility, delineate system security measures, and identify a feasible back-up system.

Hence, the competitive advantages afforded the HIS user may include fewer guest billing disputes, more time available for employees to spend with guests, improved guest services, improved employee morale, and cost savings to management.

The 1980s Guest Cycle

The 1980s guest cycle will be heavily computer-oriented. The development of fifth generation personalized information systems and easy-to-use programming languages will allow the guest to participate in self-registration, sophisticated room access systems, and self-information and settlement functions. Most of the following references are hypothetical at this point in time.

Reservations

A potential guest will simply call up the hotel and speak to the hotel's computer. The computer will have a voice synthesizer and will immediately record and process the guest's request. The interactive, formatted dialogue of the computer will give the professional reservation agent, or the guest with exact plans, an instantaneous, spoken response. Also, the computer will announce any special features the hotel may have and what, if any, entertainment or special events will be happening at the time of the guest's stay.

After accepting the guest's reservation, the computer will automatically generate and dispatch a plastic reservation hold card (Fig. 16.1), to be presented at the time of registration. This card will contain a magnetic strip coded with minimal personal data on the guest.

Registration

Guests with confirmed reservations (possessing reservation hold cards) will walk up to the electronic kiosk containing a self-registration device, a data entry pad, and a video display screen. The guest will insert the plastic registration card and a major credit card or EFT card. The self-registration machine will capture the reservation card and return

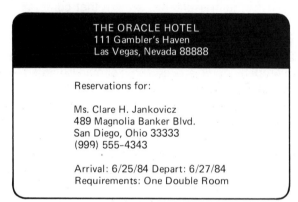

Figure 16.1. Reservation Hold Card

the credit card after making a voucher imprint. Upon insertion of both pieces of required information, a video facsimile of a registration card will be displayed on the small CRT (cathode ray tube) screen. All the guest need do is to depress the verification key, or the error key if appropriate, and the machine will proceed accordingly. Verified registration data is followed by a short series of inquiries flashed on the CRT. Inquiries into the guest's desires for specific room location, and/or other special requirements, leads directly into an automatic room assignment operation. Room assignment is performed by the computer (which is interacting with the room status package at the front office), and the room key is dispensed. The key the guest receives is not a typical one, rather it is a flat board that is perforated at one end and contains an optical characteristic recognition (OCR) code at the other (see Fig. 16.2). In addition to the key, the guest will receive a listing of hotel services, special events, and local landmarks. At this time the guest begins the occupancy phase of the guest cycle.

Room Entry

Occupancy is dependent upon room entry and security. The perforated end of the room key board is designed for guest room access. Entry into the room will be accomplished through insertion of the properly punched key and it should be noted that the computer would be capable of changing the lock codings for any door upon demand.

Guest Accounting

As the guest begins to charge purchases in the hotel operating departments, postings to the folio may be done using a register-mounted data entry pad. The OCR portion of the room key board and the amount of the charge will be entered through the key pad, which is attached to the POS terminal. The posting mechanism will incorporate some wired and wireless communication media that will be intelligible, readable postings in the folio file package. Wireless relays from the point-of-sale location to the guest's account and instantaneously alterable room locks, changed by the desk, may become a reality.

Account Reconciliation

Employing the already existing television set and the telephone found in the guest room, the guest will be able to preview and review the folio at any time during the guest cycle. The phone set would serve as the interface between the folio files and the television screen would be used to display the folio in soft copy. This access interface would be secure inasmuch as a guest could only attach the folio for one specific guest room. Prior to the guest's checking out, the folio could be inspected at the guest's leisure and any discrepancies handled in something less than a last minute, crisis situation. Should the guest have no disagreements with the statement and payment is to be made by credit card or EFT, the guest will instruct the desk to prepare the already imprinted credit card voucher for signature.

The television screen will also serve as an information base for the guest through-out the entire stay. Should the guest wish information on dining, theatre, or other entertainment, the telephone would be used to call up the proper display on the in-room

Figure 16.2. Room Key Board

television set. Hence, the guest will gain self-account appraisal and expedient checkout capabilities enabling the front desk to fully service only those customers who are exceptions.

Summary

The guest cycle of the 1980s may be more computer-oriented than anticipated. The guest cycle may be heavily dependent upon computer hardware and software and may render the hotel paperless except for government regulations and the guest's essential expense documentation. The increased technological development of already existing devices like the telephone and the advent of technological devices designed to increase the speed of relay and the comprehensibility of information, such as a voice synthesizer or radio dispatch, may be closer than the hotel operator of today realizes.

Key Concepts

> Paperless environment
> Reservation hold card
> Room key board
> Self-reservation kiosk

Questions for Discussion

1. What might the hotel computer systems of the future incorporate?

2. What trends have led the author to favor self-reservation, self-registration, and account appraisal for the guest?

3. What additional hotel devices might be added to the computer-assisted HIS?

4. What new functions might receive automation in the near future? Why?

5. Do you favor a paperless hotel? Do you think it is a feasible concept? Is it a practical idea?

Glossary

Account A means of classifying and summarizing money transactions within an accounting system.

Accountability The delegation of responsibility for financial transactions; holding specific individuals accountable for cash and/or charge transactions.

Accounting A system for recording, analyzing and summarizing the financial transactions of the firm.

Accounting cycle The period of time from when a financial transaction occurs until it is reconciled and appears on the financial report of the firm. This cycle is concerned with the proper recording analysis of all transactions.

Account payable transaction A financial procedure in which goods and services are received prior to payment for same; amount of money owed to a creditor for a previous purchase.

Account receivable load The proportion of total sales that are charged to accounts for future collection. See Credit card volume.

Account receivable summary A listing of charged sales within the hotel. Normally, a summary entry in a comprehensive report of operations.

Account receivable transaction A financial procedure in which goods and services are provided on the premise that payment will be received in the future; amounts of money owed to the business by its customers.

Account settlement The payment, by cash or credit card, of outstanding balances on a guest folio or city account. See Zeroing out.

Acoustic coupler A modem device (a modulator-demodulator unit) that converts digital signals of a terminal or computer to analogue signals that can be transmitted over a common carrier network (a telephone line).

Advance reservation See Reservations.

Algorithm A prescribed set of well-defined, unambiguous rules or procedures leading to the solution of a mathematical problem in a finite number of steps. A term given to solutions for computer problems.

Allocatable expenses Those expenditures that can be effectively apportioned or shared among various departments of a business organization.

Arranging A data-processing function whereby data elements are sorted or ordered in a predetermined sequence; similar to a filing routine.

Asset An item of monetary value and/or economic resource. May also be a service or utility that can be expressed in monetary terms. Assets constitute the resources of a business.

Audit The review, test, and verification of financial transactions in an accounting system.

Audit trail The logical order of processes involved in a proper recording of an accounting transaction; a reverse tracing of cross-reference documents to substantiate a transaction.

Average A statistical concept describing the central tendency of a data set. Various averages exist, including the mean, median, and mode, and serve as descriptors of typical observations in a sample.

Average room rate The average number of dollars derived from the sale of a room calculated by dividing total room sales by the actual number of rooms sold.

Back office That branch of the hotel responsible for coordinating all support services and managerial activities and with maintaining the ongoing status of the business.

Back office functions Those activities corresponding to the operation of the back office.

Back-of-the-house Those parts of the hotel facility with which the guest does not normally come directly into contact, for example, engineering, personnel, and accounting departments. See Back office.

Balance sheet A statement of financial condition at some specific point in time. A report presenting a measurement of assets, liabilities, and equity for a business firm.

BASIC A conversational programming language permitting the use of abbreviated English words and mathematical symbols. An acronym for Beginner's All-purpose Symbolic Instruction Code.

Batch processing A system technique in which data is first collected and coded into groups (batches) before being entered into a computer system for processing.

Bit The smallest unit of data in a digital computer. An abbreviation for binary digit.

Blocked room report A list summarizing those hotel rooms that have been reserved for a specific calendar date; depicts the density of sold rooms at some point in the reservation horizon.

Break-even analysis A financial technique used to find a point of zero profit and loss (when total costs equal revenues).

Budget A document of expected expenditures constructed from anticipated revenues and available financial resources.

Budgeting The process of preparing a budget.

Byte A binary element string operated upon as a unit and usually shorter than a computer word; a collection of bits.

Calculating A data-processing function in which an arithmetic and/or logical manipulation of data occurs.

Cancellation report A listing of those customers who held room reservations with the hotel but withdrew them prior to the point of registration.

Capital budget A budget document prepared for the capital account of a business organization.

Capturing A data-processing function that involves the recording of data from an event for the purpose of system input. Related to source documentation.

Cash dispensing terminals An electronic bank terminal designed to dispense cash or travelers checks upon validation and authorization of a commercial asset card.

Cash flow The period of time from when a good or service is sold until the actual collection of cash from the sale is available to the firm.

Cashier reconciliation The audit of a cash register and cashier to establish accurate transactional balances and procedures.

Cash operating cycle The period of time associated with a business' cash flow. More specifically it refers to the time interval between a guest charge and the hotel's receipt of cash payments.

Cash payout transaction A cash transaction in which the hotel makes a cash advance to a guest (or nonguest) account.

Cash register A business machine containing a cash drawer and possessing the capability of depicting the amount of each sale.

Cash sheet A report form carrying all cash transactions against folio accounts, cash payouts, and departmental cash sales. Also serves as a primary cross-reference document in the hotel's audit.

Cash transaction An exchange of goods and/or services for cash.

Cathode ray tube (CRT) A video display unit (a television screen). A peripheral device option in a computer system capable of presenting information in soft copy.

Central processing unit (CPU) The nucleus of a computer system. A combination of hardware and software that performs four functions: 1) controls processing, 2) fulfills arithmetic and logic operations, 3) stores data and in-structions, and 4) interfaces all other components of the system.

Central tendency A mathematical description of data that is centrally scattered about its mean. See Average.

Chart of accounts A complete listing of the names and numbers of all accounts in a ledger.

Check in The arrival and completion of a registration process by the guest.

Checkout Occurs at the completion of the guest's stay and includes settlement of his account; the departure of the guest.

Chip A piece of silicon containing numerous electronic circuits for computer system construction. May also be referred to as a silicon chip.

City account A nonguest account accorded many local businesses or special interest groups as a business promotion by the hotel. Basically, an account receivable for someone other than a registered guest.

City ledger A collection of city or nonguest accounts receivable balances; a listing of all accounts receivable owed to the hotel.

City ledger aging The time interval from when an account balance is transferred to the city ledger until its eventual collection by the hotel.

Classifying A data-processing function whereby data are placed into specific categories that provide meaning for the user.

COBOL A procedural programming language formed from English words and designed specifically for business-processing problems. An acronym for

Common Business-Oriented Language.

Coding The transformation of data into established symbols for the purpose of simplifying systematic procedures and for comprehension.

Coefficient of elasticity. The mathematical index of the elasticity of demand.

Combined network An information system in which both distributed and integrated subsystems or processes exist.

Commercial rate A special discounted room rate offered to a person who is a frequent hotel guest. Also referred to as the business rate.

Commissioned sales Sales made by a third party to which the hotel must pay a royalty or fee for the booking.

Commissions report A listing of commissioned sales and the respective agents.

Competitive pricing The construction of hotel room rates according to what the competition charges; an external rate structure criterion.

Complimentary rate A room provided to the guest at no charge. This is normally done as a promotion of business and/or goodwill.

Computer An electronic machine capable of performing data-processing and problem-solving functions.

Computer-dependent A business that bases a significantly large portion of its information and operational procedures upon the functioning of a computer system; unable to operate without computer assistance.

Computer generations The segmentation of computer development according to substantial advances in: 1) hardware, 2) software, 3) systems application, and 4) impact upon the surrounding environment.

Computeritis The belief that all aspects and operations of a firm can be computerized without regard to cost-justification or practicality.

Computer operator The person in a computer environment that is responsible for overall hardware operations and system continuity.

Computer-oriented A business that employs a computer system as a support tool in the handling of its information and operational procedures.

Computer service bureau An off-the-premises concern providing computer expertise and capabilities for a fee.

Computer system An electronic system composed of input-output devices, a memory unit, and a CPU. This system can be applied to either problem-solving and/or data-processing functions.

Conditional probability When the probability of a specific occurrence is conditioned or dependent upon the outcome of another event or occurrence.

Configuration The relative arrangement of component parts in a system.

Confirmed reservation A hotel reservation request that is firmed by phone or mail prior to a guest's arrival.

Construction costs The compilation of all pre-opening construction expenses. Normally used as a criterion in hotel room rate determination.

Contract programming Basically, computer programming for a fee. Programs that are custom-designed for a specific purpose and that are very expensive to the user. Also referred to as customized programming.

Contribution margin The difference between the selling price (sales) and the direct variable expenses (total variable costs) of any given item (or group of items).

Contribution to profitability The portion of revenues left after the subtraction of variable and fixed expenses. Can be simply stated as the contribution margin minus fixed expenses.

Control flow The branch of a computer system that oversees and directs all peripheral devices.

Control folio A hotel account record used to monitor specific transactions for a group of rooms or guests. May also be referred to as a master folio.

Conversational programming A technique enabling the user to communicate directly with the computer system, thereby enhancing response time and operating procedures. Also referred to as interactive programming.

Correlation analysis A statistical technique used to establish relationships among or within sets of data.

Cost center A hotel operating department that has minimal direct guest contact, incurs cost, and generates no direct sales. Also referred to as a non-revenue department.

Cost-effective A system in which the benefits far outweigh the costs. Also referred to as cost-justified.

Cost-justified See Cost-effective.

CPU options Refers to those variations of CPU devices available in the market; for example, minicomputer, mainframe, or microcomputer.

CPU time A measure of system usage, by the user, based upon the total amount of computer-processing time employed.

Credit See Credit entry.

Credit card volume That proportion of total sales charged to credit cards. May be a significant indicator of the cash flow position of a firm.

Credit entry The recording of financial transactions on the right-hand side of a "T" account. Credits increase liabilities and revenue accounts while decreasing asset and expense accounts.

Cross-referencing Also called cross-indexing. The identification of those source documents that can be used as support and/or verification of transactions recorded in the accounting system.

Data Raw, unevaluated facts that alone have little or no meaning, but as a group allow for more meaningful relationships and conclusions to be drawn.

Data base 1) The entire collection of information available to a computer system. 2) A structured collection of information as an entry or collection of related files treated as an entry.

Data cartridge A device for storing data. May be of a cassette tape or disc-like nature. May also be referred to as a diskette.

Data processing An operation or continuation of operations on data to achieve a desired result.

Data recorder The person in a computer environment who is responsible for compiling and preparing data for system input.

Day rate A room rate for less than an overnight accommodation. A procedure that enables the hotel to sell a given room twice in one day.

Debit See Debit entry.

Debit entry The recording of financial transactions on the left-hand side of a "T" account. Debits increase asset and expense accounts while decreasing liability and revenue accounts.

Debt A financial condition in which a person or business organization owes its creditors more money that it is capable of paying.

Degree of verification The level of investigation that is followed during an auditing procedure. Primarily a function of the frequency and/or magnitude of previous errors.

Desk agent A front office employee responsible for operating the front desk. Also referred to as a desk clerk.

Desk clerk See Desk agent.

Direct expense An expense that is incurred only when a good or service is sold. In essence, if a good or service was to be discontinued, so too would this expenditure; for example, the cost of food to a restaurant.

Disc storage A method of high-speed memory employing a rotating circular plate coated with a magnetic material. Addressable portions can be accessed at random. Also referred to as magnetic disc storage.

Display terminal A CRT or VDT unit that presents a soft copy of information on a video screen. See Cathode ray tube (CRT).

Dissemination The distribution of information along some predetermined lines of communication.

Distributed intelligence An intelligence-based network of remote terminals and central-system components.

Distributed processing A network where computer power is not centralized, but is distributed to the user.

Distributed series network A system of linked stand-alone terminals that permit multiple users to access a common CPU concurrently or to communicate with one another.

Documentation A set of written procedures detailing or authenticating the specific requirements and/or results of a system or its components.

Dump A computer term referring to a back-up copy of the system data base stored on a less expensive storage medium than the primary base.

Efficiency rate A measurement of performance designed to: 1) measure variance between a desired standard and an actual condition or 2) measure the productivity rate of a job or function.

Elastic demand An economic relationship in which the price and quantity of a good or service are inversely related.

Elasticity of demand A comparative measurement of the inverse relationship between the price and quantity of a good; a direct relationship is indicative of an inelasticity of demand. See Elastic demand.

Electronic cash register (ECR) A cash-control device whose moving parts are electronic as opposed to mechanical or manual.

Electronic data processing (EDP) An automated method for reducing the number of times data is handled in a data-processing system; equipment that processes data by electronic means (digital computers).

Electronic folio The construction and maintenance of a paper folio equivalent in a computer memory. A soft copy record of the guest's financial status with the hotel.

Electronic fund transfer (EFT) The method of payment for goods and services involving the transfer of actual cash balance between two accounts, performed electronically, at a point-of-sale.

End user The person who employs a computer system as a management tool. Also, simply referred to as a user.

Energy efficiency ratio (EER) The relationship of benefits generated as a function of the amount of energy consumed. A ratio of consumption/conversion for energy-dependent processes and devices.

Energy monitoring system A computerized system capable of monitoring and controlling environmental conditions according to specified parameters. See Energy sensor system.

Energy sensor system An energy monitoring system in which sensors are used to provide feedback on desired economic and environmental energy outcomes.

Environment Everything outside a system that either affects the operation of the system or is affected by the system's operation.

Event driven A system that remains inactive until a predetermined condition is achieved. Initiation of a system's capabilities is dependent upon the occurrence of an event.

Family plan rate A special discounted room rate offered to families; normally applied when children and parents stay in the same hotel room.

Feedback Information concerning the status of a specific situation is returned to the input by some portion of the output for corrective action.

Field developed program (FDP) A software package developed at the user's site, by a user, not by a manufacturer. Resale of an FDP by a vendor usually returns a royalty or fee to the innovative user.

File A collection of logically-arranged records.

Financial reports A group of documents depicting the profitability and solvency of a firm. See Financial statements.

Financial statements A set of commonly constructed forms that collectively detail the profitability and solvency of the firm.

Fixed costs Those expenses that are incurred regardless of sales level. May also be referred to as fixed overhead and/or nonvariable charges.

Fixed room rate The assignment of a room rate according to room square footage. A rate that is not dependent upon the number of occupants in a given room.

Flexible system A computer system in which the user can perform some software additions and/or modifications; can be user-programmed.

Floor limit The amount of charges the hotel allows a guest to incur prior to requiring payment in part or in full. Also called house limit.

Flowchart Pictoral presentation of an algorithm; a systems technique for depicting the logical procedures leading to the solution of a problem.

Folio Statement or record of a transient guest's account that contains a perpetual balance of the guest's financial obligations to the hotel. Also referred to as a guest folio.

Folio wall The physical storage location of transient guests' account folios, usually filed numerically by room number. Also referred to as a folio bucket.

FORTRAN A science-oriented programming language employing complex symbols and abbreviations. An acronym for FORmula TRANslator.

Front desk The portion of the hotel responsible for performing the check-in and checkout functions and the coordination of all guest services. Also seen as the main focal point of the front office. See Front office.

Front office The branch of the hotel responsible for coordinating all guest services, serving as a liaison between management and guest, and monitoring and controlling the guest cycle.

Front office equipment The apparatus employed by the front office to monitor and control the guest cycle and to coordinate all guest services.

Front-of-the-house Those portions of the hotel facility with which the guest comes directly in contact, for example, rooms, food, and beverage departments. See Front office.

Graphic terminal A computer system peripheral device capable of displaying output in a graphic format.

Group plan rate A special discounted hotel room rate offered to groups as an incentive to attract larger assemblages of people or to sell larger blocks of rooms.

Guaranteed reservation A reservation arrangement in which the hotel is guaranteed the room rate whether or not the guest shows up.

Guest An individual client who has registered with the hotel; a privileged status accorded hotel guests that implies certain financial and legal statuses; a person to whom hospitality is extended.

Guest account The record of a guest's financial transaction with the hotel. See Folio.

Guest accounting An effective means through which a guest's financial transactions can be monitored and controlled.

Guest cycle The conceptualization of a sequence of transactions conducted by a guest during a hotel stay; a sequence of arrival-occupancy-departure or pre-sale, point-of-sale, and post-sale activities.

Guest folio See Folio.

Guest history file A record of historical guest data for future reference and analysis.

Guest services The tangible and intangible goods and services offered by the hotel to its clientele.

Hard copy A printed version of information generated by or stored in a computer system.

Hardware The physical components that make up a computer system. Also referred to as computer equipment.

Hardware system The configuration of central system devices and peripherals that compose the overall computer network. Normally used with reference to system cabling and design and layout.

High-level language Any computer language that does not require a complete understanding of a computer's internal operations to use, or a language which is not based on a one-to-one correspondence between a command statement and a single computer operation. Examples are BASIC, COBOL, and FORTRAN languages.

High risk A guest who closely approaches, equals, or exceeds the house limit.

Hotel information system (HIS) An orderly arrangement of hotel data procedures and decision-making criteria designed to increase managerial effectiveness through the proper handling and flow of information.

House count The number of registered guests in the hotel.

Housekeeper productivity report An analysis of the efficiency, in terms of time and number of rooms completed, of housekeeping personnel.

Housekeeping A nonrevenue operating department responsible for preparing and maintaining hotel rooms for sale and for tracking room status.

Housekeeping assignment report A listing of housekeeping personnel and their specific room assignments. See Housekeeper productivity report.

House limit See Floor limit.

Hubbart formula A popular room-rating formula dependent upon accurate assumptions of operating expenses, room sales, and a desired return on investment.

Human engineering The automation of routine tasks that frees personnel to better apply their human capabilities more productively elsewhere.

Implementation The application of a tool, device, or system to achieve a desired end; also refers to putting into use or carrying out.

Income statement A report on the profitability of the firm as determined by revenue and expense items in an accounting period. Also referred to as an earnings statement.

Independent probability When the likelihood of a given occurrence is not influenced or dependent upon the outcome of any other event.

Inelastic demand An economic relationship in which the price and quantity of a good are directly related. See Inelasticity of demand.

Inelasticity of demand A comparative measurement of the direct relationship between the price and quantity of a good; determination of an indirect relationship is indicative of an elasticity of demand. See Inelastic demand.

Inflexible system A preprogrammed

computer system that does not allow the user to alter and/or addend the software; cannot be user-programmed.

Information That which adds to what is known or alleged. Information serves three basic purposes: 1) communicates knowledge, 2) provides feedback, and 3) reduces uncertainty.

Information flow The path that communication and/or documentation follow. The sequence of activities that results as a consequence of a business transaction.

In-house Refers to tasks performed on-the-premises; usually associated with on-the-premise computer processing.

In-house system A computer system that wholly operates within one facility.

Input The initial phase of a data-processing or computer-system operation.

Input data Raw, unevaluated facts entered into a data system for processing. See Data.

Input formats The various options available to users of data processing and/or computer systems, for example, punch card, CRT key pad, optical character recognition.

Input unit The component of a computer system through which instructions and data are entered.

Integrated circuit (IC) A solid state electronic component of a computer system's construction design. See Chip.

Integrated network A system configuration with a centralized, shared data base and intricate communication links among all users.

Intelligent terminal A computer hardward input/output device that contains some local memory capabilities.

Intensity of competition A measurement of the degree of direct market forces competing for a limited number of sales dollars.

Interactive program broadcasting A program format that enables the user to dial up computer-stored reservation packages onto a domestic television screen for the purpose of self-reservation inquiry.

Interactive programming See Conversational programming.

Interface The formation of a common boundary between two persons, departments, systems, or hardware components.

Internal control The verification of proper handling and documentation of financial transactions.

Intuitive pricing Charging whatever the market will bear. A pricing scheme in which a good or service is evaluated based upon what is believed people are willing to pay; not a function of costs.

Journal A chronological record of financial transactions. Shows the effect of various debit and credit entries on the overall operation.

Key rack Storage and organized index of the hotel's room keys.

Knowledge Familiarity and/or education gained through experience; an acquaintance with fact.

Late charge A charge sale, posted after the guest has checked out, that requires a late-charge billing.

Lead-through programming A computer programming format in which the operator is forced to follow a specified routine of inquiries requiring responses prior to advancing in the software. Also called drop-through programming.

Ledger A complete collection of all the accounts of an entity; a summarized posting of account debits and credits. Also referred to as a general ledger.

Liabilities Debts or financial obligations by the firm to a creditor.

Line of authority The traditional hierarchy of increasing administrative responsibilities; usually depicted in an organizational chart.

Line of credit The allowance of charged sales to a guest folio; a short-term privilege for registered guests. See House limit.

Macrolevel analysis The evaluation of an overall operation of a business enterprise or large quantities of data.

Management information system (MIS) A systematic approach to the enhancement of managerial effectiveness achieved through improved handling of the firm's most important resource: information.

Managerial reports A series of documents providing management with targeted feedback on the financial status, productive efficiency, and overall effectiveness of business operations.

Market share The percentage of the total market (in terms of units, dollars, or any other index) that is captured by a given firm.

Massage The internal manipulation of data and information by a computer system.

Master folio See Control folio.

Mean An arithmetic descriptor of central tendency. See Average.

Median The middle value in a rank-ordered (from low to high) set of data; the midpoint.

Memory unit The component part of a computer system that is composed of addressable storage locations and that serves as an intermediate buffer between input/output devices and the CPU.

Microcomputer A computer classification in which a stand-alone unit has all major CPU functions self-contained on a single printed circuit board. See Distributed intelligence.

Microlevel analysis An evaluation performed on a microcosm of the firm or a minute quantity of data.

Microprocessor A single, high-density, integrated circuit that is capable of performing complex CPU functions. See Chip.

Minicomputer A computer classification in which a stand-alone unit contains the requisite input/output, memory, and CPU components for computer capability; a centralized, compact system.

Mode The most frequently occurring observation in a set of data.

Modular The implementation of computer-assistance in modules (functional subsystems). See Distributed series network.

Module 1) A program unit that is discrete and identifiable. 2) A packaged functional hardware unit designed for use with other components.

Monolithic A total or completely integrated system. See Integrated network.

Multiple occupancy The rental of a hotel room to more than one individual guest.

Multitasking A computer system capable of satisfying many user requests at the same time; capable of executing several jobs simultaneously.

Network A structured connection of computer systems or peripheral devices, or both, each remote from the other, capable of exchanging data or information as needed.

Night audit A hotel term used to describe a specialized verification and analysis of a limited set of accounts. See Audit.

Noninteractive program broadcasting A program format in which a continuous series of displays of tourist offerings is offered to the consumer. Traditional methods of reservation inquiry are adhered to.

Normal distribution A statistical concept describing a frequency distribution that is symmetrical or bell-shaped.

No-show A descriptor for those individuals who do not arrive (show up); represents lost revenues to the hotel.

Occupancy The sale of an available hotel guest room; an intermediate phase of the guest cycle.

Occupancy load The proportion of the number of hotel rooms sold as compared to the number of hotel rooms available for sale on any given day. Also referred to as occupancy percentage.

Occupancy mix The composition/proportion of sold rooms that are singles, doubles, or multiply-occupied; also referred to as the profile of occupancy.

Occupancy percentage A ratio relating the number of hotel rooms sold to the number available for sale. See Occupancy load.

Off-line The operating mode of a computer peripheral device that is not interacting directly with the central processing unit in the system.

Off-the-premises Computing that is done off-the-property.

On-line The operating mode of a computer peripheral device that is directly interacting or connected to the central processing unit of the system; direct communication with the computer.

Operating budget See Budget.

Operating department A functional department of the hotel; a branch of the hotel normally performing only one operation or a group of specialized operations.

Operating statistics Mathematical indices of operating performances for various segments of the business; a series of industry ratios commonly understood and uniformly applied.

Operating system A structured set of software routines whose function is to control the execution sequence of programs, supervise input/output operations, and to support the entire system's resources.

Optical character recognition (OCR) An input option for a computer system.

Optimal room rate A room price that is high enough to contribute to a reasonable return on invested capital, yet low enough to attract clientele; may also be referred to as an ideal room rate.

Order entry terminal A computer peripheral used as a specialized input device.

Other equipment manufacturer (OEM) A vendor that constructs a customized system for a user, or specialized group of users, from various manufacturers' components.

Output The end result of a data-processing or problem-solving operation; data that has been processed and transferred from internal storage.

Output formats The various options available to a computer-system user; for example, magnetic tape, printed page, and punch cards.

Output information The transformation of raw data into aggregated, intelligible pieces of information or knowledge.

Output unit A system device for displaying or printing processed and/or stored information.

Overbooking The practice of committing more guest rooms than are available; a hedge against no-shows or unforeseen changes in the length of a guest's stay.

Owner's equity A capital account for owner's financial status within the firm.

Package plan rate A special discounted hotel room rate offered in conjunction with other goods and services, for example, rental cards and airline travel.

Parameter driven system A computer system configuration in which the requirements of the system's hardware and software are designed to satisfy specific user needs.

Paperless environment A computer-aided business complex in which documents and communications are maintained in soft copy except where required by law.

PBX The switchboard equipment found in the hotel's telephone department.

Percent of occupancy See Occupancy load.

Peripheral devices The computer system components located away from, but controlled by, a central processor.

Point-of-purchase Related to the point-of-sale; the time and location of a consumer's purchase. The point-of-purchase is basically the same as the point-of-sale except that it is from the consumer's perspective, not management's.

Point-of-sale (POS) The time and physical location of the sale of a good or service; provides a communication link between a remote sales location and the central (guest) accounting system. The intermediate phase of the guest cycle. See Point-of-purchase.

Point-of-sale terminal A peripheral system device employed to communicate transactions at scattered, remote locations to a centralized processor and/or data base.

Posting machine A mechanical front office device used to post charge sales to guest folios.

Postings A recording procedure that occurs subsequent to a transaction;

the transference of entries to guest folios from vouchers.

Post-sale After the original sale; final phase of the guest cycle.

Preprogrammed A computer-programming technique in which software is purchased as part of the system. Preprogrammed peripherals may be of a flexible or inflexible nature.

Pre-sale Prior to the point-of-sale; the initial phase of the guest cycle.

Price performance ratio See Cost effective.

Probability The likelihood of an event occurring; factors range from 0.0 to 1.0.

Process A particular way of accomplishing something.

Productivity rate An efficiency measure of production in terms of quality or quantity.

Profile of occupancy See Occupancy mix.

Profit center A revenue center for which expenses are calculated and profitability determined.

Programmable See Flexible system.

Programmer The person in a computer system environment who converts data and instructions into a computer-comprehendible language.

Programming The means by which the programmer communicates to the computer what instructions are to be used in data processing and/or problem solving.

Programming language The vehicle used to accurately communicate instructions to the computer.

Psychological pricing A dynamic method of pricing wherein the expectation of the customer's willingness to pay is used as an index; costs are not of paramount concern.

Random access See Random access memory.

Random-access memory (RAM) A computer memory designed so that the time to access any data item in storage is the same as for any other item. See Disc storage.

Random entry A computer input that can occur at any point in time and with unpredictable impact upon the system.

Random sample A small representation of a larger population that is selected without any definite plan or pattern.

Rate cutting The reduction in room rate as an inducement to sell an increased number of rooms; has not been found true for all occupancy-load factors within the hotel industry.

Real time A method of processing data so fast that almost no time elapses between input and output.

Record A systems term connoting a set of logically-related fields within a computer memory unit.

Recording A data-processing function wherein measurements, observations, and/or activities are documented for manipulation and storage.

Refusal report A charting of the name and/or number of guests who sought accommodations but who were denied rooms by the hotel; an accounting of excess demand.

Registration The completion of the check-in procedure, which includes the filing of guest data and room requirements; the guest's first physical contact with the hotel; the beginning of the guest cycle.

Reliability The high level of dependability and trust normally expected in an automated system environment; a measure of an electronic system's failure rate.

Report of operations A reference document providing a quick index of the hotel's revenues and occupancy statistics.

Representative sample A collection of observations believed to possess all the relevant characteristics of the population from which they were selected.

Reservation An advanced request for available space at some time in the future.

Reservation activity fee A commission paid to a reservation system broker/operator for sales directly generated by same.

Reservation hold card A machine-prepared document provided to guests with reservations, who may wish to self-register.

Reservation horizon The planning interval throughout which the hotel will be willing to accept and confirm inquiries for available space; normally, a six-month planning frame.

Reservation inquiry A specific request for types, rates, and number of rooms desired for a particular time and date; a system-formulated reservation request.

Reservation network An interfaced configuration of automated reservation hardware and software.

Responsibility center The segmenta-

tion of organizational functions according to personnel responsibilities; not based solely upon an aggregation of operations.

Retrieving A data-processing function in which data is selected and brought from a computer memory for further processing and/or display.

Revenue center An operating department that collects direct revenues for its goods or services; typically any guest service department.

Room assignment The placement of guests into specific hotel rooms; assignments usually follow a managerial desire to insure equal turnover/usage of all accommodations.

Room count sheet A permanent record of the room rack prepared nightly as a verification of room status.

Room discrepancy report A listing of room status variances that are discovered during cross-indexing of room sales and housekeeping reports.

Room inventory The number of rooms a hotel contains; the maximum number of rooms that can be made available for sale.

Room key board A futuristic design of a guest room key that is capable of serving as both a security access system and as a charge-authorization input format.

Room rack slip An indexing system used to represent room status in the room rack.

Room rate The price charged for a hotel room's use for one night or collection of nights; may or may not include food, entertainment, and/or transportation.

Room rating A procedure for constructing room rates; normally refers to the mathematical factoring of cost data as a generator of room prices.

Room sales mix An analysis of the number, types, and dollars derived from room revenues; related to occupancy mix, only price extensions are included.

Room status The present availability position of any guest room; for example, on-change or out-of-order.

Rule-of-thumb A method by which businesses construct standards based upon extensive historical data or experience; a means by which room rates can be developed.

Sampling A representative selection of a small group of observations from a larger whole.

Self-registration kiosk A free-standing machine capable of registering a guest holding a confirmed reservation and of dispensing a room key or key board.

Semi-attachment The belief that the more time or space that is given to an item, the more important that object appears to become.

Sequential filing The sorting and rank-order storage of documents by alpha, numerical, or chronological identification.

Skewness A lack of symmetry or normal curve in a frequency distribution.

Skipper A hotel guest who leaves the establishment without paying or checking out.

Sleeper A room that appears to be occupied, although it is vacant, due to a desk agent's failure to change the room status in the room rack.

Soft copy A display of information on a CRT or VDT screen.

Software The collection of programs and routines used to extend the capabilities of the computer.

Software broker The agent between a program developer and an end user.

Software system A priority arrangement of instructions and routines that command the computer-system resources.

Sorting A data-processing function in which data are categorized and classified based upon some critical quality or characteristic.

Source document Any original recording of a transaction. Basically, all those items that contribute to the recording of financial transactions, such as guest check, registration card, or voucher.

Specialty vendor A computer system vendor that develops a series of programs on a selected manufacturer's product for sale to a specialty group of end users. See Other equipment manufacturer.

Spurious A statistical conclusion that is suspect due to its being based on too small or too biased a sample.

Stand-alone terminal A computer peripheral device capable of processing all data and producing all required information in a system application.

Statistical report A collection of documents providing quantitative analyses of various aspects of the firm, such as occupancy profile, financial analysis, or productivity reports.

Statistics A collection of quantitative data assembled for analytical and interpretive purposes.

Stayover A hotel guest who remains in occupancy longer than originally planned or committed.

Storage A data-processing function in which data are placed in a select area of the system for future access and retrieval.

Subroutine A term describing the performance of a precisely-defined operation within a computer program.

Subsystem A minor arrangement of interdependent parts in one branch of a larger network or assemblage.

Switchboard See PBX.

Synergy A combined action or operation wherein the aggregate production of the component parts by far exceeds the contribution of all the individual factors composing the whole.

System An orderly arrangement of component parts in an interrelated series.

System concept See System.

System life cycle A four-phase process ranging from problem situation and environmental analysis, through design and implementation to refinement.

Systems analyst That person in a computer system environment responsible for the overall design of the system.

Text editing The alteration of inputted data to remove errors or omissions prior to processing.

Throughput A measure of system efficiency; the rate at which work can be handled by a system.

Ticket control An internal monitoring process accomplished by accounting for every serially-numbered guest check (or similar document).

Time sharing Use of a computer to process multiple requests by users.

Transactional accounting An accounting system based upon a proper chronological sequencing of transactions, postings, and financial statements.

Transcript An official or legal documentation of financial information; also, an essential reconciliation and verification audit document.

Trial balance A list of all accounts in a ledger; the proof of arithmetic accuracy in a financial account recording process (for the purpose of account statement preparation). See Audit.

Turnaround The time elapsed between the submission of input and the generation of output. See Throughput.

Turnkey A preprogrammed system designed to perform specific unalterable functions; requires no computer staff.

Uncertainty A lack of complete knowledge about the outcome of an event.

Uniform System of Accounts A standardized technique for the recording and reporting of financial transactions and for the specification of terminology.

User: See End user.

User's manual A document that describes the specific operations and maintenance requirements of all system components.

Vanilla system A one vendor system; all components in a system are produced by one manufacturer.

Variable costs Costs that vary directly proportional to sales; for example, housekeeping costs with room sales or food costs with restaurant sales.

Vendor-designed system A computer application designed for a specific user (or group of users); normally provides for some customization but does not require an EDP staff.

Verification The confirmation or establishment of accuracy within an information system; the validation of data to insure correctness.

Video display terminal (VDT) See Cathode ray tube (CRT).

Voice synthesizer A verbal system response generated by a computer from a limited syntax; voice output from a restricted vocabulary.

Voucher A written communication between one set of accounts and another; a document employed to notify a central file of charges requiring posting.

Walk-in Guest who comes to the hotel without a prior reservation; those who simply walk into a hotel seeking accommodations for the night.

Walkout See Skipper.

Zeroing out To bring an account balance to zero by having debits and credits offset one another.

Index

A

Accountability, 5, 95
Account adjustment, *see* Account settlement
Account collection
  budgeting for, 66, 67
  cash flow and, 42
  city ledger, 227
  factors affecting, 4, 49, 144
Accounting
  back-office interface for, 224–225
  budgets in, 65–72
  factors affecting hotel, 144
  financial reporting for, 63–72
  fixed room rates and, 37
  introduction of electronics for, 121–122, 146–153
  management modules for, 224–225, 227
  manual processes for, 5, 145–146; *see also* Data, paper processing of
  printer for, 164
  reports for, 227
  systems and, 96
  "T" format for, 56
  transactional, 49–57
  see also Accounting information systems *and* Auditing
Accounting cycle, 48, 49–50
  debits and credits in, 50–51
  estimates for, 30
  functioning of, 63
  zeroing out in, 57
Accounting department
  electronic posting for, 196, 197
  function of, 48
  reports from, 67
Accounting equation balance, 50, 71–72
Accounting information system, 48–60
  controls in, 57
  functioning of, 63
  overview of, 59
Accounting system, uniform, 63

Account receivable load, 85
Account receivables
  analysis of, 224
  city accounts and, 51
  control of, 227
  current assets and, 64
  display terminals and, 163
  guest accounting and, 22, 49, 51
  guest accounting module and, 193
  reservation module and, 190
Account receivable summary, 69
Account record, departmental, 227
Account settlement, 10
  accounting cycle and, 51
  computers and, 109, 149, 156
  electronic auditing for, 197, 202
  future computers and, 232, 233–234
  guest accounting module and, 193, 194, 196, 197
  line of credit and, 49
  paper processing and, 22–23, 146
  point-of-sale, 42
  posting and, 57
  transactional, 49–50
Accounts, guest
  construction of, 10, 17
  data processing in, 22–23, 99
  front office and, 17
  management module and, 222
  mistakes in, 48, 146
  see also Guest cycle
Accounts, high risk, 22
  computers and, 109, 232
  guest accounting module and, 196, 198, 202
Accounts payable
  budgeting for, 66, 67
  control over, 227
  current liabilities and, 64
  management module and, 224–225
  transactions with, 49

Accounts receivable, 22, 42, 66, 67
Acoustic coupler, 157
Actual departure report, 213
Adjustment factor, CM, 82–83
Administrative systems, 110, 111
  see also Management information systems *and* Hotel information system
Advance reservation, 19–20
  see also Reservations
Advertising
  operating expenses and, 64
  reservations and, 40, 178, 189
Agent, *see* Desk clerk
Algorithmic design, 133, 135
Allocated costs, *see* Costs, direct allocated *and* Costs, indirect allocated
Allotment report, room, 215
Analog computer, 99
Analysis
  accounting cycle, 50
  CM, 70, 82–83, 95
  computerized HIS and, 166
  contribution margin, 82–83
  correlation, 87–88
  data, *see* Data processing
  financial, 222, 223–224, 227; *see also* Accounting, Auditing, Budgets
  operations, *see* Operating departments
  post-sale, 83–86
  pre-cost, 81
  pre-sale, 80–83
  rooms management, 212, 215, 227
  statistical, *see* Statistical analysis, *and* Statistics
  subjective, 75, 79
  systems, 96, 97, 98
  see also Auditing
Analysts, systems, *see* Systems analyst
Analytical/deterministic mode, 168
APL, 134